WEST'S LAW SCHOOL ADVISORY BOARD

CURTIS J. BERGER
Professor of Law, Columbia University

JESSE H. CHOPER
Professor of Law,
University of California, Berkeley

DAVID P. CURRIE
Professor of Law, University of Chicago

YALE KAMISAR
Professor of Law, University of Michigan

MARY KAY KANE
Dean and Professor of Law, University of California,
Hastings College of the Law

WAYNE R. LaFAVE
Professor of Law, University of Illinois

ARTHUR R. MILLER
Professor of Law, Harvard University

GRANT S. NELSON
Professor of Law, University of California, Los Angeles

JAMES J. WHITE
Professor of Law, University of Michigan

CHARLES ALAN WRIGHT
Charles Alan Wright Chair in Federal Courts
The University of Texas

CONSTITUTIONAL CIVIL RIGHTS

IN A NUTSHELL

THIRD EDITION

By

NORMAN VIEIRA
Professor of Law
Southern Illinois University

WEST GROUP

ST. PAUL, MINN.
1998

Nutshell Series, In a Nutshell, the Nutshell Logo and the West Group symbol are registered trademarks of West Group. Registered in the U.S. Patent and Trademark Office.

COPYRIGHT © 1978, 1990 WEST PUBLISHING CO.
COPYRIGHT © 1998 By WEST GROUP
                      610 Opperman Drive
                      P.O. Box 64526
                      St. Paul, MN 55164–0526
                      1–800–328–9352

All rights reserved
Printed in the United States of America

Library of Congress Cataloging-in-Publication Data
Vieira, Norman.
    Constitutional civil rights in a nutshell / Norman Vieira. — 3rd ed.
      p.   cm. — (Nutshell series)
    Includes index.
    ISBN 0–314–23008–4
    1. Civil rights—United States.   I. Title.   II. Series.
KF4750.V5   1998
342.73'085—dc21   97–32604
                                                              CIP

ISBN 0–314–23008–4

PREFACE

This brief text, like others in the Nutshell series, is intended primarily for the use of law students and practitioners. In addition, it may serve as ancillary reading in appropriate undergraduate courses. The space limitations imposed by the goal of providing "a succinct exposition of the law" have made it necessary to abbreviate the discussion of some subjects and to exclude other subjects entirely. The main focus of the text is on fourteenth amendment case law, but I have generally omitted treatment of criminal procedure problems, which are ably discussed in Isreal & LaFave, Criminal Procedure in a Nutshell, and of the first amendment, which is a subject for another book. Similarly, in setting forth the statutory law, the text concentrates on certain major developments described in chapters seven and eight, but more detailed coverage of some of the statutes can be found elsewhere. See, e.g., Player, Employment Discrimination Law.

It should be obvious that for law students a text in the field of constitutional law must serve as a supplement to, and not as a substitute for, the careful reading of Supreme Court opinions. Nevertheless, students and practitioners may find a textbook helpful in understanding the cases and in analyzing them critically. With this in mind, I have at some

PREFACE

points tendered my own analysis of issues—not with any purpose to indoctrinate the reader, who must of course reach his or her own judgment, but merely to stimulate deliberation and debate. However, if a student's analytical skills are to be sharpened in this process, it is essential that close attention be given to what the Supreme Court has said and done.

I am indebted to my research assistant, Gregg Walters, for his diligent work on various parts of this book.

In order to facilitate early publication of this volume, it has been necessary to treat most of the cases decided near the end of the 1996 Term only briefly and to set June, 1997 as the cutoff date for material included in the text.

OUTLINE

	Page
PREFACE	III

Chapter I. Introduction 1
Sec.
1. The Privileges or Immunities Clause 1
2. The Application of the Bill of Rights to the States 3

Chapter II. Substantive Due Process 7
3. The Constitutionalization of "Natural Rights" 7
   From Lochner to Ferguson 7
   Defects of Lochner 10
4. "Alternatives" to Substantive Due Process 11
   The Penumbra of the Bill of Rights 11
   The Ninth Amendment 13
5. The New Substantive Due Process 15
   Roe v. Wade 15
   The Distinction Between Personal and Economic Freedoms 17
   The Standard of Review in Lochner and Roe 19
6. Scope of the New Due Process 20
   Consensual Homosexuality 22

V

OUTLINE

Page

6. Scope of the New Due Process Continued
The "Right to Die" 26
7. Post–Roe Restrictions on Abortion 29
Consent 29
Public Funding 30
Informational Requirements 33
Webster and Casey 34

Chapter III. Procedural Due Process: The Right to Be Heard 40

8. Introduction 40
9. When Due Process Applies 41
10. The Seizure of Property 46
11. Protection of Liberty 51
12. Public Employment 54
13. What Process is Due? 57
14. Irrebuttable Presumptions 60

Chapter IV. Equal Protection: Suspect Classifications 64

15. Introduction 64
16. Discrimination Against Racial Minorities .. 65
17. The Separate–But–Equal Doctrine 70
18. Brown and Its Progeny 72
19. Implementing Brown 75
The First Fifteen Years of Deliberate Speed 75
"Evasive Schemes 77
20. Swann v. Board of Education 78
The Ambiguities of Swann 80
Swann's Impact on Northern Schools 83

OUTLINE

	Page
20. Swann v. Board of Education Continued	
Congressional Reaction to Swann	87
State Legislation Against Busing	87
21. Non–Areawide Segregation	89
Partial Segregation of a Single District	90
Partial Segregation of a Multi–District Area	90
22. De Facto Segregation	93
23. Preferential Treatment of Racial Minorities	96
Early Decisions	96
From Bakke to Adarand	102
General Policy Considerations	110
24. Sex Discrimination	113
The Standard of Review	113
Compensatory Treatment	122
Family Rights	127
The Equal Rights Amendment and Unique Physical Characteristics	129
25. Differential Treatment of Indians	131
26. Wealth and Age Classifications	132
27. Discrimination Against Aliens	134
28. Illegitimacy	138

Chapter V. Equal Protection: The Focus on Specific Interests — 145

29. Introduction	145
30. Voting	146
Developing the Standard of Review	146
Property Qualifications	148
Durational Residence Requirements	149
Disqualification for Alleged Crimes	150

OUTLINE

		Page
30.	Voting Continued	
	Ballot Access and Party Affiliation	150
	Campaign Financing	153
31.	The Right to Travel	154
32.	Access to Criminal and Civil Justice	159
	Criminal Appeals	159
	Civil Justice	162
33.	Defining "Fundamental" Interests	164
34.	The Requirement of Rationality	171
	The Traditional Standard.	171
	Variations on the Traditional Rule	172
	The "Newer Equal Protection	175
35.	Reapportionment	177
	The Rule of Reynolds v. Sims	177
	Applicability of the Equal–Vote Principle	178
	Permissible Departures From Mathematical Equality	179
	Gerrymandering	181

Chapter VI. State Action		184
36.	Introduction	184
37.	The Performance of "Public Functions"	186
	The White Primary Cases	186
	Access to Private Property	187
	The Rationale and Vitality of Public Function Analysis	190
38.	Judicial Enforcement of Private Discrimination	194
39.	Significant State Involvement	198
	The Burton Case	198
	Encouraging or Aiding Private Action	199
	Regulation and Licensing	206
	The Elasticity of the Involvement Concept	209

OUTLINE

	Page
39. Significant State Involvement Continued	
Chapter VII. Congressional Enforcement of Civil Rights	211
40. Introduction	211
41. Congressional Implementation of Judicially–Declared Constitutional Rights	212
42. Congressional Modification of Judicially–Declared Constitutional Rights	216
43. Congressional Power Over Private Discrimination	221
44. Civil Rights Legislation in the Post–Brown Era	226
45. Regulating Discrimination in Employment	229
Purposeful Discrimination	229
Proof, Remedies and Procedures	235
Discriminatory Impact	240
46. The Reconstruction Statutes	244
Chapter VIII. Actions Under 42 U.S.C.A. § 1983	252
47. Personal Liability	252
The Monroe Case	252
Official Immunities	254
Federal Officials	256
Sifting Out Insubstantial Claims	257
48. Municipal Liability	258
49. Protected Interests	262
50. The Relationship Between State Law and 1983	264
"Deficiencies" in Federal Law	264
Habeas Corpus and Res Judicata	266

OUTLINE

	Page
50. The Relationship Between State Law and 1983 Continued	
Release–Dismissal Agreements	267
51. Attorney's Fees	268
APPENDIX: SELECTED CONSTITUTIONAL AND STATUTORY PROVISIONS	272
INDEX	323

TABLE OF CASES

References are to Pages

A

Abate v. Mundt, 403 U.S. 182, 91 S.Ct. 1904, 29 L.Ed.2d 399 (1971), *180*

Action v. Gannon, 450 F.2d 1227 (8th Cir.1971), *222, 225*

Adair v. United States, 208 U.S. 161, 28 S.Ct. 277, 52 L.Ed. 436 (1908), *9*

Adamson v. California, 332 U.S. 46, 67 S.Ct. 1672, 91 L.Ed. 1903 (1947), *3, 4*

Adarand Constructors, Inc. v. Pena, 515 U.S. 200, 115 S.Ct. 2097, 132 L.Ed.2d 158 (1995), *109*

Adickes v. S. H. Kress & Co., 398 U.S. 144, 90 S.Ct. 1598, 26 L.Ed.2d 142 (1970), *246*

Adkins v. Children's Hospital, 261 U.S. 525, 43 S.Ct. 394, 67 L.Ed. 785 (1923), *8*

Akron v. Akron Center for Reproductive Health, Inc., 462 U.S. 416, 103 S.Ct. 2481, 76 L.Ed.2d 687 (1983), *33, 34, 37*

Albemarle Paper Co. v. Moody, 422 U.S. 405, 95 S.Ct. 2362, 45 L.Ed.2d 280 (1975), *238, 242*

Alexander v. Holmes County Bd. of Ed., 396 U.S. 19, 90 S.Ct. 29, 24 L.Ed.2d 19 (1969), *76, 78*

Allen v. McCurry, 449 U.S. 90, 101 S.Ct. 411, 66 L.Ed.2d 308 (1980), *266*

Allen v. State Bd. of Elections, 393 U.S. 544, 89 S.Ct. 817, 22 L.Ed.2d 1 (1969), *227, 228*

Amalgamated Food Emp. Union Local 590 v. Logan Valley Plaza, Inc., 391 U.S. 308, 88 S.Ct. 1601, 20 L.Ed.2d 603, 45 O.O.2d 181 (1968), *188, 189*

Ambach v. Norwick, 441 U.S. 68, 99 S.Ct. 1589, 60 L.Ed.2d 49 (1979), *136*

TABLE OF CASES

American Party of Texas v. White, 415 U.S. 767, 94 S.Ct. 1296, 39 L.Ed.2d 744 (1974), *151, 152*

Anderson v. Celebrezze, 460 U.S. 780, 103 S.Ct. 1564, 75 L.Ed.2d 547 (1983), *152*

Anderson v. Creighton, 483 U.S. 635, 107 S.Ct. 3034, 97 L.Ed.2d 523 (1987), *255, 258*

Anderson v. Methodist Evangelical Hospital, Inc., 464 F.2d 723 (6th Cir.1972), *230*

Antelope, United States v., 430 U.S. 641, 97 S.Ct. 1395, 51 L.Ed.2d 701 (1977), *131*

Apodaca v. Oregon, 406 U.S. 404, 92 S.Ct. 1628, 32 L.Ed.2d 184 (1972), *5*

Application of (see name of party)

Aptheker v. Secretary of State, 378 U.S. 500, 84 S.Ct. 1659, 12 L.Ed.2d 992 (1964), *155*

Arlington Heights, Village of v. Metropolitan Housing Development Corp., 429 U.S. 252, 97 S.Ct. 555, 50 L.Ed.2d 450 (1977), *68, 69*

Arnett v. Kennedy, 416 U.S. 134, 94 S.Ct. 1633, 40 L.Ed.2d 15 (1974), *44, 45, 59*

Attorney General v. Soto–Lopez, 476 U.S. 898, 106 S.Ct. 2317, 90 L.Ed.2d 899 (1986), *159*

Avery v. Midland County, Tex., 390 U.S. 474, 88 S.Ct. 1114, 20 L.Ed.2d 45 (1968), *178*

B

Ball v. James, 451 U.S. 355, 101 S.Ct. 1811, 68 L.Ed.2d 150 (1981), *149*

Barron v. Baltimore, 32 U.S. 243, 7 Pet. 243, 8 L.Ed. 672 (1833), *1*

Barrows v. Jackson, 346 U.S. 249, 73 S.Ct. 1031, 97 L.Ed. 1586 (1953), *194*

Batson v. Kentucky, 476 U.S. 79, 106 S.Ct. 1712, 90 L.Ed.2d 69 (1986), *69*

Bazemore v. Friday, 478 U.S. 385, 106 S.Ct. 3000, 92 L.Ed.2d 315 (1986), *76*

Bell v. Burson, 402 U.S. 535, 91 S.Ct. 1586, 29 L.Ed.2d 90 (1971), *42, 43*

Bell v. Maryland, 378 U.S. 226, 84 S.Ct. 1814, 12 L.Ed.2d 822 (1964), *184*

TABLE OF CASES

Bell v. School City of Gary, Ind., 324 F.2d 209 (7th Cir.1963), *84, 85*

Belle Terre, Village of v. Boraas, 416 U.S. 1, 94 S.Ct. 1536, 39 L.Ed.2d 797 (1974), *168*

Bellotti v. Baird, 443 U.S. 622, 99 S.Ct. 3035, 61 L.Ed.2d 797 (1979), *29*

Benton v. Maryland, 395 U.S. 784, 89 S.Ct. 2056, 23 L.Ed.2d 707 (1969), *5*

Bernal v. Fainter, 467 U.S. 216, 104 S.Ct. 2312, 81 L.Ed.2d 175 (1984), *135, 136*

Bishop v. Wood, 426 U.S. 341, 96 S.Ct. 2074, 48 L.Ed.2d 684 (1976), *55, 56*

Bivens v. Six Unknown Named Agents of Federal Bureau of Narcotics, 403 U.S. 388, 91 S.Ct. 1999, 29 L.Ed.2d 619 (1971), *256*

Black v. Cutter Laboratories, 351 U.S. 292, 76 S.Ct. 824, 100 L.Ed. 1188 (1956), *197*

Blanchard v. Bergeron, 489 U.S. 87, 109 S.Ct. 939, 103 L.Ed.2d 67 (1989), *270*

Blum v. Stenson, 465 U.S. 886, 104 S.Ct. 1541, 79 L.Ed.2d 891 (1984), *271*

Blum v. Yaretsky, 457 U.S. 991, 102 S.Ct. 2777, 73 L.Ed.2d 534 (1982), *193, 203*

Board of County Com'rs of Bryan County, Okl. v. Brown, ___ U.S. ___, 117 S.Ct. 1382, 137 L.Ed.2d 626 (1997), *260*

Board of Curators of University of Missouri v. Horowitz, 435 U.S. 78, 98 S.Ct. 948, 55 L.Ed.2d 124 (1978), *57*

Board of Pardons v. Allen, 482 U.S. 369, 107 S.Ct. 2415, 96 L.Ed.2d 303 (1987), *53*

Board of Regents v. Roth, 408 U.S. 564, 92 S.Ct. 2701, 33 L.Ed.2d 548 (1972), *41, 51, 52, 54, 56*

Boddie v. Connecticut, 401 U.S. 371, 91 S.Ct. 780, 28 L.Ed.2d 113 (1971), *162, 163*

Boerne, City of v. Flores, ___ U.S. ___, 117 S.Ct. 2157, 138 L.Ed.2d 624 (1997), *220*

Bolling v. Sharpe, 347 U.S. 497, 74 S.Ct. 693, 98 L.Ed. 884, 53 O.O. 331 (1954), *72, 73*

Bounds v. Smith, 430 U.S. 817, 97 S.Ct. 1491, 52 L.Ed.2d 72 (1977), *161*

Bowers v. Hardwick, 478 U.S. 186, 106 S.Ct. 2841, 92 L.Ed.2d 140 (1986), *22, 23, 24, 25, 174*

TABLE OF CASES

Bray v. Alexandria Women's Health Clinic, 506 U.S. 263, 113 S.Ct. 753, 122 L.Ed.2d 34 (1993), *251*

Brewer v. Hoxie School Dist. No. 46 of Lawrence County, Ark., 238 F.2d 91 (8th Cir.1956), *222*

Brock v. Roadway Exp., Inc., 481 U.S. 252, 107 S.Ct. 1740, 95 L.Ed.2d 239 (1987), *55*

Brown v. Board of Ed., 347 U.S. 483, 74 S.Ct. 686, 98 L.Ed. 873 (1954), *72, 73, 74, 81, 83, 84, 85, 86, 87, 211, 226, 229, 244, 246, 247, 249*

Brown v. Board of Educ. of Topeka, Kan., 349 U.S. 294, 75 S.Ct. 753, 99 L.Ed. 1083 (1955), *74, 75*

Brown v. Thomson, 462 U.S. 835, 103 S.Ct. 2690, 77 L.Ed.2d 214 (1983), *181*

Buchanan v. Warley, 245 U.S. 60, 38 S.Ct. 16, 62 L.Ed. 149 (1917), *66*

Buckley v. Valeo, 424 U.S. 1, 96 S.Ct. 612, 46 L.Ed.2d 659 (1976), *153, 154*

Bullock v. Carter, 405 U.S. 134, 92 S.Ct. 849, 31 L.Ed.2d 92 (1972), *150*

Burlington, City of v. Dague, 505 U.S. 557, 112 S.Ct. 2638, 120 L.Ed.2d 449 (1992), *271*

Burns v. Ohio, 360 U.S. 252, 79 S.Ct. 1164, 3 L.Ed.2d 1209 (1959), *160*

Burns v. Richardson, 384 U.S. 73, 86 S.Ct. 1286, 16 L.Ed.2d 376 (1966), *178*

Burton v. Wilmington Parking Authority, 365 U.S. 715, 81 S.Ct. 856, 6 L.Ed.2d 45 (1961), *198, 199, 206, 209*

Bush v. Lone Star Steel Co., 373 F.Supp. 526 (E.D.Tex.1974), *238*

Bush v. Vera, ___ U.S. ___, 116 S.Ct. 1941, 135 L.Ed.2d 248 (1996), *110*

Butz v. Economou, 438 U.S. 478, 98 S.Ct. 2894, 57 L.Ed.2d 895 (1978), *256*

C

Caban v. Mohammed, 441 U.S. 380, 99 S.Ct. 1760, 60 L.Ed.2d 297 (1979), *128, 129*

Cabell v. Chavez–Salido, 454 U.S. 432, 102 S.Ct. 735, 70 L.Ed.2d 677 (1982), *136*

Calero–Toledo v. Pearson Yacht Leasing Co., 416 U.S. 663, 94 S.Ct. 2080, 40 L.Ed.2d 452 (1974), *47*

TABLE OF CASES

Califano v. Goldfarb, 430 U.S. 199, 97 S.Ct. 1021, 51 L.Ed.2d 270 (1977), *125, 126*

Califano v. Webster, 430 U.S. 313, 97 S.Ct. 1192, 51 L.Ed.2d 360 (1977), *125*

Canton, City of v. Harris, 489 U.S. 378, 109 S.Ct. 1197, 103 L.Ed.2d 412 (1989), *261*

Cardona v. Power, 384 U.S. 672, 86 S.Ct. 1728, 16 L.Ed.2d 848 (1966), *216, 218*

Carey v. Population Services, Intern., 431 U.S. 678, 97 S.Ct. 2010, 52 L.Ed.2d 675 (1977), *29*

Carolene Products Co., United States v., 304 U.S. 144, 58 S.Ct. 778, 82 L.Ed. 1234 (1938), *9*

Carrington v. Rash, 380 U.S. 89, 85 S.Ct. 775, 13 L.Ed.2d 675 (1965), *150*

Castaneda v. Partida, 430 U.S. 482, 97 S.Ct. 1272, 51 L.Ed.2d 498 (1977), *69*

Chapman v. Meier, 420 U.S. 1, 95 S.Ct. 751, 42 L.Ed.2d 766 (1975), *181, 182*

Cheatwood v. South Central Bell Tel. & Tel. Co., 303 F.Supp. 754 (M.D.Ala.1969), *234*

Cipriano v. City of Houma, 395 U.S. 701, 89 S.Ct. 1897, 23 L.Ed.2d 647 (1969), *148*

Cisneros v. Corpus Christi Independent School Dist., 467 F.2d 142 (5th Cir.1972), *81*

City of (see name of city)

Civil Rights Cases, 109 U.S. 3, 3 S.Ct. 18, 27 L.Ed. 835 (1883), *184*

Clark v. Jeter, 486 U.S. 456, 108 S.Ct. 1910, 100 L.Ed.2d 465 (1988), *143*

Classic, United States v., 313 U.S. 299, 61 S.Ct. 1031, 85 L.Ed. 1368 (1941), *211*

Cleburne v. Cleburne Living Center, 473 U.S. 432, 105 S.Ct. 3249, 87 L.Ed.2d 313 (1985), *133, 173*

Clements v. Fashing, 457 U.S. 957, 102 S.Ct. 2836, 73 L.Ed.2d 508 (1982), *152*

Cleveland Bd. of Educ. v. LaFleur, 414 U.S. 632, 94 S.Ct. 791, 39 L.Ed.2d 52 (1974), *61*

Cleveland Bd. of Educ. v. Loudermill, 470 U.S. 532, 105 S.Ct. 1487, 84 L.Ed.2d 494 (1985), *45, 55, 59*

Colautti v. Franklin, 439 U.S. 379, 99 S.Ct. 675, 58 L.Ed.2d 596 (1979), *35*

TABLE OF CASES

Columbia Broadcasting System, Inc. v. Democratic Nat. Committee, 412 U.S. 94, 93 S.Ct. 2080, 36 L.Ed.2d 772 (1973), *208*

Columbus Bd. of Ed. v. Penick, 443 U.S. 449, 99 S.Ct. 2941, 61 L.Ed.2d 666 (1979), *86*

Connecticut v. Teal, 457 U.S. 440, 102 S.Ct. 2525, 73 L.Ed.2d 130 (1982), *241*

Connor v. Finch, 431 U.S. 407, 97 S.Ct. 1828, 52 L.Ed.2d 465 (1977), *181*

Cooper v. Aaron, 358 U.S. 1, 78 S.Ct. 1401, 3 L.Ed.2d 5, 3 L.Ed.2d 19 (1958), *77*

Cornelius v. Benevolent Protective Order of Elks, 382 F.Supp. 1182 (D.Conn.1974), *249*

Craig v. Boren, 429 U.S. 190, 97 S.Ct. 451, 50 L.Ed.2d 397 (1976), *117, 118, 119, 120, 125*

Crandall v. Nevada, 73 U.S. 35, 18 L.Ed. 745 (1867), *155*

Crawford v. Board of Educ., 458 U.S. 527, 102 S.Ct. 3211, 73 L.Ed.2d 948 (1982), *87, 89*

Cruzan by Cruzan v. Director, Missouri Dept. of Health, 497 U.S. 261, 110 S.Ct. 2841, 111 L.Ed.2d 224 (1990), *26, 27*

D

Dandridge v. Williams, 397 U.S. 471, 90 S.Ct. 1153, 25 L.Ed.2d 491 (1970), *164, 165, 168*

Daniel v. Paul, 395 U.S. 298, 89 S.Ct. 1697, 23 L.Ed.2d 318 (1969), *228*

Daniels v. Williams, 474 U.S. 327, 106 S.Ct. 662, 88 L.Ed.2d 662 (1986), *42*

Davidson v. Cannon, 474 U.S. 344, 106 S.Ct. 668, 88 L.Ed.2d 677 (1986), *42*

Davis v. Bandemer, 478 U.S. 109, 106 S.Ct. 2797, 92 L.Ed.2d 85 (1986), *183*

Dayton Bd. of Ed. v. Brinkman, 443 U.S. 526, 99 S.Ct. 2971, 61 L.Ed.2d 720 (1979), *86*

Dayton Bd. of Ed. v. Brinkman, 433 U.S. 406, 97 S.Ct. 2766, 53 L.Ed.2d 851 (1977), *90, 94*

DeFunis v. Odegaard, 416 U.S. 312, 94 S.Ct. 1704, 40 L.Ed.2d 164 (1974), *111*

DeShaney v. Winnebago County Dept. of Social Services, 489 U.S. 189, 109 S.Ct. 998, 103 L.Ed.2d 249 (1989), *170, 184*

TABLE OF CASES

Diaz v. Pan Am. World Airways, Inc., 442 F.2d 385 (5th Cir. 1971), *235*

Dixon v. Alabama State Bd. of Ed., 294 F.2d 150 (5th Cir.1961), *44*

Dixon v. Love, 431 U.S. 105, 97 S.Ct. 1723, 52 L.Ed.2d 172 (1977), *59*

Doe v. Bolton, 410 U.S. 179, 93 S.Ct. 739, 35 L.Ed.2d 201 (1973), *16*

Dothard v. Rawlinson, 433 U.S. 321, 97 S.Ct. 2720, 53 L.Ed.2d 786 (1977), *234, 242*

Douglas v. California, 372 U.S. 353, 83 S.Ct. 814, 9 L.Ed.2d 811 (1963), *160, 161, 163, 167*

Dred Scott Case, 60 U.S. 393, 19 How. 393, 15 L.Ed. 691 (1856), *7*

Duncan v. Louisiana, 391 U.S. 145, 88 S.Ct. 1444, 20 L.Ed.2d 491, 45 O.O.2d 198 (1968), *4, 5*

Dunn v. Blumstein, 405 U.S. 330, 92 S.Ct. 995, 31 L.Ed.2d 274 (1972), *149, 156, 158, 158*

Dusch v. Davis, 387 U.S. 112, 87 S.Ct. 1554, 18 L.Ed.2d 656 (1967), *179*

E

Edmonson v. Leesville Concrete Co., Inc., 500 U.S. 614, 111 S.Ct. 2077, 114 L.Ed.2d 660 (1991), *205*

E.E.O.C. v. Wyoming, 460 U.S. 226, 103 S.Ct. 1054, 75 L.Ed.2d 18 (1983), *216*

Eisenstadt v. Baird, 405 U.S. 438, 92 S.Ct. 1029, 31 L.Ed.2d 349 (1972), *176*

El Paso, City of v. Simmons, 379 U.S. 497, 85 S.Ct. 577, 13 L.Ed.2d 446 (1965), *56*

Employment Div., Dept. of Human Resources of Oregon v. Smith, 494 U.S. 872, 110 S.Ct. 1595, 108 L.Ed.2d 876 (1990), *220*

Equal Employment Opportunity Commission v. Detroit Edison Co., 515 F.2d 301 (6th Cir.1975), *238*

Espinoza v. Farah Mfg. Co., Inc., 414 U.S. 86, 94 S.Ct. 334, 38 L.Ed.2d 287 (1973), *242*

Evans v. Abney, 396 U.S. 435, 90 S.Ct. 628, 24 L.Ed.2d 634 (1970), *190, 190, 196*

TABLE OF CASES

Evans v. Buchanan, 393 F.Supp. 428 (D.Del.1975), aff'd info Buchanan v. Evans, 423 U.S. 963 (1975), *91*

Evans v. Newton, 382 U.S. 296, 86 S.Ct. 486, 15 L.Ed.2d 373 (1966), *189, 190*

Examining Bd. of Engineers v. Flores de Otero, 426 U.S. 572, 96 S.Ct. 2264, 49 L.Ed.2d 65 (1976), *136*

F

F.C.C. v. Beach Communications, Inc., 508 U.S. 307, 113 S.Ct. 2096, 124 L.Ed.2d 211 (1993), *177*

Felder v. Casey, 487 U.S. 131, 108 S.Ct. 2302, 101 L.Ed.2d 123 (1988), *265*

Ferguson v. Skrupa, 372 U.S. 726, 83 S.Ct. 1028, 10 L.Ed.2d 93 (1963), *10*

Fitzpatrick v. Bitzer, 427 U.S. 445, 96 S.Ct. 2666, 49 L.Ed.2d 614 (1976), *262*

Flagg Bros., Inc. v. Brooks, 436 U.S. 149, 98 S.Ct. 1729, 56 L.Ed.2d 185 (1978), *193, 204, 205*

Foley v. Connelie, 435 U.S. 291, 98 S.Ct. 1067, 55 L.Ed.2d 287 (1978), *136*

Fordice, United States v., 505 U.S. 717, 112 S.Ct. 2727, 120 L.Ed.2d 575 (1992), *76*

Franks v. Bowman Transp. Co., Inc., 424 U.S. 747, 96 S.Ct. 1251, 47 L.Ed.2d 444 (1976), *101, 238*

Freeman v. Pitts, 503 U.S. 467, 112 S.Ct. 1430, 118 L.Ed.2d 108 (1992), *80*

Frontiero v. Richardson, 411 U.S. 677, 93 S.Ct. 1764, 36 L.Ed.2d 583 (1973), *115, 124, 125, 130*

Fuentes v. Shevin, 407 U.S. 67, 92 S.Ct. 1983, 32 L.Ed.2d 556 (1972), *40, 47, 48, 49, 50*

Fujii v. State, 38 Cal.2d 718, 242 P.2d 617 (Cal.1952), *135*

Fullilove v. Klutznick, 448 U.S. 448, 100 S.Ct. 2758, 65 L.Ed.2d 902 (1980), *107*

Furnco Const. Corp. v. Waters, 438 U.S. 567, 98 S.Ct. 2943, 57 L.Ed.2d 957 (1978), *241*

G

Gaffney v. Cummings, 412 U.S. 735, 93 S.Ct. 2321, 37 L.Ed.2d 298 (1973), *180, 181*

TABLE OF CASES

Gaston County, N. C. v. United States, 395 U.S. 285, 89 S.Ct. 1720, 23 L.Ed.2d 309 (1969), *228*

Gayle v. Browder, 352 U.S. 903, 77 S.Ct. 145, 1 L.Ed.2d 114 (1956), *73*

Geduldig v. Aiello, 417 U.S. 484, 94 S.Ct. 2485, 41 L.Ed.2d 256 (1974), *130, 131*

Georgia v. United States, 411 U.S. 526, 93 S.Ct. 1702, 36 L.Ed.2d 472 (1973), *228*

German Alliance Ins. Co. v. Lewis, 233 U.S. 389, 34 S.Ct. 612, 58 L.Ed. 1011 (1914), *8*

Gilmore v. City of Montgomery, Ala., 417 U.S. 556, 94 S.Ct. 2416, 41 L.Ed.2d 304 (1974), *77, 202*

Glona v. American Guarantee & Liability Ins. Co., 391 U.S. 73, 88 S.Ct. 1515, 20 L.Ed.2d 441 (1968), *138*

Goesaert v. Cleary, 335 U.S. 464, 69 S.Ct. 198, 93 L.Ed. 163 (1948), *113, 114*

Goldberg v. Kelly, 397 U.S. 254, 90 S.Ct. 1011, 25 L.Ed.2d 287 (1970), *57, 58, 59, 60*

Gomez v. Perez, 409 U.S. 535, 93 S.Ct. 872, 35 L.Ed.2d 56 (1973), *140*

Gomillion v. Lightfoot, 364 U.S. 339, 81 S.Ct. 125, 5 L.Ed.2d 110 (1960), *68*

Gordon v. Lance, 403 U.S. 1, 91 S.Ct. 1889, 29 L.Ed.2d 273 (1971), *179*

Goss v. Board of Ed., 444 F.2d 632 (6th Cir.1971), *83*

Goss v. Lopez, 419 U.S. 565, 95 S.Ct. 729, 42 L.Ed.2d 725 (1975), *43, 46, 51, 52, 57, 60*

Graham v. Richardson, 403 U.S. 365, 91 S.Ct. 1848, 29 L.Ed.2d 534 (1971), *134, 135*

Green v. County School Bd. of New Kent County, Va., 391 U.S. 430, 88 S.Ct. 1689, 20 L.Ed.2d 716 (1968), *76, 78*

Griffin v. Breckenridge, 403 U.S. 88, 91 S.Ct. 1790, 29 L.Ed.2d 338 (1971), *225, 250*

Griffin v. County School Bd. of Prince Edward County, 377 U.S. 218, 84 S.Ct. 1226, 12 L.Ed.2d 256 (1964), *77*

Griffin v. Illinois, 351 U.S. 12, 76 S.Ct. 585, 100 L.Ed. 891 (1956), *159, 160, 161, 163, 167*

Griffiths, Application of, 413 U.S. 717, 93 S.Ct. 2851, 37 L.Ed.2d 910 (1973), *135*

Griggs v. Duke Power Co., 401 U.S. 424, 91 S.Ct. 849, 28 L.Ed.2d 158 (1971), *240, 241*

TABLE OF CASES

Griswold v. Connecticut, 381 U.S. 479, 85 S.Ct. 1678, 14 L.Ed.2d 510 (1965), *11, 12, 13, 14*

Guest, United States v., 383 U.S. 745, 86 S.Ct. 1170, 16 L.Ed.2d 239 (1966), *155, 222, 223, 246*

Guinn v. United States, 238 U.S. 347, 35 S.Ct. 926, 59 L.Ed. 1340 (1915), *68*

Gunter v. Merchants Warren Nat. Bank, 360 F.Supp. 1085 (D.Me.1973), *47*

H

Hadley v. Junior College Dist. of Metropolitan Kansas City, Mo., 397 U.S. 50, 90 S.Ct. 791, 25 L.Ed.2d 45 (1970), *179*

Hafer v. Melo, 502 U.S. 21, 112 S.Ct. 358, 116 L.Ed.2d 301 (1991), *262*

Hale v. Iowa State Board, 302 U.S. 95, 58 S.Ct. 102, 82 L.Ed. 72 (1937), *56*

Hampton v. Mow Sun Wong, 426 U.S. 88, 96 S.Ct. 1895, 48 L.Ed.2d 495 (1976), *137*

Hanrahan v. Hampton, 446 U.S. 754, 100 S.Ct. 1987, 64 L.Ed.2d 670 (1980), *270*

Haring v. Prosise, 462 U.S. 306, 103 S.Ct. 2368, 76 L.Ed.2d 595 (1983), *267*

Harlow v. Fitzgerald, 457 U.S. 800, 102 S.Ct. 2727, 73 L.Ed.2d 396 (1982), *257, 258*

Harper v. Virginia State Bd. of Elections, 383 U.S. 663, 86 S.Ct. 1079, 16 L.Ed.2d 169 (1966), *146, 150*

Harris v. Forklift Systems, Inc., 510 U.S. 17, 114 S.Ct. 367, 126 L.Ed.2d 295 (1993), *230*

Harris v. McRae, 448 U.S. 297, 100 S.Ct. 2671, 65 L.Ed.2d 784 (1980), *31*

Hazelwood School Dist. v. United States, 433 U.S. 299, 97 S.Ct. 2736, 53 L.Ed.2d 768 (1977), *237*

Healy v. James, 408 U.S. 169, 92 S.Ct. 2338, 33 L.Ed.2d 266 (1972), *32*

Heart of Atlanta Motel, Inc. v. United States, 379 U.S. 241, 85 S.Ct. 348, 13 L.Ed.2d 258 (1964), *97, 224*

Heck v. Humphrey, 512 U.S. 477, 114 S.Ct. 2364, 129 L.Ed.2d 383 (1994), *266*

Heller v. Doe by Doe, 509 U.S. 312, 113 S.Ct. 2637, 125 L.Ed.2d 257 (1993), *174*

TABLE OF CASES

Hensley v. Eckerhart, 461 U.S. 424, 103 S.Ct. 1933, 76 L.Ed.2d 40 (1983), *271*

Hewitt v. Helms, 482 U.S. 755, 107 S.Ct. 2672, 96 L.Ed.2d 654 (1987), *269*

Hewitt v. Helms, 459 U.S. 460, 103 S.Ct. 864, 74 L.Ed.2d 675 (1983), *53*

Hill v. Stone, 421 U.S. 289, 95 S.Ct. 1637, 44 L.Ed.2d 172 (1975), *148*

Hills v. Gautreaux, 425 U.S. 284, 96 S.Ct. 1538, 47 L.Ed.2d 792 (1976), *92*

Holden v. Hardy, 169 U.S. 366, 18 S.Ct. 383, 42 L.Ed. 780 (1898), *8*

Hooper v. Bernalillo County Assessor, 472 U.S. 612, 105 S.Ct. 2862, 86 L.Ed.2d 487 (1985), *159*

Hoyt v. Florida, 368 U.S. 57, 82 S.Ct. 159, 7 L.Ed.2d 118 (1961), *113, 114*

Hudgens v. N. L. R. B., 424 U.S. 507, 96 S.Ct. 1029, 47 L.Ed.2d 196 (1976), *189*

Hudson v. Palmer, 468 U.S. 517, 104 S.Ct. 3194, 82 L.Ed.2d 393 (1984), *263*

Hughes v. Rowe, 449 U.S. 5, 101 S.Ct. 173, 66 L.Ed.2d 163 (1980), *268*

Hunter v. Erickson, 393 U.S. 385, 89 S.Ct. 557, 21 L.Ed.2d 616 (1969), *97*

Hunter v. Underwood, 471 U.S. 222, 105 S.Ct. 1916, 85 L.Ed.2d 222 (1985), *69*

Hurtado v. California, 110 U.S. 516, 4 S.Ct. 111, 28 L.Ed. 232 (1884), *5*

Hutchison v. Bank of North Carolina, N.A., 392 F.Supp. 888 (M.D.N.C.1975), *50*

I

Idaho v. Coeur d'Alene Tribe of Idaho, ___ U.S. ___, 117 S.Ct. 2028, 138 L.Ed.2d 438 (1997), *262*

Illinois State Bd. of Elections v. Socialist Workers Party, 440 U.S. 173, 99 S.Ct. 983, 59 L.Ed.2d 230 (1979), *152*

Imbler v. Pachtman, 424 U.S. 409, 96 S.Ct. 984, 47 L.Ed.2d 128 (1976), *254*

Ingraham v. Wright, 430 U.S. 651, 97 S.Ct. 1401, 51 L.Ed.2d 711 (1977), *60*

TABLE OF CASES

In re (see name of party)

International Broth. of Teamsters v. United States, 431 U.S. 324, 97 S.Ct. 1843, 52 L.Ed.2d 396 (1977), *237, 243*

International Union, United Auto., Aerospace and Agr. Implement Workers of America, UAW v. Johnson Controls, Inc., 499 U.S. 187, 111 S.Ct. 1196, 113 L.Ed.2d 158 (1991), *234*

J

Jackson v. Metropolitan Edison Co., 419 U.S. 345, 95 S.Ct. 449, 42 L.Ed.2d 477 (1974), *192, 193, 206, 207, 208, 210, 246*

Jackson v. Statler Foundation, 496 F.2d 623 (2nd Cir.1973), *202*

Jacksonville Terminal Co., United States v., 451 F.2d 418 (5th Cir.1971), *230*

Jacobs, In re, 98 N.Y. 98 (N.Y.1885), *7*

Jacobs, Rex v., 168 Eng.Rep. 830 (1817), *24*

James v. Valtierra, 402 U.S. 137, 91 S.Ct. 1331, 28 L.Ed.2d 678 (1971), *132*

J.E.B. v. Alabama ex rel. T.B., 511 U.S. 127, 114 S.Ct. 1419, 128 L.Ed.2d 89 (1994), *122*

Jefferson v. Hackney, 406 U.S. 535, 92 S.Ct. 1724, 32 L.Ed.2d 285 (1972), *67, 165*

Jenness v. Fortson, 403 U.S. 431, 91 S.Ct. 1970, 29 L.Ed.2d 554 (1971), *151*

Jimenez v. Weinberger, 417 U.S. 628, 94 S.Ct. 2496, 41 L.Ed.2d 363 (1974), *140*

Johnson v. Railway Exp. Agency, Inc., 421 U.S. 454, 95 S.Ct. 1716, 44 L.Ed.2d 295 (1975), *246, 247, 248, 265*

Johnson v. Robison, 415 U.S. 361, 94 S.Ct. 1160, 39 L.Ed.2d 389 (1974), *169*

Jones v. Alfred H. Mayer Co., 392 U.S. 409, 88 S.Ct. 2186, 20 L.Ed.2d 1189 (1968), *224, 225, 250*

Jones v. Helms, 452 U.S. 412, 101 S.Ct. 2434, 69 L.Ed.2d 118 (1981), *155*

K

Kadrmas v. Dickinson Public Schools, 487 U.S. 450, 108 S.Ct. 2481, 101 L.Ed.2d 399 (1988), *170*

Kahn v. Shevin, 416 U.S. 351, 94 S.Ct. 1734, 40 L.Ed.2d 189 (1974), *122, 123, 124, 126*

TABLE OF CASES

Karcher v. Daggett, 462 U.S. 725, 103 S.Ct. 2653, 77 L.Ed.2d 133 (1983), *180*

Katzenbach v. McClung, 379 U.S. 294, 85 S.Ct. 377, 13 L.Ed.2d 290 (1964), *223, 224*

Katzenbach v. Morgan, 384 U.S. 641, 86 S.Ct. 1717, 16 L.Ed.2d 828 (1966), *216, 217, 218, 219, 220, 221, 223*

Kelley v. Johnson, 425 U.S. 238, 96 S.Ct. 1440, 47 L.Ed.2d 708 (1976), *22*

Kentucky v. Graham, 473 U.S. 159, 105 S.Ct. 3099, 87 L.Ed.2d 114 (1985), *269*

Kentucky Dept. of Corrections v. Thompson, 490 U.S. 454, 109 S.Ct. 1904, 104 L.Ed.2d 506 (1989), *54*

Keyes v. School Dist., 413 U.S. 189, 93 S.Ct. 2686, 37 L.Ed.2d 548 (1973), *90, 91*

King v. New Rochelle Municipal Housing Authority, 442 F.2d 646 (2nd Cir.1971), *158*

Kirchberg v. Feenstra, 450 U.S. 455, 101 S.Ct. 1195, 67 L.Ed.2d 428 (1981), *127*

Kirkpatrick v. Preisler, 394 U.S. 526, 89 S.Ct. 1225, 22 L.Ed.2d 519 (1969), *180*

Kramer v. Union Free School Dist. No. 15, 395 U.S. 621, 89 S.Ct. 1886, 23 L.Ed.2d 583 (1969), *146, 147, 148, 150, 167*

Kras, United States v., 409 U.S. 434, 93 S.Ct. 631, 34 L.Ed.2d 626 (1973), *162, 163*

Kremer v. Chemical Const. Corp., 456 U.S. 461, 102 S.Ct. 1883, 72 L.Ed.2d 262 (1982), *267*

Kusper v. Pontikes, 414 U.S. 51, 94 S.Ct. 303, 38 L.Ed.2d 260 (1973), *152*

L

Labine v. Vincent, 401 U.S. 532, 91 S.Ct. 1017, 28 L.Ed.2d 288 (1971), *138, 139, 142*

Laffey v. Northwest Airlines, Inc., 366 F.Supp. 763 (D.D.C.1973), *232*

Lalli v. Lalli, 439 U.S. 259, 99 S.Ct. 518, 58 L.Ed.2d 503 (1978), *142*

Lane v. Wilson, 307 U.S. 268, 59 S.Ct. 872, 83 L.Ed. 1281 (1939), *68*

Lassiter v. Department of Social Services of Durham County, N. C., 452 U.S. 18, 101 S.Ct. 2153, 68 L.Ed.2d 640 (1981), *164*

TABLE OF CASES

Lassiter v. Northampton County Bd., 360 U.S. 45, 79 S.Ct. 985, 3 L.Ed.2d 1072 (1959), *146, 213, 218*

Lau v. Nichols, 414 U.S. 563, 94 S.Ct. 786, 39 L.Ed.2d 1 (1974), *229*

Lebron v. National R.R. Passenger Corp., 513 U.S. 374, 115 S.Ct. 961, 130 L.Ed.2d 902 (1995), *185*

Lehr v. Robertson, 463 U.S. 248, 103 S.Ct. 2985, 77 L.Ed.2d 614 (1983), *128, 129*

Leis v. Flynt, 439 U.S. 438, 99 S.Ct. 698, 58 L.Ed.2d 717 (1979), *43*

Levy v. Louisiana, 391 U.S. 68, 88 S.Ct. 1509, 20 L.Ed.2d 436 (1968), *138, 139*

Lindsey v. Normet, 405 U.S. 56, 92 S.Ct. 862, 31 L.Ed.2d 36 (1972), *165*

Lippitt v. Cipollone, 404 U.S. 1032, 92 S.Ct. 729, 30 L.Ed.2d 725 (1972), *151*

Little v. Streater, 452 U.S. 1, 101 S.Ct. 2202, 68 L.Ed.2d 627 (1981), *163*

Lloyd v. Tanner, 407 U.S. 551, 92 S.Ct. 2219, 33 L.Ed.2d 131 (1972), *188, 189*

Lochner v. New York, 198 U.S. 45, 25 S.Ct. 539, 49 L.Ed. 937 (1905), *8, 10, 11, 12, 13, 17, 18, 19, 20, 25, 26, 168*

Lockport, Town of v. Citizens for Community Action, 430 U.S. 259, 97 S.Ct. 1047, 51 L.Ed.2d 313 (1977), *179*

Logan v. Zimmerman Brush Co., 455 U.S. 422, 102 S.Ct. 1148, 71 L.Ed.2d 265 (1982), *41, 173*

Long v. District Court of Iowa, In and For Lee County, Fort Madison, Iowa, 385 U.S. 192, 87 S.Ct. 362, 17 L.Ed.2d 290 (1966), *160*

Loo v. Gerarge, 374 F.Supp. 1338 (D.Hawai'i 1974), *237*

Louisiana v. United States, 380 U.S. 145, 85 S.Ct. 817, 13 L.Ed.2d 709 (1965), *66*

Loving v. Virginia, 388 U.S. 1, 87 S.Ct. 1817, 18 L.Ed.2d 1010 (1967), *113*

Lubin v. Panish, 415 U.S. 709, 94 S.Ct. 1315, 39 L.Ed.2d 702 (1974), *150, 152*

Lucas v. Forty–Fourth General Assembly, 377 U.S. 713, 84 S.Ct. 1459, 12 L.Ed.2d 632 (1964), *178*

Lugar v. Edmondson Oil Co., Inc., 457 U.S. 922, 102 S.Ct. 2744, 73 L.Ed.2d 482 (1982), *205*

Lynch v. Household Finance Corp., 405 U.S. 538, 92 S.Ct. 1113, 31 L.Ed.2d 424 (1972), *19*

TABLE OF CASES

M

MacCollom, United States v., 426 U.S. 317, 96 S.Ct. 2086, 48 L.Ed.2d 666 (1976), *161*

Mackey v. Montrym, 443 U.S. 1, 99 S.Ct. 2612, 61 L.Ed.2d 321 (1979), *59*

Mahan v. Howell, 410 U.S. 315, 93 S.Ct. 979, 35 L.Ed.2d 320 (1973), *180*

Maher v. Roe, 432 U.S. 464, 97 S.Ct. 2376, 53 L.Ed.2d 484 (1977), *30, 31, 32, 35, 163*

Maine v. Thiboutot, 448 U.S. 1, 100 S.Ct. 2502, 65 L.Ed.2d 555 (1980), *264, 264*

Marsh v. Alabama, 326 U.S. 501, 66 S.Ct. 276, 90 L.Ed. 265 (1946), *187, 188, 189, 190, 192*

Marshall v. United States, 414 U.S. 417, 94 S.Ct. 700, 38 L.Ed.2d 618 (1974), *168*

Marston v. Lewis, 410 U.S. 679, 93 S.Ct. 1211, 35 L.Ed.2d 627 (1973), *149*

Martinez v. Bynum, 461 U.S. 321, 103 S.Ct. 1838, 75 L.Ed.2d 879 (1983), *170*

Mason v. Garris, 360 F.Supp. 420 (N.D.Ga.1973), modified info 364 F.Supp. 452 (N.D.Ga.1973), *47*

Massachusetts Bd. of Retirement v. Murgia, 427 U.S. 307, 96 S.Ct. 2562, 49 L.Ed.2d 520 (1976), *63, 133, 134, 176*

Mathews v. Diaz, 426 U.S. 67, 96 S.Ct. 1883, 48 L.Ed.2d 478 (1976), *137*

Mathews v. Eldridge, 424 U.S. 319, 96 S.Ct. 893, 47 L.Ed.2d 18 (1976), *58, 59, 60*

Mathews v. Lucas, 427 U.S. 495, 96 S.Ct. 2755, 49 L.Ed.2d 651 (1976), *140*

Mayer v. City of Chicago, 404 U.S. 189, 92 S.Ct. 410, 30 L.Ed.2d 372 (1971), *159*

Mayor of Philadelphia v. Educational Equality League, 415 U.S. 605, 94 S.Ct. 1323, 39 L.Ed.2d 630 (1974), *66*

McCarthy v. Philadelphia Civil Service Commission, 424 U.S. 645, 96 S.Ct. 1154, 47 L.Ed.2d 366 (1976), *156*

McCulloch v. State, 17 U.S. 316, 4 L.Ed. 579 (1819), *214*

McDonald v. Board of Election, 394 U.S. 802, 89 S.Ct. 1404, 22 L.Ed.2d 739 (1969), *132, 171*

McDonald v. Santa Fe Trail Transp. Co., 427 U.S. 273, 96 S.Ct. 2574, 49 L.Ed.2d 493 (1976), *102, 230*

TABLE OF CASES

McDonnell Douglas Corp. v. Green, 411 U.S. 792, 93 S.Ct. 1817, 36 L.Ed.2d 668 (1973), *235*

McGinnis v. Royster, 410 U.S. 263, 93 S.Ct. 1055, 35 L.Ed.2d 282 (1973), *175*

McGlotten v. Connally, 338 F.Supp. 448 (D.D.C.1972), *202*

McGowan v. State of Md., 366 U.S. 420, 81 S.Ct. 1101, 6 L.Ed.2d 393 (1961), *171, 172*

McKane v. Durston, 153 U.S. 684, 14 S.Ct. 913, 38 L.Ed. 867 (1894), *161*

McLaughlin v. Florida, 379 U.S. 184, 85 S.Ct. 283, 13 L.Ed.2d 222 (1964), *65*

McLaurin v. Brusturis, 320 F.Supp. 190 (E.D.Wis.1970), *248*

McLaurin v. Oklahoma State Regents for Higher Ed., 339 U.S. 637, 70 S.Ct. 851, 94 L.Ed. 1149 (1950), *71*

Meachum v. Fano, 427 U.S. 215, 96 S.Ct. 2532, 49 L.Ed.2d 451 (1976), *42, 43*

Meltzer v. Buck LeCraw, 402 U.S. 936, 402 U.S. 937, 402 U.S. 939, 402 U.S. 941, 402 U.S. 954, 402 U.S. 964, 402 U.S. 966, 91 S.Ct. 1624, 29 L.Ed.2d 107, 29 L.Ed.2d 109 (1971), *162*

Memorial Hospital v. Maricopa County, 415 U.S. 250, 94 S.Ct. 1076, 39 L.Ed.2d 306 (1974), *156, 157, 158*

Memphis, City of v. Greene, 451 U.S. 100, 101 S.Ct. 1584, 67 L.Ed.2d 769 (1981), *225*

Memphis Light, Gas and Water Division v. Craft, 436 U.S. 1, 98 S.Ct. 1554, 56 L.Ed.2d 30 (1978), *59*

Meritor Sav. Bank, FSB v. Vinson, 477 U.S. 57, 106 S.Ct. 2399, 91 L.Ed.2d 49 (1986), *230*

Metro Broadcasting, Inc. v. F.C.C., 497 U.S. 547, 110 S.Ct. 2997, 111 L.Ed.2d 445 (1990), *109*

Meyer v. Nebraska, 262 U.S. 390, 43 S.Ct. 625, 67 L.Ed. 1042 (1923), *41*

Michael H. v. Gerald D., 491 U.S. 110, 109 S.Ct. 2333, 105 L.Ed.2d 91 (1989), *25*

Michael M. v. Sonoma County Superior Court, 450 U.S. 464, 101 S.Ct. 1200, 67 L.Ed.2d 437 (1981), *118, 119, 122*

Middlesex County Sewerage Authority v. National Sea Clammers Ass'n, 453 U.S. 1, 101 S.Ct. 2615, 69 L.Ed.2d 435 (1981), *263*

Migra v. Board of Educ., 465 U.S. 75, 104 S.Ct. 892, 79 L.Ed.2d 56 (1984), *267*

Miller v. Johnson, 515 U.S. 900, 115 S.Ct. 2475, 132 L.Ed.2d 762 (1995), *110*

TABLE OF CASES

Milliken v. Bradley, 433 U.S. 267, 97 S.Ct. 2749, 53 L.Ed.2d 745 (1977), *92*

Milliken v. Bradley, 418 U.S. 717, 94 S.Ct. 3112, 41 L.Ed.2d 1069 (1974), *90, 92*

Mills v. Habluetzel, 456 U.S. 91, 102 S.Ct. 1549, 71 L.Ed.2d 770 (1982), *143*

Minneapolis & St. L.R. Co. v. Bombolis, 241 U.S. 211, 36 S.Ct. 595, 60 L.Ed. 961 (1916), *5*

Minnesota v. Clover Leaf Creamery Co., 449 U.S. 456, 101 S.Ct. 715, 66 L.Ed.2d 659 (1981), *177*

Mississippi University for Women v. Hogan, 458 U.S. 718, 102 S.Ct. 3331, 73 L.Ed.2d 1090 (1982), *126, 217*

Missouri v. Jenkins, 515 U.S. 70, 115 S.Ct. 2038, 132 L.Ed.2d 63 (1995), *92*

Missouri ex rel. Gaines v. Canada, 305 U.S. 337, 59 S.Ct. 232, 83 L.Ed. 208 (1938), *71, 104*

Mitchell v. Forsyth, 472 U.S. 511, 105 S.Ct. 2806, 86 L.Ed.2d 411 (1985), *258*

Mitchell v. W. T. Grant Co., 416 U.S. 600, 94 S.Ct. 1895, 40 L.Ed.2d 406 (1974), *47, 48, 49, 50, 51, 59*

Mobile v. Bolden, 446 U.S. 55, 100 S.Ct. 1490, 64 L.Ed.2d 47 (1980), *68*

Monell v. Department of Social Services of City of New York, 436 U.S. 658, 98 S.Ct. 2018, 56 L.Ed.2d 611 (1978), *253, 258, 259*

Monroe v. Pape, 365 U.S. 167, 81 S.Ct. 473, 5 L.Ed.2d 492 (1961), *245, 252, 253, 258, 263*

Moore v. East Cleveland, Ohio, 431 U.S. 494, 97 S.Ct. 1932, 52 L.Ed.2d 531 (1977), *21*

Moose Lodge No. 107 v. Irvis, 407 U.S. 163, 92 S.Ct. 1965, 32 L.Ed.2d 627 (1972), *185, 197, 198, 199, 206, 207, 208, 210*

Morris v. Cizek, 503 F.2d 1303 (7th Cir.1974), *248*

Morrison, State v., 25 N.J.Super. 534, 96 A.2d 723 (N.J.Co.1953), *24*

Morrissey v. Brewer, 408 U.S. 471, 92 S.Ct. 2593, 33 L.Ed.2d 484 (1972), *57*

Morton v. Mancari, 417 U.S. 535, 94 S.Ct. 2474, 41 L.Ed.2d 290 (1974), *131*

Muller v. Oregon, 208 U.S. 412, 28 S.Ct. 324, 52 L.Ed. 551 (1908), *8*

Munro v. Socialist Workers Party, 479 U.S. 189, 107 S.Ct. 533, 93 L.Ed.2d 499 (1986), *151*

TABLE OF CASES

N

National Collegiate Athletic Ass'n v. Tarkanian, 488 U.S. 179, 109 S.Ct. 454, 102 L.Ed.2d 469 (1988), *206*

Nebbia v. New York, 291 U.S. 502, 54 S.Ct. 505, 78 L.Ed. 940 (1934), *9*

New Jersey Welfare Rights Organization v. Cahill, 411 U.S. 619, 93 S.Ct. 1700, 36 L.Ed.2d 543 (1973), *140*

Newman v. Piggie Park Enterprises, Inc., 390 U.S. 400, 88 S.Ct. 964, 19 L.Ed.2d 1263 (1968), *268*

Newport, City of v. Fact Concerts, Inc., 453 U.S. 247, 101 S.Ct. 2748, 69 L.Ed.2d 616 (1981), *261*

Newton, Town of v. Rumery, 480 U.S. 386, 107 S.Ct. 1187, 94 L.Ed.2d 405 (1987), *267*

New York City Transit Authority v. Beazer, 440 U.S. 568, 99 S.Ct. 1355, 59 L.Ed.2d 587 (1979), *172*

Nixon v. Condon, 286 U.S. 73, 52 S.Ct. 484, 76 L.Ed. 984 (1932), *190*

Nixon v. Fitzgerald, 457 U.S. 731, 102 S.Ct. 2690, 73 L.Ed.2d 349 (1982), *256*

Nixon v. Herndon, 273 U.S. 536, 47 S.Ct. 446, 71 L.Ed. 759 (1927), *186*

Nordlinger v. Hahn, 505 U.S. 1, 112 S.Ct. 2326, 120 L.Ed.2d 1 (1992), *177*

Norris v. Alabama, 294 U.S. 587, 55 S.Ct. 579, 79 L.Ed. 1074 (1935), *97*

North Dakota State Bd. v. Snyder's Drug Stores, Inc., 414 U.S. 156, 94 S.Ct. 407, 38 L.Ed.2d 379 (1973), *9*

North Georgia Finishing, Inc. v. Di–Chem, Inc., 419 U.S. 601, 95 S.Ct. 719, 42 L.Ed.2d 751 (1975), *47, 48, 49, 50, 205*

Norwood v. Harrison, 413 U.S. 455, 93 S.Ct. 2804, 37 L.Ed.2d 723 (1973), *77, 201*

Nyquist v. Mauclet, 432 U.S. 1, 97 S.Ct. 2120, 53 L.Ed.2d 63 (1977), *137*

O

O'Brien v. Skinner, 414 U.S. 524, 94 S.Ct. 740, 38 L.Ed.2d 702 (1974), *150*

Occidental Life Ins. Co. of California v. E.E.O.C., 432 U.S. 355, 97 S.Ct. 2447, 53 L.Ed.2d 402 (1977), *240*

TABLE OF CASES

Oregon v. Mitchell, 400 U.S. 112, 91 S.Ct. 260, 27 L.Ed.2d 272 (1970), *213, 215, 219*

Orr v. Orr, 440 U.S. 268, 99 S.Ct. 1102, 59 L.Ed.2d 306 (1979), *127*

Ortwein v. Schwab, 410 U.S. 656, 93 S.Ct. 1172, 35 L.Ed.2d 572 (1973), *163*

Owen v. City of Independence, Mo., 445 U.S. 622, 100 S.Ct. 1398, 63 L.Ed.2d 673 (1980), *261*

Owens v. Okure, 488 U.S. 235, 109 S.Ct. 573, 102 L.Ed.2d 594 (1989), *264*

P

Palko v. Connecticut, 302 U.S. 319, 58 S.Ct. 149, 82 L.Ed. 288 (1937), *3, 4*

Palmer v. Thompson, 403 U.S. 217, 91 S.Ct. 1940, 29 L.Ed.2d 438 (1971), *77*

Palmore v. Sidoti, 466 U.S. 429, 104 S.Ct. 1879, 80 L.Ed.2d 421 (1984), *66*

Paradise, United States v., 480 U.S. 149, 107 S.Ct. 1053, 94 L.Ed.2d 203 (1987), *106, 110*

Parham v. Hughes, 441 U.S. 347, 99 S.Ct. 1742, 60 L.Ed.2d 269 (1979), *128*

Parham v. J. R., 442 U.S. 584, 99 S.Ct. 2493, 61 L.Ed.2d 101 (1979), *53*

Pasadena City Bd. of Ed. v. Spangler, 427 U.S. 424, 96 S.Ct. 2697, 49 L.Ed.2d 599 (1976), *94*

Patsy v. Board of Regents of State of Fla., 457 U.S. 496, 102 S.Ct. 2557, 73 L.Ed.2d 172 (1982), *253*

Patterson v. McLean Credit Union, 491 U.S. 164, 109 S.Ct. 2363, 105 L.Ed.2d 132 (1989), *246*

Paul v. Davis, 424 U.S. 693, 96 S.Ct. 1155, 47 L.Ed.2d 405 (1976), *41, 51, 52, 53, 263*

Pembaur v. City of Cincinnati, 475 U.S. 469, 106 S.Ct. 1292, 89 L.Ed.2d 452 (1986), *259*

Pennhurst State School and Hospital v. Halderman, 451 U.S. 1, 101 S.Ct. 1531, 67 L.Ed.2d 694 (1981), *215, 263*

Perez v. United States, 402 U.S. 146, 91 S.Ct. 1357, 28 L.Ed.2d 686 (1971), *223*

Perkins v. Matthews, 400 U.S. 379, 91 S.Ct. 431, 27 L.Ed.2d 476 (1971), *228*

TABLE OF CASES

- Perry v. Sindermann, 408 U.S. 593, 92 S.Ct. 2694, 33 L.Ed.2d 570 (1972), *54, 55*
- Peterson v. City of Greenville, 373 U.S. 244, 83 S.Ct. 1119, 10 L.Ed.2d 323 (1963), *195, 200, 201*
- Philadelphia, City of v. Pennsylvania Human Relations Commission, 7 Pa.Cmwlth. 500, 300 A.2d 97 (Pa.Cmwlth.1973), *235*
- Phillips v. Martin Marietta Corp., 400 U.S. 542, 91 S.Ct. 496, 27 L.Ed.2d 613 (1971), *230, 231, 233*
- Phoenix, City of v. Kolodziejski, 399 U.S. 204, 90 S.Ct. 1990, 26 L.Ed.2d 523 (1970), *149*
- Pickett v. Brown, 462 U.S. 1, 103 S.Ct. 2199, 76 L.Ed.2d 372 (1983), *143*
- Pierce v. Society of the Sisters, 268 U.S. 510, 45 S.Ct. 571, 69 L.Ed. 1070 (1925), *31, 32, 192*
- Pierson v. Ray, 386 U.S. 547, 87 S.Ct. 1213, 18 L.Ed.2d 288 (1967), *254, 255*
- Planned Parenthood of Central Missouri v. Danforth, 428 U.S. 52, 96 S.Ct. 2831, 49 L.Ed.2d 788 (1976), *29, 30*
- Planned Parenthood of Southeastern Pennsylvania v. Casey, 505 U.S. 833, 112 S.Ct. 2791, 120 L.Ed.2d 674 (1992), *36, 37, 38, 39*
- Plessy v. Ferguson, 163 U.S. 537, 16 S.Ct. 1138, 41 L.Ed. 256 (1896), *70, 71, 72, 74*
- Plyler v. Doe, 457 U.S. 202, 102 S.Ct. 2382, 72 L.Ed.2d 786 (1982), *169, 170*
- Poelker v. Doe, 432 U.S. 519, 97 S.Ct. 2391, 53 L.Ed.2d 528 (1977), *31*
- Polk County v. Dodson, 454 U.S. 312, 102 S.Ct. 445, 70 L.Ed.2d 509 (1981), *203*
- Preiser v. Rodriguez, 411 U.S. 475, 93 S.Ct. 1827, 36 L.Ed.2d 439 (1973), *266*
- Price, United States v., 383 U.S. 787, 86 S.Ct. 1152, 16 L.Ed.2d 267 (1966), *245*
- Public Utilities Commission of District of Columbia v. Pollak, 343 U.S. 451, 72 S.Ct. 813, 96 L.Ed. 1068 (1952), *207*
- Pulliam v. Allen, 466 U.S. 522, 104 S.Ct. 1970, 80 L.Ed.2d 565 (1984), *256, 269*

R

- Railway Exp. Agency v. People of State of N.Y., 336 U.S. 106, 69 S.Ct. 463, 93 L.Ed. 533 (1949), *171*

TABLE OF CASES

Reed v. Reed, 404 U.S. 71, 92 S.Ct. 251, 30 L.Ed.2d 225 (1971), *114, 116, 127*

Regents of University of California v. Bakke, 438 U.S. 265, 98 S.Ct. 2733, 57 L.Ed.2d 750 (1978), *102, 104*

Regents of University of Michigan v. Ewing, 474 U.S. 214, 106 S.Ct. 507, 88 L.Ed.2d 523 (1985), *57*

Reitman v. Mulkey, 387 U.S. 369, 87 S.Ct. 1627, 18 L.Ed.2d 830 (1967), *199, 200, 205, 249*

Rendell–Baker v. Kohn, 457 U.S. 830, 102 S.Ct. 2764, 73 L.Ed.2d 418 (1982), *193, 203*

Rex v. _____ (see opposing party)

Reynolds v. Sims, 377 U.S. 533, 84 S.Ct. 1362, 12 L.Ed.2d 506 (1964), *177, 178, 179, 181, 183*

Rhodes v. Stewart, 488 U.S. 1, 109 S.Ct. 202, 102 L.Ed.2d 1 (1988), *270*

Richardson v. Belcher, 404 U.S. 78, 92 S.Ct. 254, 30 L.Ed.2d 231 (1971), *40, 165*

Richardson v. Ramirez, 418 U.S. 24, 94 S.Ct. 2655, 41 L.Ed.2d 551, 72 O.O.2d 232 (1974), *150*

Richmond, City of v. Croson Co., 488 U.S. 469, 109 S.Ct. 706, 102 L.Ed.2d 854 (1989), *106, 108*

Riverside, City of v. Rivera, 477 U.S. 561, 106 S.Ct. 2686, 91 L.Ed.2d 466 (1986), *254, 270*

Robel, United States v., 389 U.S. 258, 88 S.Ct. 419, 19 L.Ed.2d 508 (1967), *12*

Roberts v. LaVallee, 389 U.S. 40, 88 S.Ct. 194, 19 L.Ed.2d 41 (1967), *160*

Robertson v. Wegmann, 436 U.S. 584, 98 S.Ct. 1991, 56 L.Ed.2d 554 (1978), *265*

Roe v. Wade, 410 U.S. 113, 93 S.Ct. 705, 35 L.Ed.2d 147 (1973), *15, 16, 17, 19, 20, 21, 22, 23, 24, 25, 30, 34, 36, 37, 38*

Rogers v. Lodge, 458 U.S. 613, 102 S.Ct. 3272, 73 L.Ed.2d 1012 (1982), *68*

Rome, City of v. United States, 446 U.S. 156, 100 S.Ct. 1548, 64 L.Ed.2d 119 (1980), *214*

Romer v. Evans, ___ U.S. ___, 116 S.Ct. 1620, 134 L.Ed.2d 855 (1996), *174*

Rosario v. Rockefeller, 410 U.S. 752, 93 S.Ct. 1245, 36 L.Ed.2d 1 (1973), *151, 152*

Rosenfeld v. Southern Pac. Co., 444 F.2d 1219 (9th Cir.1971), *234*

TABLE OF CASES

Ross v. Moffitt, 417 U.S. 600, 94 S.Ct. 2437, 41 L.Ed.2d 341 (1974), *161*

Rostker v. Goldberg, 453 U.S. 57, 101 S.Ct. 2646, 69 L.Ed.2d 478 (1981), *119, 120, 122*

Runyon v. McCrary, 427 U.S. 160, 96 S.Ct. 2586, 49 L.Ed.2d 415 (1976), *247, 249*

S

Sailors v. Board of Ed. of Kent County, 387 U.S. 105, 87 S.Ct. 1549, 18 L.Ed.2d 650 (1967), *179*

Salyer Land Co. v. Tulare Lake Basin Water Storage Dist., 410 U.S. 719, 93 S.Ct. 1224, 35 L.Ed.2d 659 (1973), *149, 179*

San Antonio Independent School Dist. v. Rodriguez, 411 U.S. 1, 93 S.Ct. 1278, 36 L.Ed.2d 16 (1973), *133, 161, 167, 168, 170, 171*

San Francisco Arts & Athletics, Inc. v. United States Olympic Committee, 483 U.S. 522, 107 S.Ct. 2971, 97 L.Ed.2d 427 (1987), *209*

Santosky v. Kramer, 455 U.S. 745, 102 S.Ct. 1388, 71 L.Ed.2d 599 (1982), *59*

Scheuer v. Rhodes, 416 U.S. 232, 94 S.Ct. 1683, 40 L.Ed.2d 90 (1974), *254, 255*

Schlesinger v. Ballard, 419 U.S. 498, 95 S.Ct. 572, 42 L.Ed.2d 610 (1975), *124*

School Dist. of Abington v. Schempp, 374 U.S. 203, 83 S.Ct. 1560, 10 L.Ed.2d 844 (1963), *15, 192*

Screws v. United States, 325 U.S. 91, 65 S.Ct. 1031, 89 L.Ed. 1495 (1945), *245*

Seminole Tribe of Florida v. Florida, 517 U.S. 609, 116 S.Ct. 1114, 134 L.Ed.2d 252 (1996), *262*

Serfass v. United States, 420 U.S. 377, 95 S.Ct. 1055, 43 L.Ed.2d 265 (1975), *6*

Shapiro v. Thompson, 394 U.S. 618, 89 S.Ct. 1322, 22 L.Ed.2d 600 (1969), *155, 157, 158, 164, 167*

Shaw v. Hunt, ___ U.S. ___, 116 S.Ct. 1894, 135 L.Ed.2d 207 (1996), *110*

Shaw v. Reno, 509 U.S. 630, 113 S.Ct. 2816, 125 L.Ed.2d 511 (1993), *110*

Shelley v. Kraemer, 334 U.S. 1, 68 S.Ct. 836, 92 L.Ed. 1161 (1948), *194, 195, 196, 197, 198*

TABLE OF CASES

- Simmons v. Eagle Seelatsee, 244 F.Supp. 808 (E.D.Wash.1965), aff'd info Simmons v. Chief Eagle Seelatsee, 384 U.S. 209, 86 S.Ct. 1469, 16 L.Ed.2d 480 (1966), *131*
- Skinner v. Oklahoma, 316 U.S. 535, 62 S.Ct. 1110, 86 L.Ed. 1655 (1942), *145, 167*
- Slaughter–House, 83 U.S. 36, 21 L.Ed. 394 (1872), *1, 2, 3*
- Smith v. Allwright, 321 U.S. 649, 64 S.Ct. 757, 88 L.Ed. 987 (1944), *186, 187*
- Smith v. Bennett, 365 U.S. 708, 81 S.Ct. 895, 6 L.Ed.2d 39 (1961), *160*
- Smith v. Organization of Foster Families For Equality and Reform, 431 U.S. 816, 97 S.Ct. 2094, 53 L.Ed.2d 14 (1977), *59*
- Smith v. Wade, 461 U.S. 30, 103 S.Ct. 1625, 75 L.Ed.2d 632 (1983), *253*
- Sniadach v. Family Finance Corp., 395 U.S. 337, 89 S.Ct. 1820, 23 L.Ed.2d 349 (1969), *46, 47, 49, 205*
- Sosna v. Iowa, 419 U.S. 393, 95 S.Ct. 553, 42 L.Ed.2d 532 (1975), *157, 158*
- South Carolina v. Katzenbach, 383 U.S. 301, 86 S.Ct. 803, 15 L.Ed.2d 769 (1966), *212, 213, 215, 216, 221*
- Southeastern Promotions, Ltd. v. Conrad, 420 U.S. 546, 95 S.Ct. 1239, 43 L.Ed.2d 448 (1975), *32*
- Speiser v. Randall, 357 U.S. 513, 78 S.Ct. 1332, 2 L.Ed.2d 1460 (1958), *32*
- Spencer v. Kugler, 404 U.S. 1027, 92 S.Ct. 707, 30 L.Ed.2d 723 (1972), *94*
- Sprogis v. United Air Lines, Inc., 444 F.2d 1194 (7th Cir.1971), *231*
- Stanley v. Illinois, 405 U.S. 645, 92 S.Ct. 1208, 31 L.Ed.2d 551 (1972), *61, 63*
- Stanton v. Stanton, 429 U.S. 501, 97 S.Ct. 717, 50 L.Ed.2d 723 (1977), *116*
- Stanton v. Stanton, 421 U.S. 7, 95 S.Ct. 1373, 43 L.Ed.2d 688 (1975), *116*
- Starns v. Malkerson, 401 U.S. 985, 91 S.Ct. 1231, 28 L.Ed.2d 527 (1971), *158*

State v. _____ (see opposing party)

State of (see name of state)

- St. Louis, City of v. Praprotnik, 485 U.S. 112, 108 S.Ct. 915, 99 L.Ed.2d 107 (1988), *260*
- St. Mary's Honor Center v. Hicks, 509 U.S. 502, 113 S.Ct. 2742, 125 L.Ed.2d 407 (1993), *236*

TABLE OF CASES

Stone v. Powell, 428 U.S. 465, 96 S.Ct. 3037, 49 L.Ed.2d 1067 (1976), *266*

Storer v. Brown, 415 U.S. 724, 94 S.Ct. 1274, 39 L.Ed.2d 714 (1974), *151*

Strauder v. West Virginia, 100 U.S. 303, 10 Otto 303, 25 L.Ed. 664 (1879), *65, 70, 132*

Suffling v. Bondurant, 339 F.Supp. 257 (D.N.M.1972), *158*

Sugar v. Curtis Circulation Co., 383 F.Supp. 643 (S.D.N.Y.1974), *51*

Sugarman v. Dougall, 413 U.S. 634, 93 S.Ct. 2842, 37 L.Ed.2d 853 (1973), *136*

Sullivan v. Little Hunting Park, Inc., 396 U.S. 229, 90 S.Ct. 400, 24 L.Ed.2d 386 (1969), *224*

Supreme Court of Virginia v. Consumers Union of United States, Inc., 446 U.S. 719, 100 S.Ct. 1967, 64 L.Ed.2d 641 (1980), *256, 269*

Swann v. Charlotte–Mecklenburg Bd. of Ed., 402 U.S. 1, 91 S.Ct. 1267, 28 L.Ed.2d 554 (1971), *78, 79, 80, 81, 82, 83, 84, 85, 90, 93, 95, 96, 98, 99, 100*

Sweatt v. Painter, 339 U.S. 629, 70 S.Ct. 848, 94 L.Ed. 1114 (1950), *71*

T

Takahashi v. Fish and Game Commission, 334 U.S. 410, 68 S.Ct. 1138, 92 L.Ed. 1478 (1948), *135*

Tancil v. Woolls, 379 U.S. 19, 85 S.Ct. 157, 13 L.Ed.2d 91 (1964), *98*

Tashjian v. Republican Party of Connecticut, 479 U.S. 208, 107 S.Ct. 544, 93 L.Ed.2d 514 (1986), *153*

Tate v. Short, 401 U.S. 395, 91 S.Ct. 668, 28 L.Ed.2d 130 (1971), *160, 161*

Taylor v. Louisiana, 419 U.S. 522, 95 S.Ct. 692, 42 L.Ed.2d 690 (1975), *114*

Tenney v. Brandhove, 341 U.S. 367, 71 S.Ct. 783, 95 L.Ed. 1019 (1951), *254*

Terrace v. Thompson, 263 U.S. 197, 44 S.Ct. 15, 68 L.Ed. 255 (1923), *135*

Terry v. Adams, 345 U.S. 461, 73 S.Ct. 809, 97 L.Ed. 1152 (1953), *187*

TABLE OF CASES

Texas Dept. of Community Affairs v. Burdine, 450 U.S. 248, 101 S.Ct. 1089, 67 L.Ed.2d 207 (1981), *236*

Texas State Teachers Ass'n v. Garland Independent School Dist., 489 U.S. 782, 109 S.Ct. 1486, 103 L.Ed.2d 866 (1989), *270*

Thompson v. School Bd. of City of Newport, 465 F.2d 83 (4th Cir.1972), *81*

Thornburg v. Gingles, 478 U.S. 30, 106 S.Ct. 2752, 92 L.Ed.2d 25 (1986), *215*

Thornburgh v. American College of Obstetricians and Gynecologists, 476 U.S. 747, 106 S.Ct. 2169, 90 L.Ed.2d 779 (1986), *33, 34, 37*

Town of (see name of town)

Trans World Airlines, Inc. v. Hardison, 432 U.S. 63, 97 S.Ct. 2264, 53 L.Ed.2d 113 (1977), *244*

Trimble v. Gordon, 430 U.S. 762, 97 S.Ct. 1459, 52 L.Ed.2d 31 (1977), *142, 143*

Truax v. Corrigan, 257 U.S. 312, 42 S.Ct. 124, 66 L.Ed. 254 (1921), *9*

Twining v. New Jersey, 211 U.S. 78, 29 S.Ct. 14, 53 L.Ed. 97 (1908), *2*

U

United Air Lines, Inc. v. Evans, 431 U.S. 553, 97 S.Ct. 1885, 52 L.Ed.2d 571 (1977), *238*

United Broth. of Carpenters and Joiners v. Scott, 463 U.S. 825, 103 S.Ct. 3352, 77 L.Ed.2d 1049 (1983), *251*

United Jewish Organizations of Williamsburgh, Inc. v. Carey, 430 U.S. 144, 97 S.Ct. 996, 51 L.Ed.2d 229 (1977), *100, 182*

United States v. _____ (see opposing party)

United States Dept. of Agriculture v. Moreno, 413 U.S. 528, 93 S.Ct. 2821, 37 L.Ed.2d 782 (1973), *172*

United States Dept. of Agriculture v. Murry, 413 U.S. 508, 93 S.Ct. 2832, 37 L.Ed.2d 767 (1973), *61, 63*

United States R.R. Retirement Bd. v. Fritz, 449 U.S. 166, 101 S.Ct. 453, 66 L.Ed.2d 368 (1980), *176*

United Steelworkers of America v. Weber, 443 U.S. 193, 99 S.Ct. 2721, 61 L.Ed.2d 480 (1979), *106*

TABLE OF CASES

V

Vacco v. Quill, ___ U.S. ___, 117 S.Ct. 2293, 138 L.Ed.2d 834 (1997), *28*

Vance v. Bradley, 440 U.S. 93, 99 S.Ct. 939, 59 L.Ed.2d 171 (1979), *133*

Village of (see name of village)

Virginia, United States v., ___ U.S. ___, 116 S.Ct. 2264, 135 L.Ed.2d 735 (1996), *120*

Vitek v. Jones, 445 U.S. 480, 100 S.Ct. 1254, 63 L.Ed.2d 552 (1980), *53*

Vlandis v. Kline, 412 U.S. 441, 93 S.Ct. 2230, 37 L.Ed.2d 63 (1973), *59, 61*

W

Wards Cove Packing Co., Inc. v. Atonio, 490 U.S. 642, 109 S.Ct. 2115, 104 L.Ed.2d 733 (1989), *242*

Washington v. Davis, 426 U.S. 229, 96 S.Ct. 2040, 48 L.Ed.2d 597 (1976), *67, 94*

Washington v. Glucksberg, ___ U.S. ___, 117 S.Ct. 2258, 138 L.Ed.2d 772 (1997), *26, 27, 28*

Washington v. Seattle School Dist. No. 1, 458 U.S. 457, 102 S.Ct. 3187, 73 L.Ed.2d 896 (1982), *88*

Washington, County of v. Gunther, 452 U.S. 161, 101 S.Ct. 2242, 68 L.Ed.2d 751 (1981), *230*

Weber v. Aetna Cas. & Sur. Co., 406 U.S. 164, 92 S.Ct. 1400, 31 L.Ed.2d 768 (1972), *139*

Webster v. Reproductive Health Services, 492 U.S. 490, 109 S.Ct. 3040, 106 L.Ed.2d 410 (1989), *34, 35, 36*

Weeks v. Southern Bell Tel. & Tel. Co., 408 F.2d 228 (5th Cir.1969), *234*

Weinberger v. Salfi, 422 U.S. 749, 95 S.Ct. 2457, 45 L.Ed.2d 522 (1975), *62, 63*

Weinberger v. Wiesenfeld, 420 U.S. 636, 95 S.Ct. 1225, 43 L.Ed.2d 514 (1975), *123, 125*

Wells v. Edwards, 409 U.S. 1095, 93 S.Ct. 904, 34 L.Ed.2d 679 (1973), *179*

Wengler v. Druggists Mut. Ins. Co., 446 U.S. 142, 100 S.Ct. 1540, 64 L.Ed.2d 107 (1980), *126*

TABLE OF CASES

Wesberry v. Sanders, 376 U.S. 1, 84 S.Ct. 526, 11 L.Ed.2d 481 (1964), *180*

West Coast Hotel Co. v. Parrish, 300 U.S. 379, 57 S.Ct. 578, 81 L.Ed. 703 (1937), *9*

West Peachtree Tenth Corp., United States v., 437 F.2d 221 (5th Cir.1971), *226*

Whalen v. Roe, 429 U.S. 589, 97 S.Ct. 869, 51 L.Ed.2d 64 (1977), *21*

Whitcomb v. Chavis, 403 U.S. 124, 91 S.Ct. 1858, 29 L.Ed.2d 363 (1971), *182*

White v. Regester, 412 U.S. 755, 93 S.Ct. 2332, 37 L.Ed.2d 314 (1973), *180, 181, 182*

White v. Weiser, 412 U.S. 783, 93 S.Ct. 2348, 37 L.Ed.2d 335 (1973), *180*

Wickard v. Filburn, 317 U.S. 111, 63 S.Ct. 82, 87 L.Ed. 122 (1942), *223*

Will v. Michigan Dept. of State Police, 491 U.S. 58, 109 S.Ct. 2304, 105 L.Ed.2d 45 (1989), *261*

Williams v. Illinois, 399 U.S. 235, 90 S.Ct. 2018, 26 L.Ed.2d 586, 52 O.O.2d 281 (1970), *160*

Williams v. Rhodes, 393 U.S. 23, 89 S.Ct. 5, 21 L.Ed.2d 24, 45 O.O.2d 236 (1968), *151*

Williams v. Standard Oil Co., 278 U.S. 235, 49 S.Ct. 115, 73 L.Ed. 287 (1929), *8*

Williams, United States v., 341 U.S. 70, 71 S.Ct. 581, 95 L.Ed. 758 (1951), *245*

Williamson v. Lee Optical, 348 U.S. 483, 75 S.Ct. 461, 99 L.Ed. 563 (1955), *10*

Willingham v. Macon Tel. Pub. Co., 507 F.2d 1084 (5th Cir.1975), *231, 232*

Willner v. Committee on Character and Fitness, 373 U.S. 96, 83 S.Ct. 1175, 10 L.Ed.2d 224 (1963), *44*

Wilson v. Garcia, 471 U.S. 261, 105 S.Ct. 1938, 85 L.Ed.2d 254 (1985), *264*

Wisconsin v. Constantineau, 400 U.S. 433, 91 S.Ct. 507, 27 L.Ed.2d 515 (1971), *51, 52*

Wood v. Strickland, 420 U.S. 308, 95 S.Ct. 992, 43 L.Ed.2d 214 (1975), *257*

Wright v. Emporia, 407 U.S. 451, 92 S.Ct. 2196, 33 L.Ed.2d 51 (1972), *77*

Wygant v. Jackson Bd. of Educ., 476 U.S. 267, 106 S.Ct. 1842, 90 L.Ed.2d 260 (1986), *105, 107*

TABLE OF CASES

Y

Yick Wo v. Hopkins, 118 U.S. 356, 6 S.Ct. 1064, 30 L.Ed. 220 (1886), *66*

Youngberg v. Romeo, 457 U.S. 307, 102 S.Ct. 2452, 73 L.Ed.2d 28 (1982), *53*

Z

Zablocki v. Redhail, 434 U.S. 374, 98 S.Ct. 673, 54 L.Ed.2d 618 (1978), *25, 168*

Zemel v. Rusk, 381 U.S. 1, 85 S.Ct. 1271, 14 L.Ed.2d 179 (1965), *155*

Zinermon v. Burch, 494 U.S. 113, 110 S.Ct. 975, 108 L.Ed.2d 100 (1990), *263*

Zobel v. Williams, 457 U.S. 55, 102 S.Ct. 2309, 72 L.Ed.2d 672 (1982), *158*

Zuch v. Hussey, 366 F.Supp. 553 (E.D.Mich.1973), *226*

CONSTITUTIONAL CIVIL RIGHTS
IN A NUTSHELL
THIRD EDITION

*

CHAPTER I

INTRODUCTION

The Supreme Court decided at an early date that the fifth amendment restriction on the taking of private property, and by implication the other restrictions in the Bill of Rights, applied only to the federal government. *Barron v. Baltimore* (S.Ct. 1833). However, the fourteenth amendment prohibits the states from abridging "the privileges or immunities of citizens of the United States," from depriving any person of life, liberty or property without due process, and from denying any person the equal protection of the laws. These provisions can receive content from the Bill of Rights and thereby extend its coverage to the states.

§ 1. THE PRIVILEGES OR IMMUNITIES CLAUSE

Although it has been urged that the privileges or immunities clause was the most logical vehicle for enforcing the Bill of Rights against the states, that clause was drained of much of its effectiveness by the ruling in the *Slaughter–House Cases* (S.Ct. 1873). It was there held that only privileges and immunities of national, not state, citizenship were protected by this provision. Privileges of national citizenship include "the right to pass freely" among the states, to petition Congress, to vote for national offices, to enter public lands, to be physically protected while in the custody of a federal marshall, and "to inform the United States authorities of violation of its laws." *Twining v. New Jersey* (S.Ct. 1908). However, most civil rights were deemed to be incidents of state citizenship and hence not within the reach of the privileges clause.

The narrow interpretation in the *Slaughter–House Cases* was clearly intended to promote interests of federalism by preventing a radical transference of power from the states to the federal government, which the majority believed would be implicit in a contrary result. A broad interpretation of privileges or immunities, it was thought, "would constitute this court a perpetual censor upon [state] legislation" and would "bring within the power of Congress [to enforce the amendment] the entire domain of civil rights heretofore belonging exclusively to the states." The due process and equal protection clauses were less imposing, the opinion implied, because the former would apply only to procedural matters and the latter would reach only racial discrimination.

If due process and equal protection had been confined to the meaning which *Slaughter–House* prophesied, the fourteenth amendment's impact on federalism would have been attenuated. But these provisions have been construed far more generously than the Court foresaw. As a result, many of the apprehended consequences for federal-state relations have come to pass, albeit not under the rubric of the privileges or immunities clause. It may in fact be, as some writers have suggested, that the privileges clause failed because other provisions succeeded in accomplishing what might have been its objectives. At any rate, the *Slaughter–House* view of privileges and immunities has prevailed, but the overriding concern for principles of federalism ultimately gave way to pressures for enforcing the Bill of Rights against the states.

§ 2. THE APPLICATION OF THE BILL OF RIGHTS TO THE STATES

The modern day debate over the applicability of the Bill of Rights to the states was initiated by *Palko v. Conn.* (S.Ct.1937) and *Adamson v. Calif.* (S.Ct.1947). In *Palko* the Court announced that the fourteenth amendment absorbs only those provisions of the Bill of Rights which are "implicit in the concept of ordered liberty" and without which "a fair and enlightened system of justice would be impossible." Dissenting from that position in the *Adamson* case, Mr. Justice Black argued that the fourteenth amendment was intended to incorporate the Bill of Rights in its entirety and thereby avoid the subjective judgments required under *Palko*. Mr. Justice Frankfurter, defending *Palko*, replied that total incorporation was both overinclusive and underinclusive in relation to fundamental fairness: the Bill of Rights protects some relatively insignificant matters, such as the right to jury trials in suits for more than $20, and fails to protect other interests of high importance. In Frankfurter's view the fourteenth amendment did not embrace all of the guarantees of the first eight amendments and was not limited to those guarantees. His analysis had both the virtues and deficiencies of great flexibility; it maximized the opportunity for reaching optimum results in a particular case but provided little control over the misuse of judicial power. (See § 3.) A final view, expressed in dissent in *Adamson,* would combine elements of the Black and Frankfurter positions by incorporating the first eight amendments plus those unenumerated freedoms which are essential to individual liberty. (Murphy and Rutledge, JJ., dissenting.)

Ironically, neither *Palko* nor the *Adamson* dissents represent the current approach to the Bill of Rights. Instead the Court, by its actions if not always its words, has adopted a process of selective incorporation. Under that approach, those portions of the Bill of Rights which are "fundamental to the American scheme of justice" bind the states through the fourteenth amendment. *Duncan v. La.* (S.Ct.1968). The issue is not, as *Palko* stated, whether "a civilized system could be imagined" without a particular provision but whether the provision "is necessary to an *Anglo–American* regime of ordered liberty." Applying selective incorporation, the Court has held the states to be bound by the first, fourth and sixth amendments, as well as by the eighth amendment's prohibition against cruel and unusual punishment, and the fifth amendment's privilege against self-incrimination and protections against double jeopardy and the expropriation of private property. See *Benton v. Md.* (1969), *Duncan v. La.,* and cases cited therein. The seventh amendment and the requirement of a grand jury indictment have been held inapplicable to the states, *Minneapolis & St. Louis R. Co. v. Bombolis* (S.Ct.1916), *Hurtado v. Calif.* (S.Ct.1884), while the applicability of other amendments has yet to be determined.

Even after a given provision is held to apply to the states, a question remains as to whether the same standards used to enforce the provision in federal cases should also control state cases. The Court has answered that question affirmatively, refusing to inquire into whether particular aspects of a federal rule are essential to ordered liberty, *Benton v. Md.,* although occasionally an individual Justice of a different persuasion has cast a decisive vote because other members of the Court were evenly divided on their interpretation of the Bill of Rights. See *Apodaca v. Oregon* (S.Ct.1972) (nonunanimous jury verdicts permitted in state but apparently not in federal cases, despite the rejection by 8 Justices of the concept of dual standards). Thus, under the majority approach, a determination that jeopardy attaches at a given moment in a federal case would seem to mean that it also attaches at that moment in a state case for purposes of enforcing the double jeopardy clause, even though it may not be a matter of fundamental significance whether jeopardy begins when a jury is empaneled or when the first witness is sworn. Indeed this matter almost certainly is not fundamental, for one rule applies in federal bench trials and the other in federal jury trials. *Serfass v. U.S.* (S.Ct.1975). The argument for applying the same standards to state and federal cases is that a contrary approach would involve "impermissible subjective judgments," lack of predictability and increased friction between the state and federal judicial systems. Yet the theory of selective incorporation accepts, not altogether consistently, the subjectivity which is implicit in a case-by-case determination of which portions of the Bill of Rights are applicable to the states. In any event, the Bill of Rights is now to a very large extent binding upon state governments and the next question—to be addressed in the following chapter—is whether substantive freedoms not enumerated in the first eight amendments may also be protected by the due process clause.

CHAPTER II

SUBSTANTIVE DUE PROCESS

§ 3. THE CONSTITUTIONALIZATION OF "NATURAL RIGHTS"

From Lochner to Ferguson. The notion that all persons "are endowed by their Creator" with certain rights which are immune from government interference has deep roots in American and European history. But it is hardly surprising in a country with a written Constitution that there would be insistent demands for a Bill of Rights and that a natural law philosophy for protecting other interests would have to find some constitutional base if it was to be secure. During the late nineteenth century, the due process clause was pressed into service for the purpose of establishing substantive rights not specifically enumerated in the Constitution. At first the doctrine of substantive due process was largely confined to a few state courts. See *In re Jacobs* (1885). In the Supreme Court the doctrine was resisted until about 1890, except for a casual dictum by Chief Justice Taney in the infamous *Dred Scott Case* (S.Ct.1857). However, pressure for judicial intervention persisted among influential members of the bar who had formed, as one writer put it, "a sort of juristic sewing circle for mutual education in the gospel of *laissez faire*." Eventually the Court capitulated and ushered in the era of *Lochner v. New York* (S.Ct.1905) by holding that a statute which limited the working hours of employees in a bakery violated the due process clause.

Under the *Lochner* regime, courts freely substituted their judgments for those of the legislature on a wide variety of subjects. Labor laws were held to impair the liberty of contract, taxes were invalidated, and rates established by public utility agencies were struck down as confiscatory. The results were not always destructive of regulatory authority, "but this only emphasized the fact that the Court, and not the legislature, became the final judge of what might be law." R. Jackson, The Struggle For Judicial Supremacy, 70 (1941). Women's working hours could be regulated, *Muller v. Ore* (S.Ct.1908), but their rates of pay could not. *Adkins v. Children's Hosp.* (S.Ct.1923). Men had a constitutional right to work for more than 10 hours a day in a bakery, *Lochner v. N.Y.*, but they could be prohibited from working more than 8 hours in a coal mine. *Holden v. Hardy* (1898). Prices might or might not be regulated, depending on whether courts believed the matter was "affected with a public interest." Fire insurance companies and tobacco warehouses apparently met this "test," e.g. *German Alliance Ins. Co. v. Lewis* (S.Ct.1914), but gasoline distributors and employment agencies did not. E.g. *Williams v. Standard Oil Co.* (S.Ct.1929). In the field of labor-management relations the government could not protect employees against being discharged for joining a union, *Adair v. U.S.* (S.Ct.

1908), and could not refuse to protect employers against picketing or boycotts by employees. *Truax v. Corrigan* (S.Ct.1921).

This untenable line of decisions came to a precipitate halt during the New Deal years. In one field after another—labor law, price control, taxation—the law turned 180 degrees. E.g. *West Coast Hotel Co. v. Parrish* (S.Ct.1937) (minimum wage law upheld); *Nebbia v. N.Y.* (S.Ct.1934) (regulation of milk prices sustained). The doctrine of substantive due process, which had once threatened vast areas of social and economic legislation, became a "last resort of constitutional arguments." The controlling rule was that legislation which neither intruded upon the Bill of Rights nor restricted the political processes was to be upheld unless under all reasonably conceivable facts the law was "of such a character as to preclude the assumption that it rests upon some rational basis." *U.S. v. Carolene Products Co.* (S.Ct.1938). Applying that standard the Court sustained, for example, (a) state right-to-work statutes, (b) the regulation of advertising vehicles, and (c) laws limiting the debt-adjusting business to lawyers and the operation of corporate pharmacies to firms having majority shares owned by pharmacists. See *North Dakota State Board v. Snyder's Drug Stores* (S.Ct.1973) and cases cited therein. In each of these instances arguments could easily be mounted against the wisdom of the legislation. It was enough, however, that the issue was a debatable one. In fact, some opinions went even further, implying that the Court would not review such regulation at all. *Ferguson v. Skrupa* (S.Ct. 1963); *Williamson v. Lee Optical Co.* (S.Ct.1955). But in either event, economic and social legislation became virtually immune from attack on substantive due process grounds.

Defects of Lochner. It is important in assessing the doctrine of substantive due process to consider the factors which brought *Lochner* into disrepute. The problem was not merely the inconsistency of result in the Court's actions; this indeed seems only symptomatic of the real difficulty. The root problem was the absence of adequate standards for determining which of the values not explicitly safeguarded by the constitutional text are nevertheless entitled to *special* protection under the fourteenth amendment. It is one thing to apply a general requirement of reasonableness to cases resting solely on the due process clause and to provide heightened protection for specifically guaranteed freedoms, such as religious liberty or free speech; it is quite another matter to give special solicitude to some values which have no constitutional roots, while denying it to others. Strict scrutiny is relatively easy to justify in cases implicating the Bill of Rights, given the express mandate of the first eight amendments. Furthermore, the language and history of the amendments provide useful guidance for avoiding the excesses of *Lochner* though, to be sure, it is difficult enough to fix the proper scope of those amendments. But if certain unenumerated liberties are to receive special constitutional protection while others are not, some basis must be found for determining which freedoms are entitled to such protection and which are entrusted to the fortunes of the political processes. It was this challenge which the *Lochner* Court never met and which persists even today.

§ 4. "ALTERNATIVES" TO SUBSTANTIVE DUE PROCESS

The Penumbra of the Bill of Rights. In 1965, after substantive due process had been in repose for more than a quarter of a century, *Griswold v. Conn.* (S.Ct.1965) held that a criminal prohibition against the use of devices by married couples for the purpose of preventing contraception violated the constitutionally protected right of privacy. The Court insisted that its decision did not rest independently on the due process clause but was based on implications in the Bill of Rights, which were made applicable to the states through the fourteenth amendment. The underlying theory was that the first eight amendments contain peripheral as well as explicit guarantees, and that zones of privacy can be found in the "penumbras" of the first, third, fourth, fifth, and ninth amendments. Since these guarantees—including the right of married persons to practice contraception—were discovered in the constitutional text, the Court believed it was not, as in *Lochner,* acting as a super-legislature to determine the wisdom of laws in the social and economic field.

The immediate question raised by *Griswold* was whether the peripheral rights theory is significantly different from substantive due process. Providing fourteenth amendment protection for specific freedoms in the Bill of Rights can easily be distinguished from what was done in *Lochner*. But if those freedoms are read so expansively as to protect whatever five Justices deem to be "fundamental," the approach may simply achieve in two steps what *Lochner* accomplished in one. Thus commentators noted that the contract clause and the fifth amendment ban on taking property without compensation could be construed under the penumbra approach as conferring an implied right to enter contracts and to enjoy the use of property free from inappropriate government interference. Plainly, such a loose construction of the specific guarantees of the Constitution would make the penumbra theory a functional equivalent of *Lochner* and would yield largely the same results. On the other hand, there is ample precedent for giving constitutional shelter to unenumerated liberties which are implicit in the Bill of Rights. Freedom of association, for instance, is protected by the first amendment, even though it finds no mention in the text. *U.S. v. Robel* (S.Ct. 1967). And so the question reduces itself to whether *Griswold's* reading of the Bill of Rights was so extravagant as to resurrect the doctrine of substantive due process in disguise.

In any event, the invalidation of Connecticut's contraception statute did not require the heavy-handed judicial intervention in legislative policy-making which was characteristic of the *Lochner* era. Given the widespread availability of contraceptives in the state and the lawfulness of their possession and sale for some purposes, it is doubtful that the anti-use ban could reasonably promote the asserted government purpose of discouraging illicit sexual relations; people who would otherwise ignore the prohibitions against adultery and fornication were hardly likely to be inhibited by the additional prohibition on use, which was conceded to be almost totally unenforceable. In short, this "uncommonly silly law" could be struck down without imposing an extraordinary burden of justification on the political processes because there was no convincing evidence that the law—or its invalidation—would have any appreciable impact on the level of illicit sexual activity which was Connecticut's purported concern.

The Ninth Amendment. More than any other provision in the Constitution, the ninth amendment seems to invite judicial acceptance of the notion of natural law. It states that "The enumeration in the Constitution, of certain rights, shall not be construed to deny or disparage others retained by people." But the amendment is silent on the crucial question of which unenumerated liberties are retained by the people or how courts can go about making that determination. Reliance on the ninth amendment as a source of substantive rights therefore involves the same problem of lack of standards as *Lochner,* and it has been said that "on analysis they turn out to be the same thing." *Griswold v. Conn.* (Black, J., dissenting). Moreover, it is not at all clear that the ninth amendment was intended to safeguard individual freedoms rather than "states' rights." There is substantial evidence that the amendment grew out of the fear that, without it, the denial of certain federal powers in the Bill of Rights might be misunderstood to imply the delegation of other powers to the national government. This construction of the ninth amendment, as importing principles of federalism rather than of personal liberty, is buttressed by the fact that, unlike various safeguards for individual rights, the amendment has no parallel in the state constitutions. Finally, even if individuals were its intended beneficiaries, the amendment may have been designed only to facilitate the finding of implied guarantees—such as freedom of association—in the first eight amendments, rather than to generate new guarantees independent of those amendments.

A somewhat more modest interpretation of the ninth amendment views it, not as a source of substantive rights, but as a guide to the meaning of the fourteenth amendment. Thus Mr. Justice Goldberg argued in *Griswold* that "the Ninth Amendment simply lends strong support to the view that the 'liberty' protected by the ... Fourteenth Amendment ... is not restricted to rights specifically mentioned in the first eight amendments." This suggestion, however, merely returns one to the question of substantive due process and raises the same issues. Furthermore, if the ninth amendment was intended to safeguard states' rights, it seems ironic that the amendment should be employed "to broaden the powers of [the Supreme] Court or [of] any other department of 'the general government.'" *Griswold v. Conn.* (Black, J., dissenting). Admittedly such a "somersault of history" would not be unprecedented, as the establishment clause of the first amendment shows; the latter clause was evidently intended to prevent federal interference with state establishments of religion, and yet it now has the opposite effect of prohibiting such establishments. Nevertheless, it may be easier to justify the transmutation of the establishment clause, since all state establishments of religion had been dissolved long before the fourteenth amendment was ratified, and so the framers of that amendment were arguably not concerned with protecting official churches. *School Dist. v. Schempp* (S.Ct.1963) (Brennan, J., concurring). Perhaps they also were wholly unconcerned with principles of federalism, but this at least is a more difficult proposition to substantiate.

§ 5. THE NEW SUBSTANTIVE DUE PROCESS

Roe v. Wade. The penumbra theory was designed to avoid any necessity for reviving the doctrine of substantive due process. Reliance on the ninth amendment on the other hand was intended, not to avoid, but to justify a revival of that doctrine. In *Roe v. Wade* (S.Ct.1973), the Court faced similar options upon a challenge to an anti-abortion statute and based its decision squarely on due process. It ruled that the right of privacy "founded in the Fourteenth Amendment's concept of personal liberty ... is broad enough to encompass a woman's decision whether or not to terminate her pregnancy." Noting that "abortion laws are of relatively recent vintage" and that they impose serious detriment on pregnant women, the Court announced that only a *compelling* interest "in maintaining medical standards and protecting potential life" could justify government regulation. This meant that beginning at the end of the first trimester the state could regulate abortion in the interest of maternal health, and that beginning with the viability of the fetus—the point at which an unborn child is "potentially able to live outside the mother's womb, albeit with artificial aid"—abortions could be prohibited in order to protect potential life, provided the mother's health would not be endangered. A compelling interest standard also meant that first trimester abortions could neither be proscribed nor confined to accredited hospitals and made subject to approval by special committee. *Doe v. Bolton* (S.Ct. 1973).

The choice of viability as the constitutionally permissible point for protecting the unborn is at the heart of the abortion decisions and has been sharply criticized. E.g. Ely, The Wages of Crying Wolf: A Comment on Roe v. Wade, 72 Yale L.J. 920 (1973). It is difficult to see how either the woman's interests or those of the fetus significantly change at viability. The fact, stressed by the Court, that the fetus can survive outside the womb would be relevant if premature birth were the alternative to abortion. But what *Roe* seems to contemplate by authorizing certain prohibitions against abortion is that some women will be compelled to carry their fetuses for many weeks. If this compulsion is justified in the interest of permitting a viable fetus to develop into an infant, it is unclear why a similar compulsion could not be justified to permit an embryo to develop into, first, a viable fetus and, then, an infant. Conversely, if the interest in potential life warrants no interference with a woman's desire to terminate her pregnancy before viability, it is not apparent why that interest should prevail after viability. In the present state of medical science the rule in *Roe* allows pregnant women considerable time to seek an abortion, but the development of new life-support systems could render fetuses viable—and abortions constitutionally unprotected—at a much earlier point in the pregnancy.

A broader question arising from the abortion cases is whether the new substantive due process is meaningfully different from the discredited regime of *Lochner v. New York*. The argument usually advanced for renewed judicial intervention relies on the distinction between personal and economic liberties. But this argument assumes that the defect of *Lochner* was in the values it protected. If, as suggested above, a major deficiency was in the standard of judicial review, it is important to consider whether *Roe* has cured that deficiency.

The Distinction Between Personal and Economic Freedoms. Some courts and commentators have urged an active judicial role in cases of "personal" liberties, notwithstanding the lessons of *Lochner,* which they deem to be applicable only to economic liberties. The argument for distinguishing between personal and economic rights has rested on (1) the "greater importance" of personal freedoms to the individual, (2) the greater impact of these freedoms on the processes of government (3) the lack of judicial expertise in economic matters and (4) the lack of time available to the Supreme Court for supervising economic controversies in addition to discharging its other duties.

Whether any of these points can adequately distinguish *Lochner* is open to serious question. No doubt, personal freedoms are frequently more important than economic ones. But that surely is not universally true. The freedom to practice one's profession—whether it be law, carpentry or baking pastries—would probably rank as high in a national scheme of values as the "personal" right to attend private academies or to march in a parade. And occupational restraints may substantially affect the opportunity and capacity for self-government. Such restraints often deny access to professional associations which are importantly involved in the political process; more generally, it is difficult without economic resources to exercise political or other personal rights in an effective way. Nor is it self-evident that judicial capabilities would be more severely strained by economic matters than by school segregation, political gerrymandering or the intricacies of fetal development. One can argue, as Learned Hand did, that the limits of judicial competence require a general deference to the legislative branches, but it is hard to insist that economic cases are so inherently complex that courts must reject them while nevertheless accepting complicated litigation from a variety of other fields. Of course these cases will add to the burden of the

Court's work, but so too does any other area of legal dispute. Since the Supreme Court continues regularly to assume new tasks, as well as to resume old ones, time pressures cannot, without more, justify the exclusion of economic controversies.

Perhaps for these reasons, the Court seems to have despaired of the tenuous distinction between economic and personal freedoms, finding that "the dichotomy between personal liberties and property rights is a false one" and that such a distinction would be almost impossible to apply. *Lynch v. Household Fin. Corp.* (S.Ct.1972). The Court argued that "The right to enjoy property without unlawful deprivation, no less than the right to speak or the right to travel, is, in truth, a 'personal' right.... In fact, a fundamental interdependence exists between the personal right to liberty and the personal right to property. Neither could have meaning without the other." Many commentators have agreed with that position, differing among themselves only on whether it implies a more active judicial role in economic cases or a more modest one than has been taken in non-economic cases.

The Standard of Review in Lochner and Roe. Despite some stylistic differences between the opinions in *Roe* and *Lochner,* the two cases employed essentially the same test of constitutionality. *Lochner,* it is true, purported to apply a rationality test, while *Roe* candidly asserted a power to invalidate reasonable regulations which lack compelling justification. But the extent of actual judicial control over legislative policymaking was basically the same in each case. What *Lochner* did in fact was little different from what *Roe* said and did, so far as the constitutional standard was concerned.

The requirement of compelling justification has been called "strict in theory and fatal in fact." Gunther, Forward, 86 Harv.L.Rev. 1, 8 (1972). By contrast, a demand merely for rationality leaves the legislative branches a wide range of choices in formulating state or national policy. Yet, as recent cases demonstrate, such a demand need not be enforced so loosely as to eliminate meaningful judicial oversight. See Gunther; § 34, infra. A reasonableness test is also consistent with precedent since the Court, in repudiating *Lochner,* did not formally abandon the requirement of rationality, but simply applied it so tolerantly that for many years few pieces of legislation failed to pass muster. In short, the Court rejected *Lochner's* misapplication of the rule of reasonableness, not the rule itself. The question then raised by *Roe* was when government action would require a compelling, rather than only a rational, justification.

§ 6. SCOPE OF THE NEW DUE PROCESS

The volatile history of substantive due process cautions against issuing any elaborate formula for measuring the law's reach in this area. Although one can speculate as to which freedoms might be given special protection in the near future, an analysis of the long term must await the disposition of claims which will be brought to test the elasticity of the new due process. Cf. *Moore v. City of East Cleveland* (S.Ct.1977) (zoning ordinance which precluded a homeowner from residing with the offspring of more than one of her children found to be arbitrary and unreasonable, but four Justices urged that the ordinance was entitled to less than "the usual judicial deference").

It is clear, however, that the potential reach of the new substantive due process would be vast if the rationale of the *Roe* opinion were given its full breadth. The Court's argument was essentially that (1) the constitutional right of privacy "has some extension" to activities relating to marriage, procreation and family relationships, (2) anti-abortion laws impose a detriment on pregnant women and (3) the right of privacy is therefore spacious enough to encompass a woman's decision to terminate her pregnancy. Without pausing to examine the glaring non sequitur in the suggestion that a right of abortion can be inferred from the fact that *some* burdens on family relationships are unconstitutional, it is apparent that the force of the Court's argument could reach into many other areas of private life in which the law places a substantial detriment on family autonomy. In two of these areas—the regulation of homosexual acts and infringements on the "right to die"—the Court has begun to address the scope of the new due process. See also *Whalen v. Roe* (S.Ct.1977) (upholding a requirement that the state be furnished with copies of all prescriptions of certain drugs for retention in a centralized computer file); *Kelley v. Johnson* (S.Ct.1976) (employing a rationality test to reject a due process attack on a regulation of the length of policemen's hair).

Consensual Homosexuality. *Bowers v. Hardwick* (S.Ct.1986) illustrates the problem with the new substantive due process. That case arose out of the arrest of Michael Hardwick for engaging in an oral homosexual act in the bedroom of his home in violation of a Georgia statute prohibiting oral and anal sex between any two persons. After the district attorney decided not to continue the prosecution in the absence of additional evidence, Hardwick filed suit seeking a declaratory judgment that the statute was unconstitutional. On review, the Supreme Court ruled that as applied to homosexual conduct the Georgia statute did not violate the constitutional right of privacy. In so ruling, the *Hardwick* case clearly repudiated the basic reasoning of *Roe v. Wade*. The *Roe* Court had relied on historical and prudential arguments to invalidate state controls on abortion. *Hardwick* paid lip service to historical arguments and ignored prudential ones.

The *Hardwick* opinion stated that "sodomy was a criminal offense at common law" and that "proscriptions against that conduct have ancient roots." The Court thereby sought to distinguish the historical analysis in *Roe v. Wade,* which had struck down broad proscriptions on abortion after noting that "abortion laws are of relatively recent vintage." However, the common law controls on homosexual conduct encompassed considerably less than the

Hardwick opinion implies. In *Rex v. Jacobs* (Eng. 1817), one of the earliest reported cases on sodomy, the court specifically held that the criminal prohibition against sodomy did not apply to oral sex. The holding of the *Jacobs* case was widely accepted, and as a result it was said that there is "almost complete accord" among commentators that "at common law commission of the crime [against nature] required penetration per anum and that penetration per os did not constitute the offense." *State v. Morrison* (N.J.1953). Since the *Hardwick* case arose out of an incident of oral sex, the Court's insistence upon focusing on the Georgia statute *as applied* should have led to a recognition that "proscriptions against that conduct" do not have the "ancient roots" claimed by Justice White. Indeed, it is hard to resist the conclusion that criminal sanctions against oral sex, like the sanction in *Roe v. Wade,* "are of relatively recent vintage."

The *Hardwick* opinion also rejected the policy reasons articulated in *Roe v. Wade.* In *Roe,* the Court relied not only on historical considerations but even more emphatically on the substantial "detriment that the [abortion law] would impose upon the pregnant woman" and on the limited interests of the state during early stages of pregnancy. The *Hardwick* case plainly rejected this focus on detriment and utilitarian state interests, finding it sufficient that Georgia's sodomy law, as applied, rests on "majority sentiments about the morality of homosexuality...." Yet the state interest in preserving majoritarian moral values, which was recognized in

Hardwick, had also been implicated in *Roe v. Wade.* The moral values expressed in the two cases— abhorrence of homosexual sodomy in one and of abortion in the other—are not identical, but the Court has suggested no reason why anti-abortion values are less deserving of government expression than anti-sodomy values. Moreover, *Roe v. Wade* involved important state interests in protecting potential life and maternal health, which had no counterpart in the *Hardwick* case. Given comparable moral values and the larger utilitarian interests present in the abortion cases, it seems implausible to suggest that Georgia put forward a stronger claim for regulation than had been advanced in *Roe v. Wade.*

Of course, it is more difficult to compare the detriment imposed in the two cases, since the activities regulated by abortion and sodomy laws are totally different. It seems clear, however, that the burden imposed by the Georgia statute, if fully enforced, would be very substantial. For a person who is exclusively homosexual rather than bisexual, compliance with Georgia law would mean a continuing abstinence from sexual intercourse. If such abstinence were tolerable—even in less extreme form—for heterosexuals, there would be few occasions for abortion except in cases of rape. Perhaps those who doubt that the burden of complying with sodomy laws is comparable to that imposed by abortion laws should ask themselves how many individuals would elect to have abortions if the inevitable result of the abortion procedure were to make sexual intercourse impossible in the future. Not surprisingly, the Court made no suggestion in *Hardwick* that the burden of complying with sodomy laws is less substantial than the burden imposed by abortion laws.

The conflict between *Hardwick* and *Roe* points up the difficulty which has inhered in the philosophy of *Lochner v. New York* from the very beginning. The values of the judges have changed: the old struggle to measure the scope of the liberty of contract has given way to a search for the compelling point in the life of a fetus. But the crucial problem of devising standards for determining which unenumerated freedoms are entitled to special protection remains as intractable as ever. Neither history nor personal detriment can explain why abortion is entitled to such protection, but consensual homosexuality is not. And there is little reason to believe that the problem of inadequate standards, which continues to resist solution after 85 years of judicial effort, will be overcome in the foreseeable future. Compare *Zablocki v. Redhail*, (S.Ct.1978) (giving "critical examination" to a "significant" restriction on the right to marry) with *Michael H. v. Gerald D.* (S.Ct.1989) (finding no liberty interest in the relationship of a natural father to a child whose mother was married to and cohabiting with another man at the time of the child's conception and birth) (plurality opinion). Unfortunately, in the absence of adequate standards or a return to a general requirement of rationality for unenumerated freedoms (see Gunther; § 34, infra), substantive due process may remain as unprincipled as it was during the season of *Lochner v. New York.*

The "Right to Die". In *Cruzan v. Director, Missouri Dept. of Health* (S.Ct.1990), the Court addressed the question whether a person in a persistent·vegetative state has a constitutional right to have food and hydration equipment withdrawn upon request of her parents. State law required Cruzan's parents to establish by "clear and convincing evidence" their daughter's wish to terminate artificial feeding, and the issue in the Supreme Court was whether that evidentiary requirement was unconstitutional. The Court assumed without deciding that competent adults have "a constitutionally protected liberty interest in refusing lifesaving hydration and nutrition." Nevertheless, Missouri's elevated standard of proof was held to be constitutionally valid because of the state's legitimate interests in preserving life, protecting personal choice, and preventing abuse of discretion by surrogate decisionmakers: "An erroneous decision to withdraw life-sustaining treatment [would not be] susceptible of correction."

A few years later, *Washington v. Glucksberg* (S.Ct.1997) brought the issue of physician-assisted suicide before the Supreme Court. In that case, a state law made it a felony for physicians or others knowingly to cause or aid a suicide. A federal court of appeals, sitting *en banc*, held that the ban on assisted suicide was unconstitutional "as applied to terminally ill competent adults who wish to hasten their deaths with medication prescribed by their physicians." On review, the Supreme Court rejected a due process challenge, finding that the statute was not unconstitutional on its face or as applied. All nine Justices agreed with that result, although only five of them embraced the majority opinion written by Chief Justice Rehnquist. The Court attempted to limit heightened scrutiny under the due process clause to matters deeply rooted in history and tradition, and *Cruzan* was distinguished on the ground that the assumed right to reject lifesaving food and hydration was based on a "long tradition protecting the decision to refuse unwanted medical treatment." Although a determination to commit suicide might "be just as personal and profound as the decision to refuse unwanted medical treatment, it has never enjoyed similar legal protection." Thus, it was not simply the personal or important nature of an activity that was thought to trigger heightened scrutiny, but rather the historical practice of according it legal protection. Because of the "consistent and almost universal tradition that has long rejected the asserted right" to assisted suicide, the Court rejected any heightened level of scrutiny and proceeded to apply a rationality test.

The *Glucksberg* Court found that a number of legitimate state interests were served by the ban on assisted suicide. Included among these were the state's interests in (1) preserving human life, (2) protecting the integrity of the medical profession, (3) shielding vulnerable groups like the elderly and disabled from abuse, prejudice or neglect, and (4) avoiding a gradual slide "down the path to voluntary and perhaps even involuntary euthanasia."

The Court said that a ban on assisted suicide was reasonably related to the promotion of those interests and hence was constitutionally valid. These same interests were deemed sufficient, in a companion case, to withstand a challenge based on the equal protection clause. See *Vacco v. Quill* (S.Ct. 1997) (upholding a New York law which permitted the removal of life-sustaining equipment, but prohibited assisted suicide).

The decision in *Washington v. Glucksberg* clearly rejected any generalized constitutional right of assisted suicide. However, it was not necessary to decide "whether suffering patients have a constitutionally cognizable interest in obtaining relief from [suffering] in the last days of their lives," since state law permitted doctors to prescribe such relief even if it hastened a patient's death. (O'Connor, J., concurring.) Moreover, the Court's ruling does not prevent the states from creating a statutory right to assisted suicide. *Glucksberg*, like other post-*Roe* cases, rejected a heightened standard of scrutiny, but it permits the legislative debate to go forward. As Justice O'Connor stated in her concurring opinion, "There is no reason to think the democratic process will not strike the proper balance between the interests of terminally ill, mentally competent individuals who would seek to end their suffering and the State's interests in protecting those who might seek to end life mistakenly or under pressure."

§ 7. POST-ROE RESTRICTIONS ON ABORTION

Even if the new substantive due process is ultimately held to modest proportions, it does not necessarily follow that *Roe* will be narrowly applied in cases of abortion or procreation. Cf. *Carey v. Population Services Int'l* (S.Ct.1977) (invalidating, for lack of any compelling justification, a statutory ban on the sale of contraceptives by anyone other than a licensed pharmacist or the sale to an individual under 16 years of age). After 1973 many states adopted measures which (a) required spousal or parental consent for abortion, (b) prohibited nontherapeutic abortions in public hospitals and barred the use of government revenues to pay for them or (c) imposed informational requirements on abortion procedures. Recent statutes have also mandated medical tests, designed to protect viable fetuses, and attempted to require spousal notification before abortion.

Consent. Requirements of spousal consent and of parental approval for abortions performed on minors under the age of 18 were reviewed in *Planned Parenthood of Missouri v. Danforth* (S.Ct. 1976). Both requirements were set aside for conferring arbitrary veto power, though the Court left open the possibility that a minor might be denied an abortion unless a judge found that she had the capacity to give informed consent or that the abortion would serve her best interests. See *Bellotti v. Baird* (S.Ct.1979) (if a state generally requires a minor to secure parental consent, "it also must provide an alternative procedure whereby authorization for the abortion can be obtained" when the minor is sufficiently mature and informed or shows that an abortion would be in her best interest) (plurality opinion). A court hearing for minors could protect the rights which *Roe* bestowed upon adults, while also responding to the fact that children who range in age from 12 to 17 cannot be presumed to have the maturity needed to make a reasoned decision in this matter. But an ex parte proceeding cannot assure the representation of all interested parties, and a bilateral proceeding could deprive minors of freedom of choice.

Requirements of spousal consent posed a difficult problem since they introduced third party interests which *Roe* did not consider. But in light of the importance which *Roe* attached to the right to terminate a pregnancy, it was difficult to find a legal basis for enforcing a husband's desire to have a child over a woman's desire not to have one. However, the states might still be free to insist that a husband be given notice of a pregnancy in order to enable him to "participate in the decision whether his wife should have an abortion." *Planned Parenthood.* And recent decisions recognizing government power to favor childbirth over abortion (see pp. 30–31) may cause the question of paternal rights to be revisited.

Public Funding. The Court's treatment of provisions denying medicaid payments for nontherapeutic abortions is harder to explain than its disposition of consent requirements. *Maher v. Roe* (S.Ct. 1977) held that states may single out nontherapeutic abortions for exclusion from the pregnancy coverage of a government-financed health care program even though benefits would be paid under the program when pregnancies were carried to term. The opinion distinguished between "direct state interference with protected activity and state encouragement of an alternative activity," and it reasoned that the state had created no obstacle to abortion. An analogy was drawn to *Pierce v. Society of Sisters* (S.Ct.1925) which protected the right to attend private schools but did not guarantee public funding of those schools. The Court then invoked the same arguments to sustain a prohibition against nontherapeutic abortions in city hospitals. *Poelker v. Doe,* (S.Ct.1977). See also *Harris v. McRae* (S.Ct.1980), upholding the Hyde Amendment, which prohibited the use of federal funds to reimburse the costs of abortion under the Medicaid program except where the mother's life was endangered or either rape or incest was involved.

The principal thrust of the *Maher* opinion was that the case involved no *state-created* restriction on abortion since the government had not caused the plaintiffs' economic distress. However, one need not embrace the theory that states are obliged to supply medical services (see § 33) in order to take exception to a policy under which such services are provided selectively on the basis of how constitutional rights are exercised. *Maher* distinguished between "direct interference" with abortion and "encouragement of an alternative," but there is less than meets the eye in the distinction between imposing a burden and withholding a benefit. The fact that a state has no duty to establish a university, for example, does not mean that it can withhold from dissident groups the benefit of using campus facilities. *Healy v. James* (S.Ct.1972). There is, after all, a difference between refusing to provide government service to anyone—which might be justified on fiscal grounds—and refusing to provide it to those who exercise their constitutional liberties in a way the state disapproves. The *Maher* case placed great emphasis on the acknowledged power of government to confine its support of education to the public schools. But what was at stake in *Maher* was not a decision to restrict taxpayer funds to public institutions, with abortion and childbirth treated alike; it was a decision to exclude from state assistance certain constitutionally protected activity which is in official disfavor, while financing alternative activity that the state approves. Arguably a more apt analogy than *Pierce* would be found in a state policy to support all schools except those that advocate abandonment of a system of free enterprise. The Court has often rebuffed attempts to condition government benefits upon the manner in which constitutional rights are exercised, though the case law is not entirely uniform. E.g. *Southeastern Promotions Ltd. v. Conrad* (S.Ct.1975) (use of a municipal theater); *Speiser v. Randall* (S.Ct. 1958) (entitlement to a tax exemption). Perhaps in the end the *Maher* decision will be viewed as an expedient political compromise, given the intensity of opposition to the use of taxpayer funds for abortions. But it is not a decision that inspires confidence in the new substantive due process.

Informational Requirements. In *Akron v. Akron Center For Reproductive Health* (S.Ct.1983), the Court struck down local regulations that required an attending physician to inform a patient of the development of her fetus, the date of possible viability, the physical and emotional complications that might result from abortion and the names of agencies that could give assistance or information about birth control, adoption and childbirth. The Court acknowledged the government's interest in protecting maternal health and said a regulation would be upheld when reasonably designed to further that interest. But "regulations designed to influence the woman's informed choice between abortion and childbirth" were thought to be unjustified, and the provisions before the Court were found to place unreasonable " 'obstacles in the path of the doctor upon whom [the woman is] entitled to rely for advice....' "

The Court addressed informational requirements again in *Thornburgh v. American College of Obstetricians and Gynecologists* (S.Ct.1986). Pennsylvania had enacted a statute which required women seeking an abortion to be given certain information, including: (1) a description of the medical risks associated with the abortion procedure and with carrying the pregnancy to term, (2) the "fact that there may be detrimental physical and psychological effects which are not accurately foreseeable," and (3) the fact that medical benefits and child support payments might be available to her. The Court struck down the statute, stating that the mandated information seemed to be "nothing less than an outright attempt to wedge the Commonwealth's message discouraging abortion into the privacy of the informed-consent dialogue between the woman and her physician." The Court said the requirement that women be told the possible detrimental effects of abortion, which was not imposed for other medical procedures, was "the antithesis of informed consent" and revealed "the anti-abortion character of the statute and its real purpose."

Neither *Akron* nor *Thornburgh* explained why the mandatory disclosure of accurate and generally relevant information would not serve legitimate functions of informed consent. And if the function of informed consent was served, it is not clear why the legislature's anti-abortion motives, even assuming a court's capacity to discern such motives, should invalidate the statute. No doubt, the disclosure of information might cause a patient to reconsider her decision; that is the very purpose of an informed consent requirement. But even if the legislature seeks to discourage abortion, it is not apparent why this should be impermissible when discouragement takes the form of an informed consent requirement, though not impermissible when it takes the form of denying public funds for abortion. Perhaps predictably, the Court reconsidered the issue of informed consent a few years later. See pg. 37 infra.

Webster and Casey. In *Webster v. Reproductive Health Services* (S.Ct.1989), the Supreme Court was invited to reassess the *Roe* decision and permit the states to protect potential human life. The Court found it unnecessary "to revisit the holding of *Roe*," but its opinion appeared to signal an acceptance of a greater degree of government regulation of abortion than earlier cases had allowed.

The *Webster* case involved a Missouri statute which provided in part that a physician, intending to perform an abortion on any woman whom he had reason to believe was at least 20 weeks pregnant, must first ascertain whether the fetus was viable by performing "such medical examinations and tests as are necessary to make a finding of [the fetus'] gestational age, weight, and lung maturity." The statute also prohibited the use of public employees and facilities to perform or assist abortions not necessary to save the life of the mother. Although the latter prohibition applied to all facilities and equipment owned or leased by the state, as well as to all state employees, the Court upheld the restriction, relying on *Maher v. Roe* and its progeny. The Court also upheld the viability-testing provision, which a three-member plurality read to create a "presumption of viability at 20 weeks, which the physician must rebut with [appropriate] tests indicating that the fetus is not viable prior to performing an abortion." This regulation of the method for determining viability seemed to conflict with the ruling in *Colautti v. Franklin* (S.Ct.1979) that the determination of viability "'must be a matter for the judgment of the responsible attending physician.'" The regulation was nevertheless upheld because, in the plurality's view, it was "reasonably designed to ensure that abortions are not performed where the fetus is viable."

The *Webster* case suggested that the states would have some significant power to enforce regulations designed for the protection of potential life, although the parameters of that power were not clear. In *Planned Parenthood v. Casey* (S.Ct.1992), the Court revisited the subject of abortion restrictions but again left the limits of state power uncertain. *Casey* addressed the validity of several provisions of a Pennsylvania statute regulating abortion before viability. The statute required that a woman seeking an abortion give informed consent for the procedure, and it prescribed a 24–hour waiting period between receipt of the information and performance of an abortion. The statute also required minors to obtain a parent's consent for abortion or, alternatively, the approval of a court. A married woman was required to sign a statement indicating that she had notified her husband of the pregnancy, unless someone else had impregnated her or she believed that such notification would lead to a physical assault upon her. The Supreme Court struck down the requirement of spousal notification and upheld all of the other statutory provisions.

Only a minority of the Court expressed agreement with the decision in *Roe v. Wade*. Justices O'Connor, Kennedy and Souter wrote a joint opinion which noted that the "immediate question is not the soundness of *Roe's* resolution of the issue, but the precedential force that must be accorded to its holding." The opinion relied heavily on the principle of stare decisis in declining to overrule *Roe*: "So to overrule under fire in the absence of the most compelling reason to reexamine a watershed decision would subvert the Court's legitimacy." Instead, the joint opinion applied an "undue burden" test, while purporting to reaffirm "the essential holding of *Roe*." Under this approach, Pennsylvania's requirement of spousal notification was invalid because it exposed married women to non-physical abuse, such as verbal harassment, or the loss of financial support, and thereby placed a substantial obstacle—or undue burden—on access to abortion.

Yet *Casey's* professed concern for stare decisis did not deter the Court from overruling other abortion decisions that had embraced the principles of *Roe v. Wade*. The Pennsylvania statute contained provisions for informed consent, which were not significantly different from those struck down in *Thornburgh v. American College of Obstetricians and Gynecologists* (S.Ct.1986). But because of the state's legitimate interest in assuring that patients receive accurate and relevant information about medical procedures, *Casey* sustained these provisions and expressly overruled the contrary holdings in *Thornburgh* and *Akron v. Akron Center for Reproductive Health* (S.Ct.1983). For similar reasons, *Casey* upheld the requirement of a 24–hour waiting period, noting that important personal decisions may be "more informed and deliberate if they follow some period of reflection." *Akron's* earlier ruling to the contrary was overturned.

Casey was also highly selective about which aspects of *Roe* were "essential" and would therefore be reaffirmed. The Court recognized a woman's right to have an abortion before viability without undue government interference. But much of *Roe* was explicitly or implicitly repudiated. Chief Justice Rehnquist wrote in dissent that "The joint opinion, following its newly-minted variation on stare decisis, retains the outer shell of *Roe v. Wade* ... but beats a wholesale retreat from the substance of that case." He pointed out that the joint opinion rejected *Roe's* trimester framework and, even more significantly, *Roe's* insistence that regulations of early-stage abortions must be subjected to strict scrutiny. *Casey's* repudiation of important rulings in *Roe* and its progeny made it difficult to argue convincingly that respect for stare decisis dictated the result reached in the joint opinion, or that the legitimacy of judicial decisionmaking would be seriously undermined by a contrary result.

The effect that *Casey* will have on access to abortion remains uncertain. It is not at all clear what will be deemed an "undue burden," even assuming that this test of constitutionality—endorsed by only three Justices in *Casey*—commands the support of a majority of the Court. The joint opinion in *Casey* found that a requirement of spousal notification would constitute an undue burden because of the risk of non-physical or economic duress. Yet, the same opinion concluded that a requirement of parental consent did not pose an undue burden, despite the obvious risk of both economic *and* physical duress from some parents. To be sure, Pennsylvania provided a judicial by-pass procedure for minors as a way to ameliorate that risk. But many minors will find it difficult or impossible to utilize a judicial by-pass. If the requirement of a court appearance for a 14–year-old is not a "substantial obstacle" within the meaning of *Casey*, it is difficult to predict which abortion regulations will survive the new level of scrutiny and which will not. What has become increasingly evident, however, is that our experience with the new substantive due process has been strikingly similar to the experience years ago with the old substantive due process.

CHAPTER III

PROCEDURAL DUE PROCESS: THE RIGHT TO BE HEARD

§ 8. INTRODUCTION

It is often observed that the basic function of procedural due process is to afford "an opportunity to be heard ... 'at a meaningful time and in a meaningful manner,'" thereby promoting fairness and accuracy in the resolution of disputes. *Fuentes v. Shevin* (S.Ct.1972). This function has been sharply distinguished from that of the due process cases discussed in the previous chapter (see §§ 3–5), which reviewed substantive judgments of the legislative branches. E.g. *Richardson v. Belcher* (S.Ct.1971). Since procedural due process confers a right to be heard rather than a right ultimately to prevail, judicial action in this field usually does not threaten a state's substantive goals unless prescribed procedures are inordinately costly. Moreover, courts can reasonably claim considerable expertise on the question of what procedural safeguards are needed to assure fair treatment and reliability of result. Commentators have accordingly argued that "several of the common objections to an enlarged judicial review lose much of their persuasiveness ... where the challenge is not to remake substantive policy, but to supervise the procedures through which laws are enforced upon individuals." Kadish, Methodology and Criteria in Due Process Adjudication: A Survey and Criticism, 66 Yale L.J. 319, 358 (1957). But see, Easterbrook, Substance and Due Process, 1982 Sup.Ct.Rev. 85.

§ 9. WHEN DUE PROCESS APPLIES

The threshold problem is to determine the point at which due process guarantees attach. By the terms of the fifth and fourteenth amendments, it is the deprivation of "life, liberty, or property" which activates those guarantees, but it is obviously difficult to fix the meaning of liberty or property. Liberty interests have been described, not very helpfully, as "those privileges long recognized as essential to the orderly pursuit of happiness by free men," *Meyer v. Neb.* (S.Ct.1923), a property interest requires "a legitimate claim of entitlement" to a benefit, as opposed to an abstract need or unilateral expectation of it. *Board of Regents v. Roth* (S.Ct. 1972). The Court has said that "these interests attain ... constitutional status by virtue of [having] been judicially recognized and protected by state law" or by the Bill of Rights and that procedural due process applies "whenever the State seeks to remove or significantly alter that protected status." *Paul v. Davis* (S.Ct.1976). See also *Logan v. Zimmerman Brush Co.* (S.Ct.1982) (finding a property interest in "a state-created right to redress discrimination" under Fair Employment Practices Act). Of course, many cases involve overlapping interests in property and liberty. E.g. *Bell v. Burson* (S.Ct. 1971) (protecting against suspension of a driver's license, which would affect both property rights and the liberty to use the highways). Similarly, matters of substance and procedure may overlap, as they do for instance when the type of hearing which is available depends on the interests at stake in the case. (See § 13.)

A legitimate claim of entitlement may be based on explicit law or official practice. However, entitlement analysis plainly rejects the view that "*any* grievous loss visited upon a person by the State is sufficient to invoke the procedural protection of the Due Process Clause." *Meachum v. Fano* (S.Ct. 1976) (transfer of prisoners to a new correctional facility with less favorable living conditions does not implicate a property or liberty interest unless state law or practice conditions transfers upon specific conduct or events). Some losses do not constitute a "deprivation" within the meaning of the fourteenth amendment. See *Daniels v. Williams* (S.Ct.1986) and *Davidson v. Cannon* (S.Ct.1986) (negligent conduct by a government official, though causing personal injury, does not constitute a deprivation of liberty). Furthermore, even deprivations admittedly falling within the boundaries of property or liberty can be effected without a hearing in certain emergency situations (see § 10) and in cases involving losses that are "de minimis." The Court's opinions have done relatively little to clarify the latter term. One revealing decision holds that suspension of students from public schools for a few days is not de minimis, *Goss v. Lopez* (S.Ct.1975), and observers have expressed concern that the same rule might apply to a host of other actions such as minor reductions in government services, the reassignment of public employees or the denial of a pay raise or promotion. Wilkinson, Goss v. Lopez: The Supreme Court as School Superintendent, 1975 Supreme Court Review 25 (1975). But even if these matters occasion more than de minimis losses, a hearing will not be required unless the affected parties can legitimately claim entitlement to the benefits in question. See *Leis v. Flynt* (S.Ct.1979) (the opportunity of out-of-state attorneys to represent local defendants does not involve a cognizable property or liberty interest). If instead the state retains general discretion to alter the level of benefits—rather than making such alterations contingent upon particular events—a hearing is apparently unnecessary. See *Meachum*. Compare *Bell v. Burson*, which required a hearing on a motorist's possible liability for an accident before his driver's license and vehicle registration could be suspended, because "the statutory scheme [made] liability an important factor in the State's determination to deprive an individual of his licenses...."

The entitlement doctrine may help to explain the distinction which is often drawn between the termination of benefits and the denial of an initial application. Applicants for admission to a state university, for example, will ordinarily be unable to show any legitimate claim of entitlement to the limited number of openings available there. On the other hand an enrolled student, having expended funds in reliance upon the customary policy permitting academically qualified individuals to continue their studies until they earn a degree, stands in an entirely different position. Cf. *Dixon v. Alabama State Board of Educ.* (5th Cir.1961). This is not to say that an initial applicant will never be entitled to a hearing. Persons denied admission to the bar on the basis of character have a right to be heard, *Willner v. Comm. on Character and Fitness* (S.Ct. 1963), and the same may hold true for a six-year-old who is denied admission to the first grade. In both cases the denial arguably undermines reasonable expectations, prompted by state policies, that applicants will not be excluded without cause. Viewed this way, the entitlement doctrine seems designed to serve a three-fold purpose: (1) to provide a means for determining which interests warrant procedural safeguards; (2) to protect parties who change their position in justified reliance on official action; and (3) to maximize state control over the creation of protected interests.

It has sometimes been suggested that a state, not only can decide which property and liberty interests to create, but may also limit the procedures available to protect those interests. Thus in *Arnett v. Kennedy* (S.Ct.1974), three members of the Court insisted that an employee could not claim due process protection for his federal job, despite assurances in the controlling statute that the job would be terminated only for cause, because the same statute had expressly limited procedural rights: "Only by bifurcating the very sentence of the Act of Congress which conferred [job protection] could it be said that he had an expectancy of that substantive right without the procedural limitations which Congress attached to it.... Where the grant of a substantive right is inextricably intertwined with the limitations on the procedures which are to be employed in determining that right, a litigant ... must take the bitter with the sweet." (Rehnquist, J., announcing the judgment of the Court.) But whether the procedures were defined in the same statute or in a previously enacted statute could hardly be decisive. The notion that litigants "must take the bitter with the sweet" expresses the view that discretion not to create protected interests, and hence to withhold procedural safeguards, carries with it the "lesser" power to create the interests without the safeguards. In the end this approach, though advanced originally in the context of public employment, could enable the states to tie almost all benefits to procedural limitations for their termination. A majority of the Court, declaring that rights of procedural due process are conferred by the Constitution and cannot be curtailed by legislative action, rejected that approach in *Arnett*.

The view of *Arnett's* majority was reaffirmed in *Cleveland Board of Educ. v. Loudermill* (S.Ct.1985) which squarely rejected a claim that, because the very statute that created a property right in continued employment also specified the procedures for dismissal, an employee was entitled to no more process than the statute provided. See also *Goss v. Lopez* (hearing required for brief suspension from public school notwithstanding a state statute that authorized the principal to suspend students for 10 days or less). It is possible, nevertheless, that states will attempt to define substantive rights in such a way as automatically to restrict available procedures. The legislature might provide, for instance, that all resident children have a right to attend school "until the principal finds that they have violated a disciplinary rule." Perhaps the Court would ignore a procedural limitation even when it is part of the defined substantive right; but the difficulty of reconciling such a decision with state autonomy over the creation of protected interests exposes a weakness of the entitlement doctrine and illustrates the potential for conflict among the three objectives described in the above paragraph.

§ 10. THE SEIZURE OF PROPERTY

Until 1969 it was widely assumed that prejudgment seizures of property without notice or hearing were constitutionally permissible so long as the dispossessed party had the protection of a post-seizure adjudication of the merits. *Sniadach v. Family Finance Corp.* (S.Ct.1969) repudiated this assumption, at least in the context of garnishment of a person's wages. It held that, because such garnishment would deprive an employee of the use of his or her salary pending disposition of the case, a prior hearing was constitutionally required.

Fuentes v. Shevin (S.Ct.1972) applied the *Sniadach* rationale to replevin statutes which permitted a secured installment seller to obtain a sheriff's aid in repossessing consumer goods under a writ issued by a court clerk without notice, hearing, or judicial supervision. A closely divided Court, with two of its members not participating, ruled that even a temporary deprivation of a possessory interest in personal property required a prior adversary hearing. Exceptions were spelled out only for "extraordinary situations" involving a government-initiated seizure, an important public interest and a need for swift action. See, e.g., *Calero–Toledo v. Pearson Yacht Leasing Co.* (S.Ct.1974) (upholding official seizure without notice of a vessel used to transport contraband). The apparently broad ruling in *Fuentes* threatened traditional ex parte creditor remedies, a number of which were in fact declared unconstitutional by lower courts. E.g. *Mason v. Garris* (N.D.Ga.1973) (foreclosure of mechanic's lien); *Gunter v. Merchants Warren Nat'l Bank* (D.Me.1973) (attachment of real estate).

The scope of *Fuentes* was tested in *Mitchell v. W.T. Grant Co.* (S.Ct.1974) against a statute which authorized a judge, upon the filing of an affidavit and bond, to issue a writ of sequestration to enforce a vendor's lien on personal property. The Court acknowledged the debtor's property interest under the due process clause but held that seizure without a prior adversary hearing was constitutionally permissible to protect a creditor against the dissipation of assets and to forestall self-help. The opinion was careful to note the differences between the procedures it approved and those struck down in *Fuentes:* the statutory scheme in *Mitchell* required more than conclusory allegations, provided judicial supervision, and guaranteed an immediate post-seizure hearing at which the creditor would have the burden of proving entitlement to the writ. These safeguards, which are analogous to those surrounding the issuance of a search warrant, were thought, to reduce the risk of erroneous seizure to a level that was tolerable in light of countervailing interests. Nevertheless *Fuentes* was viewed by many, including its author, as having been implicitly overruled by *Mitchell*.

The apparent conflict between *Fuentes* and *Mitchell* set the stage for *North Ga. Finishing, Inc. v. Di–Chem, Inc.* (S.Ct.1975), which was expected to clarify the law in this area. In *Di–Chem* a garnishment statute was applied against a corporate bank account by state courts, which distinguished *Sniadach* on the ground that wages were subject to a special rule. Mr. Justice White, writing for the Supreme Court on review, said that the approach below had "failed to take account of *Fuentes v. Shevin* " and that the Court was "no more inclined now than we have been in the past to distinguish among different kinds of property in applying the Due Process Clause." The opinion proceeded to evaluate the garnishment statute by comparing it with the procedures in *Mitchell,* even though the latter case had emphasized the creditor's coexisting interest in the very property sought to be seized, and this element was absent in *Di–Chem*. The garnishment law fell, apparently because it had "none of the saving characteristics" of the statute in *Mitchell:* a writ could be issued without participation by a judge, upon wholly conclusory allegations, and there was no provision for a prompt hearing at which the creditor would be required to show probable cause.

Mr. Justice Blackmun, in a dissent which attempted to capture the meaning of this series of cases, said: "The Court now has embarked on a case-by-case analysis (weighted heavily in favor of *Fuentes* and with little hope under *Mitchell*) of the respective state statutes in this area." It would surely be ironic if Mr. Justice White, who delivered the opinion in *Mitchell,* became responsible for subordinating that decision to *Fuentes,* which he previously viewed as representing "no more than ideological tinkering with state law." However it should be noted that *Di–Chem,* while purporting to rely on *Fuentes,* conspicuously refrained from mandating a pre-seizure hearing. Instead, the Court stressed the need for an "early" hearing and reaffirmed the *Mitchell* analysis which had precipitated the original doubts concerning the vitality of *Fuentes.* Moreover the failure to require a prior adversary hearing in *Di–Chem* also casts a shadow on *Sniadach* since both cases involved garnishments, and the Court has evidently rejected the suggestion of a special rule for wages. The implication may well be that the pre-seizure hearings prescribed in *Fuentes* and *Sniadach* are unnecessary when a statute has "the saving characteristics" of *Mitchell*. Arguably this approach would protect a creditor against the deterioration of property, for which he might otherwise have no remedy, and would protect a debtor by assuring an immediate post-seizure hearing and by holding out the promise of compensating him through forfeiture of the creditor's bond; but it would not prevent erroneous seizures of property.

Even assuming the primacy of *Mitchell,* some important questions remain unanswered by this series of decisions. First, it is still possible that a narrow reading of *Mitchell* could limit its rationale to secured transactions. However, *Di–Chem* conspicuously refused to invoke such a limitation, and it identified the constitutional defect in *Fuentes* as the failure to provide "a hearing *or other safeguard* against mistaken repossession." This revision of *Fuentes* in the guise of reaffirmation, together with *Di–Chem's* use of the *Mitchell* analysis in the absence of any security interest, makes it doubtful that alternatives to a pre-seizure hearing will be confined to secured transactions. Second, it is unclear precisely what "other safeguard" is constitutionally essential when a prior hearing is not provided. The saving characteristics of *Mitchell* may be sufficient, but since *Fuentes* and *Di–Chem* had none of those characteristics, it is open to question whether all or only some of the characteristics are necessary. Compare *Hutchison v. Bank of North Carolina* (M.D.N.C.1975) (lack of participation by a judge in the issuance of a writ of attachment held to be constitutionally insignificant) with *Sugar v. Curtis Circulation Co.* (S.D.N.Y.1974) (absence of one of the *Mitchell* characteristics deemed fatal.)

§ 11. PROTECTION OF LIBERTY

The most important procedural due process cases focusing specifically on liberty have dealt with injury to reputation or with physical restraints. *Wisconsin v. Constantineau* (S.Ct.1971) struck down a statute which authorized municipal officials to forbid the dispensation of intoxicating liquor to certain "excessive drinkers" by posting notices in retail outlets. The Court found that "the label or characterization given a person by 'posting', though a mark of serious illness to some, is to others such a stigma or badge of disgrace that procedural due process requires notice and an opportunity to be heard." Subsequent cases indicated that due process guarantees would be triggered by defamation in the course of suspending a student, *Goss v. Lopez* (S.Ct.1975), or refusing to renew a teacher's contract, *Board of Regents v. Roth,* if the defamatory matter is publicly disclosed.

Each of the foregoing cases went before the Court in the posture of a demand for a hearing or for the invalidation of laws that denied a hearing. *Paul v. Davis* (S.Ct.1976) arose out of the circulation by city police of a flyer which labeled the plaintiff "an active shoplifter." In its defamatory aspects the case was almost identical to the posting in *Constantineau,* but the complaint sought damages as well as other relief under a federal statute providing civil remedies for the violation of constitutional rights, including procedural rights. (See chapter 8, discussing 42 U.S.C.A. § 1983.) Faced with the prospect of numerous actions for damages in federal courts, as opposed to a single suit to enjoin statutory enforcement, the Court chose to construe the earlier cases as narrowly as possible. *Constantineau* was read as protecting the right to purchase liquor in common with the rest of the citizenry. *Roth* and *Goss* were likewise understood to involve, not simply reputation, but eligibility to teach and attend school. Injury to reputation alone was held not to implicate a liberty interest within the meaning of the due process clause.

But it is not at all clear why a state's decision to permit consumption of liquor should create protected interests, while a decision to safeguard personal reputation through libel laws does not. *Paul v. Davis* noted that state law did not extend "any legal guarantee of present enjoyment of reputation" but merely provided "a forum for vindication of ... interests [in reputation] by means of damages actions." The same holds true, however, for a great many state-created interests. Certainly Florida did not undertake to guarantee the existence of Ms. Fuentes' personal property; it merely stood ready to provide relief against interference with her use of that property, including interference effected through a wrongfully secured writ of replevin. The Court has offered no persuasive reason for finding the distinction between a guarantee and a remedy to be crucial in libel cases, though irrelevant in property cases. Perhaps *Paul v. Davis* rests on some principled basis, rather than on an intuitive sense that federal courts should not be burdened with claims which state courts have adequately handled in the past, but it is difficult to find such a basis in the opinion.

The Court has been more consistent in its treatment of the liberty interests implicated in cases of physical restraint, notwithstanding the availability of state remedies for such restraint. *Parham v. J.R.* (S.Ct.1979) found that children as well as adults have a liberty interest in being free from bodily restraint, and the Court prescribed an appropriate hearing to determine whether a parental decision to have a child institutionalized for mental health care is warranted. See also *Vitek v. Jones* (S.Ct.1980) (transfer of prisoners to a mental hospital constitutes a deprivation of liberty requiring procedural safeguards). Even after a person has been committed pursuant to a proper hearing, he or she retains a liberty interest in safe conditions and in some freedom of movement. *Youngberg v. Romeo* (S.Ct.1982). Finally, prisoners have sometimes been held to acquire a liberty interest in parole release, *Board of Pardons v. Allen* (S.Ct.1987), or in remaining among the general prison population rather than being subjected to administrative segregation. *Hewitt v. Helms* (S.Ct.1983). The Court has said that states create a liberty interest in a prison context by adopting regulations which use "explicitly mandatory language" that limits official discretion and gives rise to an "objective expectation." *Kentucky Dept. of Corrections v. Thompson* (S.Ct.1989) (no liberty interest in receiving visitors in prison when regulations contain a nonexhaustive list of visitors who "may" be excluded).

§ 12. PUBLIC EMPLOYMENT

Since public employment incorporates aspects of both liberty and property, much of the discussion above is applicable here and need not be repeated. (See §§ 10–11.) However, *Board of Regents v. Roth* and *Perry v. Sindermann* (S.Ct.1972), a companion case, require some elaboration. In *Roth* an instructor at a state university, who was informed upon completing a one-year contract that the agreement would not be renewed, sued to compel the university to explain the reasons for its action and afford him a hearing. The Court ruled that under these circumstances the instructor had no legitimate claim of entitlement to be employed beyond the one-year term specified in his contract and that a hearing on the decision of non-renewal was therefore not required. This result seemed calculated to enable public employers to hire workers for a probationary period without incurring the costs of individualized hearings or the risk that unqualified employees might be retained in order to avoid those costs.

In *Sindermann,* an instructor who had been employed by a state college for 10 years, was also denied renewal of a one-year contract, but he alleged that his college had a "de facto tenure program" under which he was assured continued employment in the absence of "sufficient cause." The Court said that an explicit tenure provision would support a claim of entitlement and that a de facto tenure system with similar mutual "understandings" would have the same effect. Although *Sindermann* did not specify the time at which a hearing must take place, it appears that the government's interest in the speedy removal of inefficient or insubordinate employees may justify the postponement of an evidentiary hearing until after the discharge occurs, at least if the employee is allowed to respond to charges informally before termination and is entitled to reinstatement with back pay in the event of his ultimate vindication. See *Cleveland Board of Educ. v. Loudermill* (S.Ct. 1985), ruling that a pretermination hearing need only (1) afford the employee "an opportunity to present his side of the story" and (2) determine "whether there are reasonable grounds to believe that the charges against the employee are true and support the proposed action." See also *Brock v. Roadway Express* (S.Ct.1987), calling for similar procedures to protect an employer's property interest in opposing a government-ordered reinstatement of discharged employees.

How meaningful an employee's right to a hearing will be is another question. The existence of a property interest in cases like *Sindermann* "must be decided by reference to state law." *Bishop v. Wood* (S.Ct.1976). Consequently, there is a risk that states may interpret their laws narrowly to defeat any legitimate entitlement, and federal courts can provide only limited review of state law to determine whether such an interpretation is untenable or "manifestly wrong." See e.g. *Hale v. Iowa State Board* (S.Ct.1937). An even more serious threat to procedural due process arises out of the Court's assertion that when state law is construed to create a property interest in employment "the power to change or clarify that [law] will remain in the hands" of the legislative body. *Bishop*. Since the Court did not indicate that the power in question could be exercised only against future employees, this statement suggests that the government can achieve in two steps what it cannot accomplish in one. If an employee like Sindermann is entitled to a hearing, the state can apparently modify its substantive law to destroy his "entitlement" and then discharge him without a hearing. Such a power critically impairs the basic policy of protecting "those claims upon which people rely in their daily lives, reliance that," according to *Roth,* "must not be arbitrarily undermined." In the end, public employees who rely on official assurances of job security may be protected only until the government chooses to withdraw those assurances, and employees who rely on contractual guarantees might fare no better. See *El Paso v. Simmons* (S.Ct.1965), holding the constitutional prohibition against state impairment of contractual obligations not to be violated where the state had altered an agreement which was not "central" to the contract.

§ 13. WHAT PROCESS IS DUE?

In most of the cases discussed above the Court was content to decide whether "some kind of hearing" was constitutionally required. Nevertheless, "once it is determined that due process applies, the question remains what process is due." *Morrissey v. Brewer* (S.Ct.1972). It is generally recognized that due process "calls for such procedural protections as the particular situation demands" and that the type of hearing required is determined by a balancing of interests. *Morrissey*.

Two extremes of formal and informal proceedings can be illustrated by *Goldberg v. Kelly* (S.Ct.1970) and *Goss v. Lopez*. The latter case stated that a public school student threatened with suspension for 10 days or less need only be afforded notice of the charges against him and "an opportunity to present his side of the story." This admittedly "rudimentary" hearing was deemed sufficient because, given the volume of disciplinary suspensions, "even truncated trial-type procedures might well overwhelm administrative facilities in many places and by diverting resources, cost more than it would save in educational effectiveness." See also *Regents of the Univ. of Michigan v. Ewing* (S.Ct.1985); *Board of Curators of the Univ. of Missouri v. Horowitz* (S.Ct.1978) (academic dismissals, as opposed to disciplinary ones, do not require a hearing before the school's decisionmaking body). On the other hand, *Goldberg v. Kelly* held that a welfare recipient is entitled to a full evidentiary hearing before his benefits can be terminated. Prescribed elements of the hearing include (1) timely notice detailing the reasons for the proposed termination of benefits, (2) an opportunity to confront adverse witnesses and present evidence and arguments, (3) representation by retained counsel, if desired, (4) an impartial decisionmaker, (5) a ruling based strictly on the evidence presented at the hearing, and (6) a statement of reasons for that ruling.

Lower courts proceeded to apply *Goldberg* to various government benefits other than welfare, but *Mathews v. Eldridge* (S.Ct.1976) eventually signaled a halt to that development. *Eldridge* involved the termination of social security disability benefits on the basis of written reports without a prior evidentiary hearing. The Court said that a determination of requisite procedures called for consideration of the private and governmental interests at stake and of the relative risks of incurring error through various procedural mechanisms. In holding that the procedures which had been employed, together with the availability of a post-termination evidentiary hearing, were constitutionally sufficient, *Eldridge* distinguished *Goldberg* on two grounds—that less hardship may result from loss of disability benefits, which are not predicated on need, and that an adversary hearing is less important where documentary evidence may be dispositive of the case. The Court emphasized that a contrary ruling in *Eldridge* would entail substantial costs to the government because of "the increased number of hearings and the expense of providing benefits to ineligible recipients pending decision." Implicit in the Court's analysis is the view that legal procedures should be designed to minimize the sum of two types of costs: (1) expenditures arising out of the operation of the fact-finding machinery and (2) the damage caused by diminishing the accuracy of the dispute-resolving process. See *Memphis Light, Gas and Water Division v. Craft* (S.Ct.1978) (requiring notice to consumers of the procedure for challenging a contested bill from a city's utility company); *Santosky v. Kramer* (S.Ct.1982) (requiring clear and convincing evidence to terminate parental rights).

No elaborate discussion is needed to show that *Goldberg* has been narrowly confined. Taken together with *Arnett* and *Mitchell,* which also accepted substitutes for a prior evidentiary hearing, the *Eldridge* case suggests a significant shift in direction: deprivations of property or liberty interests may be permitted to *precede* a full hearing if some minimal safeguards are afforded before the deprivation. See *Cleveland Board of Educ. v. Loudermill* (S.Ct.1985); *Mackey v. Montrym* (S.Ct.1979) (allowing automatic suspension of driver's license for refusal to take a breathalyzer test where a prompt post-suspension hearing is available). See also *Smith v. Organization of Foster Families for Equality and Reform* (S.Ct.1977) (permitting the removal of children from a foster home after an informal conference but prior to an adversary hearing); *Dixon v. Love* (S.Ct.1977) (allowing revocation of a driver's license for repeated traffic offenses, with an opportunity for "written objection" to suspected clerical errors and for a complete post-revocation hearing). The reason for the Court's shift in direction is not that the factors used to strike a proper balance have changed but that they are being evaluated differently. The costs of a prior adversary hearing are now accorded greater weight, and its advantages less weight, than during *Goldberg's* brief reign. Cf. *Goss v. Lopez* (rejecting the need for an evidentiary hearing because of costs, and permitting "students whose presence poses a continuing danger to persons or property or [to] the academic processes" to be removed before any hearing at all); *Ingraham v. Wright* (S.Ct.1977) (relying on the adequacy of common law remedies to sustain corporal punishment in public schools without a hearing, although a liberty interest was admittedly implicated). The ease with which the judicial shift has been made illustrates the vulnerability of decisions that rest on ad hoc balancing, but of course this vulnerability extends also to the *Eldridge* case itself.

§ 14. IRREBUTTABLE PRESUMPTIONS

From 1972 to 1974 the Supreme Court struck down a number of government classifications which created conclusive or irrebuttable presumptions. The theory of the cases was that such a classification effectively denies individuals the right to be heard on the validity of the presumption as applied to them. Irrebuttable presumptions were therefore

§ 14   *THE RIGHT TO BE HEARD*   61

held unconstitutional when they were not "necessarily or universally true in fact."

Vlandis v. Kline (S.Ct.1973) provides a good example. That case involved a Connecticut rule that treated as "nonresidents" for tuition purposes during the entire period of university enrollment (a) all unmarried students whose legal address for any part of the year preceding their application for admission was outside Connecticut and (b) all married students whose legal address at the time of application was outside Connecticut. The Court declared that "since Connecticut purports to be concerned with residence in allocating the rates for tuition and fees at its university system, it is forbidden by the Due Process Clause to deny an individual the resident rates on the basis of a permanent and irrebuttable presumption of nonresidence, when that presumption is not necessarily or universally true in fact, and when the State has reasonable alternative means of making the crucial determination. Rather, standards of due process require that the State allow such an individual the opportunity to present evidence showing that he is a bona fide resident entitled to the in-state rates." A similar analysis led to the invalidation of presumptions that women in the fifth month of pregnancy are unable to teach, *Cleveland Bd. of Educ. v. LaFleur* (S.Ct.1974), and that unwed fathers are incompetent to raise their children. *Stanley v. Ill.* (S.Ct.1972). See also *U.S. Department of Agriculture v. Murry* (S.Ct.1973), striking down the exclusion from food stamp eligibility of "any household which includes a member who has reached his eighteenth birthday and who is [or during the previous year was] claimed as a dependent child for Federal income tax purposes by a taxpayer who is not a member of an eligible household."

The difficulty with the irrebuttable presumption doctrine is that virtually all regulations rely on classifications which contain some measure of inaccuracy. For example, applicants for admission to law school are usually required to have a college degree. However, the assumption that persons having no degree are unqualified for law training and practice is surely not "necessarily or universally true." Yet individual hearings or examinations to determine the actual potential of such persons might be no more accurate than the presumption itself, as the current controversy over the merits of the Law School Admission Test demonstrates.

Perhaps because of its open-ended quality, the doctrine of irrebuttable presumptions has now been sharply curtailed. The occasion for retrenchment was *Weinberger v. Salfi* (S.Ct.1975), which dealt with a provision of the Social Security Act that denied benefits to a surviving spouse and stepchildren whose familial relationship to a deceased wage earner existed for less than nine months before his death. The duration-of-relationship requirement was designed to prevent payments in the case of a sham marriage undertaken for the purpose of qualifying for benefits, but of course marriages preceding a wage earner's death by less than nine months are not "necessarily or universally" fraudulent. Nevertheless the statutory presumption was sustained. The Court distinguished *Stanley* and *LaFleur* as involving constitutionally protected interests, and it apparently limited the applicability of *Vlandis* to classifications which "purport to speak in terms of the bona fides of the parties ... but then make plainly relevant evidence of such bona fides inadmissible." In other social welfare cases an irrebuttable presumption will be impermissible only if it is not rationally related to legitimate governmental goals. E.g. *Murry*. Under this approach a state can readily avoid the impact of the pre-*Salfi* decisions by employing rational presumptions which do not impair any constitutionally protected status and do not purport to be concerned with factors made "inadmissible." Indeed, this approach affords little independent significance to irrebuttable presumption analysis since statutory classifications must survive essentially the same degree of scrutiny in order to satisfy the demands of the equal protection clause (§§ 33–34). See *Massachusetts Board of Retirement v. Murgia* (S.Ct.1976) (applying equal protection standards to uphold the mandatory retirement of state police officers at age 50, and making no mention of the *Vlandis* line of cases despite the conclusive statutory presumption of physical unfitness). The principal difference between equal protection and irrebuttable presumption analysis now seems to be that the remedy for unconstitutional presumptions is an individualized hearing which focuses on the degree to which the plaintiff's claim comports with the perceived purpose of the classification.

CHAPTER IV

EQUAL PROTECTION: SUSPECT CLASSIFICATIONS

§ 15. INTRODUCTION

Courts have long acknowledged that the government can treat different classes of people in different ways. If all persons "similarly situated" with respect to a permissible state purpose are treated alike, there is no denial of equal protection. But few classifications are perfectly tailored to their objectives. More often a classification is overinclusive, in that it reaches some people who are not similarly situated with respect to the government's purpose, or underinclusive, in that it fails to reach some people who are similarly situated, or both. Thus the evacuation of Japanese–Americans for security reasons during World War II was at once overinclusive and underinclusive since many members of the class posed no genuine threat and some non-members did pose a threat. The question of how far over or under the proper level of inclusion a classification can lawfully be has engaged judicial attention for the better part of a century.

The traditional standard of equal protection has required only that classifications be reasonably related to a permissible governmental purpose. (See

§ 34.) However, the history of the fourteenth amendment justified close judicial scrutiny of classification by race, and eventually attempts were made to apply similar scrutiny to other areas. The upshot has been a demand for more than a reasonable relation when government touches upon specially protected interests or classifies along "suspect" lines. The latter developments are the subject of this chapter, while the former will be traced in chapter five.

§ 16. DISCRIMINATION AGAINST RACIAL MINORITIES

It is widely agreed that "the central purpose of the Fourteenth Amendment was to eliminate racial discrimination emanating from official sources in the States." *McLaughlin v. Fla.* (S.Ct.1964). Accordingly, such discrimination has been subjected to exacting scrutiny under the equal protection clause and is held invalid unless shown to have been *necessary* to an *overriding* governmental purpose, not merely rationally related to a legitimate purpose. *McLaughlin.* Laws which on their face purposefully discriminate against racial minorities— whether in voting, housing, employment or other fields—are generally easy to invalidate. For example, statutes excluding blacks from eligibility for jury duty were struck down unanimously in *Strauder v. West Va.* (S.Ct.1879), and the same result was reached when blacks were excluded by law from residence on any block occupied by a white majority. *Buchanan v. Warley* (S.Ct.1917). Even racial classifications which are designed to protect against private biases have been unanimously invalidated. See *Palmore v. Sidoti* (S.Ct.1984), overturning a custody decree that was based on a desire to avoid the problems which racially mixed households might pose for young children: "The effects of racial prejudice, however real, cannot justify a racial classification removing an infant child from the custody of its natural mother," who had entered into an interracial marriage.

Laws which are facially neutral but discriminatorily applied are likewise unconstitutional, although proof of deliberate discrimination is sometimes difficult to establish in these situations. *Yick Wo v. Hopkins* (S.Ct.1886) found impermissible discrimination where all of some 200 Chinese applicants were denied permits to operate certain laundries, while virtually every non-Chinese applicant was granted one. See also *Louisiana v. U.S.* (S.Ct.1965) (discriminatory application of a requirement that voters be able to interpret the state and federal constitutions). In *Mayor of Philadelphia v. Educational Equality League* (S.Ct.1974), on the other hand, the evidence was "too fragmentary and speculative" to show that an official had discriminated by selecting 2 blacks and 11 whites for service on a panel chosen from a population which was 34% black; because panel members were required to have designated qualifications, the Court said it could not assume that the high proportion of whites was due to unlawful racial exclusions.

As the latter case suggests, proof that a statute has a disproportionate impact on members of a particular race does not necessarily constitute a prima facie showing of unlawful discrimination. Thus the Court rejected a challenge to a welfare grant program which was more generous to some needy groups than to others. Evidence that blacks and Mexican–Americans were disproportionately represented in the less favored categories did not establish the invalidity of the program: "Given the heterogeneity of the Nation's population, it would be only an infrequent coincidence that the racial composition of each grant class was identical to that of the others. The acceptance of appellant's constitutional theory would render suspect each difference in treatment among the grant classes, however lacking in racial motivation and however otherwise rational the treatment might be. Few legislative efforts to deal with the difficult problems posed by current welfare programs could survive such scrutiny, and we do not find it required by the Fourteenth Amendment." *Jefferson v. Hackney* (S.Ct. 1972). This conclusion was reaffirmed in *Washington v. Davis* (1976), which held that official action having racially differentiated effects is not unconstitutional under the fourteenth amendment unless the action can "ultimately be traced to a racially discriminatory *purpose.*" (Emphasis added.) A rule requiring close scrutiny of all government classifications that burden one race more than another, the Court said, would imperil "a whole range of tax, welfare, public service, regulatory, and licensing statutes." See also *Mobile v. Bolden* (S.Ct.1980) (plurality opinion); *Rogers v. Lodge* (S.Ct.1982) (suggesting that the fifteenth amendment likewise requires proof of a discriminatory purpose).

Nevertheless an important differential impact may be evidence of purposeful discrimination and sometimes is sufficient in itself to establish such discrimination. For example, grandfather clauses denying black people an equal opportunity to vote and "onerous procedural requirements" based upon such clauses seem discriminatory in both purpose and effect and have been held unconstitutional. *Guinn v. U.S.* (S.Ct.1915) (grandfather clause offering special protection to those eligible to vote in 1866 and their descendants); *Lane v. Wilson* (S.Ct. 1939) (provision giving prospective voters only 12 days to register, while exempting persons who had voted when an unconstitutional grandfather clause was in effect). Similarly, *Gomillion v. Lightfoot* (S.Ct.1960) ruled that a change in city boundaries from a square to a 28–sided figure, which excluded 99% of the black voters and no white voter, constituted racial discrimination violative of the fifteenth amendment. But "absent a pattern as stark as that in *Gomillion* ..., impact alone is not determinative, and the Court must look to other evidence." *Village of Arlington Heights v. Metropolitan Housing Development Corp.* (S.Ct.1977) (perceiving insufficient manifestations of racial motivation in the denial of a rezoning petition). The factors to be considered in determining the existence of an invidious purpose include the historical background of the challenged action, any procedural or substantive departures from the normal course of conduct, and the legislative or administrative history of the action. *Arlington Heights*. If the evidence is adequate to establish a prima facie case of purposeful discrimination, the burden shifts to the state to "demonstrate that the law would have been enacted without that factor." *Hunter v. Underwood* (S.Ct. 1985) (invalidating a provision in the Alabama constitution that disenfranchised persons convicted of crimes involving moral turpitude, because the provision was originally motivated by a racially discriminatory purpose and had subsequently had a racially discriminatory impact). See also *Castaneda v. Partida* (S.Ct.1977) (finding discriminatory selection of jurors and citing a statement in *Arlington Heights* that a less extreme statistical pattern is needed in such cases "because of the nature of the jury selection task").

It is often difficult, however, to determine precisely what showing is needed to create a prima facie case. *Batson v. Kentucky* (S.Ct.1986) illustrates the difficulty. The *Batson* case examined the evidentiary burden cast upon a criminal defendant who claims to have been denied equal protection through the prosecutor's use of peremptory challenges to exclude members of his race from the jury that convicted him. Since minority group members might be challenged for either legitimate or racially motivated reasons, the Court was able to define in only the most general terms the standard under which a defendant may establish a prima facie case of purposeful discrimination: "[T]he defendant must first show that he is a member of a cognizable racial group ... and that the prosecutor has exercised peremptory challenges to remove from the venire members of the defendant's race.... Finally, the defendant must show that these facts and any other relevant circumstances raise an inference that the prosecutor used that practice to exclude the veniremen from the petit jury on account of their race."

§ 17. THE SEPARATE–BUT–EQUAL DOCTRINE

Despite the unmistakable call for racially equal treatment which the *Strauder* case issued in 1880, the Court proceeded to uphold official segregation of the races before the end of the century. In *Plessy v. Ferguson* (S.Ct.1896), it ruled that a statute requiring "equal but separate" railway accommodations for whites and blacks was compatible with *Strauder's* construction of the fourteenth amendment as mandating "that all persons, whether colored or white, shall stand equal before the laws of the States...." The Court rejected Justice Harlan's dissenting view that "our constitution is color-blind" and chose to interpret segregation as a mutual separation of the races which branded neither group inferior, so long as equal facilities were provided for each. Unfortunately the majority's rationale overlooked the fact that segregation was imposed by whites, who were politically and economically dominant, and that in its historical context state-enforced racial separation would almost certainly be understood to imply the inferiority of blacks. *Plessy* also ignored the likelihood that separate facilities would be unequal in fact and that case-by-case proof of inequality would be extremely expensive.

The legal attack on the separate-but-equal doctrine began with a series of suits to compel the admission of blacks to state professional schools. In *Missouri ex rel. Gaines v. Canada* (S.Ct.1938), the Court invalidated a plan under which Missouri provided a law school for whites only and financed the legal education of black citizens at out-of-state institutions. That decision was followed by *Sweatt v. Painter* (S.Ct.1950) and *McLaurin v. Okla.* (S.Ct. 1950). *Sweatt* held that even an in-state "Negro law school" was constitutionally insufficient if it failed to provide an education equal in both tangible and intangible respects to that offered to whites. The Court noted differences between the law schools in question in the "reputation of the faculty, experience of the administration, position and influence of the alumni, standing in the community, traditions and prestige...." *McLaurin* ruled that blacks who were admitted to a state university could not be consigned to separate sections of the classroom, library and cafeteria; such restrictions impaired the "ability to study, to engage in discussions, and exchange views with other students...." These decisions, relying as they did on a wide variety of intangible factors not readily subject to equalization, made it virtually impossible to satisfy the requirement that separate facilities be equal if they were to survive attack under the fourteenth amendment. The obvious next step would be a frontal assault on the separate-but-equal doctrine in primary and secondary education.

§ 18. BROWN AND ITS PROGENY

Brown v. Board of Educ. (S.Ct.1954) addressed the question whether purposefully segregated public schools are inherently unequal. The Court, in answering that question affirmatively, reasoned that the separation of black children "solely because of their race generates a feeling of inferiority as to their status in the community that may affect their hearts and minds in a way unlikely ever to be undone...." Because a sense of inferiority "affects the motivation of a child to learn" and tends to retard educational development, the *Plessy* rule was found to have no place "in the field of public education," and state-imposed segregation in that field violated the equal protection clause. The same day *Bolling v. Sharpe* (S.Ct.1954) invalidated school segregation in the District of Columbia, but since the equal protection clause has no direct application to the federal government, the Court relied on fifth amendment due process: "Segregation in public education is not reasonably related to any proper governmental objective, and thus it imposes on Negro children in the District of Columbia a burden that constitutes an arbitrary deprivation of their liberty in violation of the Due Process Clause." Soon afterwards, the school cases were applied by per curiam rulings to public parks, buses, golf courses and other government facilities. E.g., *Gayle v. Browder* (S.Ct.1956).

The "meaning of *Brown*" has been a subject of contention ever since the case was decided. To some readers, the opinion seemed to rest simply on the physical separation of black and white children, with its inherent inequality, and hence to apply to de facto as well as de jure segregation. Others interpreted *Brown* and *Bolling* to bar government classification by race. Under the latter interpretation, racial factors could not be considered in official decisionmaking, and so "benign" as well as invidious racial classifications would be constitutionally proscribed. It is unlikely, however, that *Brown* was intended to pass upon either the abstract question of racial separation per se or that of classification by race.

The *Brown* case dealt specifically and exclusively with state-enforced segregation on the basis of race. The validity of neighborhood school plans was assumed rather than decided in the implementation order, which called upon lower courts to "consider" the revision of attendance zones "into compact units to achieve a system of determining admission to the public schools on a nonracial basis...." *Brown v. Board of Educ.* (S.Ct.1955). In any event, the question of fortuitous segregation resulting from racially neutral student assignment plans was simply not presented in *Brown,* and the Court made no effort to reach it.

But if *Brown* did not address itself to racial separation in the abstract, neither did it deal abstractly with racial classification. A ban on all racial distinctions would obliterate *Plessy* rather than rule it out of place in the field of education and would render wholly gratuitous the discussion of separation and inherent inequality which comprised much of the opinion. Admittedly, the per curiam decisions which followed the school cases gave greater credence to the theory that racial classification was unconstitutional per se. Because racial distinctions were common to all the cases and because there was little evidence of inherent inequality in those decided per curiam, some writers argued that *Brown* and its progeny prohibited all government classification by race. However, the per curiam cases raised only the issue of state power to exclude blacks from public facilities on racial grounds when allegedly equal facilities were available to them; those cases surely did not call for a ruling as to whether official classification by race is inevitably unconstitutional in every context without regard to its purpose or effect. Accordingly, these decisions should be interpreted together with the school cases to proscribe official *segregation* of public facilities *by racial classification.* This construction leaves open the questions raised by racial classifications designed to integrate public facilities or to compensate for past invidious discrimination.

§ 19. IMPLEMENTING BROWN

The First Fifteen Years of Deliberate Speed. The difficult task of enforcing the school decisions began with the second *Brown* case. The issue there concerned "the manner in which relief is to be accorded" against segregation in the public schools. *Brown II* held that gradual relief was constitutionally sufficient but said that courts should act "with all deliberate speed." *Brown v. Board of Educ.* (S.Ct.1955).

For the next 10 years the speed was painfully deliberate. By 1964 only about ⅛ of the southern school districts had desegregated, and a large proportion of these were in border states or were districts in which only a token number of blacks went to school with whites. In the deep South less than 1% of the black children attended integrated schools.

During the second decade of desegregation the other two branches of government came to the aid of the Court. First, Congress authorized the termination of federal spending for any program administered in a racially discriminatory way, and it empowered the Attorney General to bring or intervene in school desegregation suits. Then the Department of Health, Education and Welfare issued desegregation guidelines which local school districts were required to follow as a condition of eligibility to receive federal aid unless they were already complying with judicial orders to desegregate. These pressures had a dramatic effect on the number of one-race schools in the South.

At the same time the Court reasserted its own pressure for desegregation. *Green v. County School Board* (S.Ct.1968) ruled that de jure segregated school systems have an affirmative obligation to achieve desegregation, not merely to refrain from enforcing segregation. The board of education in that case had adopted a freedom-of-choice plan in 1965, but after three years under the plan no white child had chosen to go to the "Negro school" and 85% of the black children had remained in that school. The Court instructed the board "to take whatever steps might be necessary to convert to a unitary system in which racial discrimination would be eliminated root and branch." A freedom-of-choice plan would be permissible only "where it offers real promise of aiding a desegregation program to effectuate conversion of a state-imposed dual system to a unitary non-racial system...." Shortly thereafter, the Court said that all motions for additional time to desegregate should be denied because the "deliberate speed" formula was no longer constitutionally acceptable: "Under explicit holdings of this Court the obligation of every school district is to terminate dual school systems at once and to operate now and hereafter only unitary schools." *Alexander v. Holmes County Board of Educ.* (S.Ct.1969). The "affirmative duty to desegregate" has "no application" to nonschool facilities like the 4–H and Homemakers Clubs, *Bazemore v. Friday* (S.Ct.1986), but it does apply to colleges and universities. See *U.S. v. Fordice* (S.Ct.1992) (a state cannot "leave in place policies rooted in its prior officially-segregated system that serve to maintain the racial identifiability of its universities if those policies can be practicably eliminated without eroding sound educational policies").

"Evasive Schemes." Beginning with *Cooper v. Aaron* (S.Ct.1958), which dealt with hostility generated by official opposition to integration, a wide variety of state activities that impede desegregation have been declared unconstitutional. *Griffin v. County School Board of Prince Edward County* (S.Ct.1964) invalidated an attempt to avoid desegregation "by a combination of closed public schools and county grants to white children" attending private schools. But government assistance to segregated private academies has been held unconstitutional even in the absence of public school closures. *Norwood v. Harrison* (S.Ct.1973) (state loan of textbooks to private school students); *Gilmore v. City of Montgomery* (S.Ct.1974) (exclusive access by private schools to city recreational facilities). On the other hand, the closure of public facilities without government assistance to private ones is permissible despite proof that the action is "motivated by a desire to avoid integration." *Palmer v. Thompson* (S.Ct. 1971) (upholding a decision to close municipal swimming pools and distinguishing *Griffin* on the ground that the state had there "pretended to close" public schools "only to run them under a 'private' label"). Finally, the creation of new school districts in a de jure segregated system has been ruled unlawful where, by altering the ratio of black to white students, it hindered the process of disestablishment. *Wright v. Emporia* (S.Ct.1972).

§ 20. SWANN v. BOARD OF EDUCATION

Although the *Green* and *Alexander* cases imposed an affirmative obligation on de jure segregated schools to convert to a "unitary system," those cases gave no clear indication of what was meant by that term. *Swann v. Charlotte–Mecklenburg Board of Educ.* (S.Ct.1971) was reviewed for the express purpose of "defining in more precise terms than heretofore the scope of the duty of school authorities and district courts" to disestablish dual school systems. The arguments in the lower courts had dealt with numerous remedial problems, each of which provoked heated debate. And so the Supreme Court set out 18 months after it decided *Alexander v. Board of Educ.* to determine what it was that the latter case had ordered the schools to do "at once." Because *Swann* contains the most detailed statement to date of the duty to desegregate, and because of the important implications it holds for schools in the North and West, the case requires considerable discussion.

Swann addressed what it called "four problem areas"—the use of racial quotas, the elimination of one-race schools, racial gerrymandering of attendance zones and the use of transportation facilities for remedial purposes. Its unanimous rulings in those areas are easy to state, if not necessarily to comprehend. First, the Court decided that no particular degree of racial balance or mixing is required, and it appeared to approve the use of mathematical quotas only as "a starting point in shaping a remedy to correct past constitutional violations." Beyond this, it cautiously defined the permissible "starting point" merely by noting that since a remedial decree must be judged by its effectiveness, an awareness of the racial composition of a school system would be a helpful place to begin. Second, *Swann* ruled that a small number of one-race schools was not in itself a mark of de jure segregation. However, school officials were admonished to "make every effort to achieve the greatest possible degree of actual desegregation, taking into account the practicalities of the situation," and the burden of proving that any one-race schools are not "the result of present or past discriminatory action" was placed on the state. For those students remaining in predominantly one-race schools, a remedy of sorts was prescribed in the form of a majority-to-minority transfer provision allowing students to transfer from a school in which their race was in the majority to one in which it was in the minority. Third, the Court sanctioned racial gerrymandering designed to reduce segregation, though it noted that "there are limits" to the permissible use of this device. Fourth, the opinion approved the use of busing for desegregation but added that objections to transportation "may have validity when the time or distance of travel is so great as to risk either the health of the children or significantly impinge on the educational process." Finally, the Court recognized that shifting demographic patterns might cause continuing changes in the racial composition of schools, and it stated that this would not necessitate judicial intervention so long as the state itself did not attempt to control those patterns. See *Freeman v. Pitts* (S.Ct.1992); *Oklahoma City Board of Educ. v. Dowell* (S.Ct.1991) (a desegregation decree should be dissolved if the school board has "complied in good faith" with the decree and "the vestiges of past discrimination have been eliminated to the extent practicable").

The Ambiguities of Swann. Although the principal aim of *Swann* was to give content to the mandate for "unitary school systems" and to define acceptable ways for complying with it, the ambiguous opinion which apparently was needed to preserve unanimity made only limited progress on these issues. The discussion of the problem of one-race schools provides a good example of the Court's equivocation. At first *Swann* appeared clearly to reject a requirement to eliminate one-race schools, stating that the existence of a small number of such schools "is not in and of itself the mark of a system which still practices segregation by law." But the permissibility of southern one-race schools was drawn into question when the opinion added a virtually insurmountable condition: in scrutinizing desegregation plans, courts must place on school officials the burden of proving that the composition of one-race schools "is not the result of present *or past* discriminatory action on their part." (Emphasis added.) On analysis, the task of proving that one-race schools are not causally related to past policies of segregation—policies which for years encouraged massive resistance to integration and which caused schools to be constructed in such areas and of such sizes as to assure that they would remain segregated—seems, if taken seriously, to be utterly unmanageable. And if that burden could be sustained, it is hard to see what *Swann* would teach about the lawfulness of one-race schools. It had not been assumed that *Brown* required corrective action where the racial composition of schools did not result from present or past discrimination by government. *Swann's* express authorization for one-race schools is therefore difficult to understand, or to reconcile with any meaningful demand for disproof of past and present discriminatory causation. Unfortunately, if a choice must be made between the authorization given and the condition imposed, one would have to expect continued conflict in the lower courts and a prolongation of the uncertainty which *Swann* was designed to curtail.

Ambivalence and ambiguity also characterized the Court's treatment of specific remedies and its sketchy description of the unitary school system. Racially gerrymandered school zones are allowable on an "interim" basis but "there are limits" to how far a court may go in that regard. What those limits are remains something of a mystery, for *Swann* had nothing whatever to say on that subject. Busing is likewise an acceptable corrective tool, but since objections to it on the basis of health or educational considerations "may have validity," no one can know how much busing the law requires. Compare *Cisneros v. Corpus Christi Ind. School Dist.* (5th Cir.1972) (rejecting substantial busing and ordering district courts to "minimize student transportation") with *Thompson v. School Board of*

Newport News (4th Cir.1972) (approving mandatory busing of two hours per day). Nor is much known about the dividing line between unitary and dual school systems. In determining the existence of a dual system, an important matter to consider, according to *Swann,* is whether the pattern of school construction facilitates racial separation. But neighborhood school plans may facilitate segregation either intentionally or unintentionally, and *Swann* did not suggest that such plans are unconstitutional per se. Instead, it stated that upon a "proper" showing the district court may take construction patterns into account. Judges are apparently expected to recognize a proper showing when they see it. Similarly, school construction in the future must not serve to perpetuate or reestablish a dual system, but the crucial question as to when racial separation constitutes a dual system remains largely unanswered.

In a series of important rulings *Swann* did resolve three points: (1) schools need not be racially balanced; (2) officials must seek "to achieve the greatest possible degree of actual desegregation;" and (3) the drive for maximum desegregation must give due regard to "the practicalities of the situation." The first two points will provide some guidance to lower courts, but this is substantially offset by the inexplicit nature of the third. One can only guess what weight will be accorded to the "practicalities" and whether the latter term refers merely to considerations of health and learning, which the Court mentioned in connection with busing, or also embraces such matters as economic costs and white flight into private or suburban schools. It is not surprising, therefore, to find a circuit court declaring that "Respectfully, we read *Swann* ... as primarily a command to all school authorities in states where *de jure* segregation was once the rule, to do a better job of mixing the races and teaching staffs than they have heretofore done." *Goss v. Board of Educ.* (6th Cir.1971). At most we learn from *Swann* that a considerable degree of racial mixing will ordinarily be required in the desegregation process and that some busing and racially gerrymandered school zones may be employed in that process. What we do not know is how *Swann's* very general guidelines should be translated into concrete action. That so little should be known after such a prodigious effort is a measure of the difficulty of defining the affirmative duty to convert to a unitary system.

Swann's Impact on Northern Schools. Even after allowances are made for all the ambiguities of the opinion, *Swann* has the potential to strike northern school segregation with greater force than any decision since the first *Brown* case. Its holding does not appear to reach fortuitous racial imbalance (see § 22) but it clearly applies in the North to the extent that schools there have a recent history of de jure segregation.

The northern impact of *Swann* is a direct result of the newly defined scope of the duty to desegregate. For many years, it was generally thought that the obligation of dual school systems could be satisfied by the cessation of discriminatory practices and the assignment of students and faculty on a nonracial basis. Under *Swann,* however, those measures are constitutionally sufficient only if they seek "the greatest possible degree actual desegregation" consistent with the practicalities. The gulf between ending discrimination on the one hand and seeking maximum desegregation on the other hand carries major implications for the North and West where school segregation policies, though usually assumed to be covert, have often been no less overt than those once enforced in southern school districts. What has tended to make the segregation cases relatively difficult to apply outside the South is not simply the cloak of legality employed elsewhere, but also the apparently limited scope of constitutionally mandated relief under the second *Brown* case. So long as a dual school system was deemed to become unitary by ending its discriminatory practices, northern schools which had abolished overt discrimination by 1954 were effectively insulated from legal attack. But if, as *Swann* declares, the fourteenth amendment demands more than the abolition of existing discriminatory practices, there is no reason to assume that these schools have met their constitutional obligations.

Bell v. School City of Gary (7th Cir.1963), one of the early northern school cases, shows just how much difference the new desegregation standards could make. The plaintiffs in *Bell* tried to establish that the school board was purposefully sponsoring segregation or that it had a duty to correct even fortuitous racial separation in the public schools. The latter claim was held to be legally unfounded, and the former ran into insurmountable barriers of proof. But under the duty to desegregate described in *Swann,* the plaintiffs could prevail without proving that Gary was then engaged in purposeful school segregation. For it was conceded that the board of education had operated a dual system until 1947 and although the practice had been formally abolished, there was no evidence that every effort had been made to achieve "the greatest possible degree of actual desegregation" which *Swann* requires. In short, the application of *Swann* to the Gary school system could have eliminated the need to prove contemporaneous discriminatory practices, since the system had never been brought into compliance with the constitutional command.

If *Bell* were a unique case of de jure segregation outside the South, the new dimension in *Swann* would have only marginal importance for most of the country. But dual school systems were once far more prevalent in the North and West than is generally supposed. Racially segregated schools were authorized in Wyoming and New Mexico until 1954, and Indiana permitted such schools until 1949. In other states dual school systems were prohibited by statute but were nevertheless maintained under local practice, sometimes to the very eve of the *Brown* case. U.S. Comm. on Civil Rights, Racial Isolation in the Public Schools 42–43 (1967). Of course, as the examination into past practice is extended further back in time, more regions will be found to have operated officially segregated school systems; but even if the inquiry is limited to the recent past, a substantial amount of racial separation in the North may be vulnerable to attack without proof of a continuing intent to discriminate. See *Dayton Board of Educ. v. Brinkman* (S.Ct.1979) ("the measure of the post-*Brown I* conduct of a school board under an unsatisfied duty to liquidate a dual system is the effectiveness, not the purpose, of the actions in decreasing or increasing the segregation caused by the dual system"); *Columbus Board of Educ. v. Penick* (S.Ct.1979) (finding of purposeful segregation in 1954 and of subsequent segregative effects of school board action is enough to warrant a systemwide remedy).

To be sure, laws requiring or permitting segregation outside the South were repealed before *Brown v. Board of Education* and in some instances had been dormant for a number of years before repeal. But the fact that a northern state repealed its segregation provisions a few years before rather than a few years after *Brown* should not be critical unless during the interval the effects of the earlier policy were eradicated in the manner which is required of states in the South. The date of repeal may disclose something about the current effects of the statute, but it is a rough indicator at best, suggesting little more than that recent discriminatory practices are more likely to have a continuing impact than remote ones. Since there is ample evidence that the effects of segregation have not yet dissipated in the South, more than 30 years after

Brown, there is small cause for assuming that such effects were quickly washed away in the North.

Congressional Reaction to Swann. In 1974 Congress sought to impose statutory limits on federally mandated busing. The Education Amendments Act provided that no court or agency of the United States shall "require the transportation of any student to a school other than the school closest or next closest to his place of residence" or shall "require ... the transportation of any student if such transportation poses a risk to the health of such student or constitutes a significant impingement on the educational process with respect to such student." However, these provisions were prefaced by a significant disclaimer, stating that they "are not intended to modify or diminish the authority of the courts of the United States to enforce the fifth and fourteenth amendments." In light of this disclaimer the statute might well be construed to leave intact all judicial powers to remedy unlawful segregation, thereby avoiding the question of constitutional validity. Under that interpretation, the restrictions on busing would express a congressional preference for other remedies but would not foreclose court-ordered busing to enforce constitutional rights.

State Legislation Against Busing. Some states have enacted legislation designed to forestall mandatory busing that extends beyond the parameters required under federal law. Two cases involving such legislation reached the Court in 1982. *Crawford v. Board of Educ.* (S.Ct.1982) dealt with an amendment to the California constitution which prohibited state courts from ordering mandatory pupil assignment or transportation unless a federal court would be permitted to order it as a remedy for a violation of the equal protection clause. Although the amendment was adopted by voter referendum after state court decisions called for "reasonable steps" to alleviate racial imbalance, the Supreme Court found no violation of the fourteenth amendment: "It would be paradoxical to conclude that by adopting the Equal Protection Clause of the Fourteenth Amendment, the voters of the State thereby had violated it." The Court emphasized that the California provision "does not embody a racial classification.... It simply forbids state courts to order pupil school assignment or transportation in the absence of a Fourteenth Amendment violation."

A contrary result was reached in *Washington v. Seattle School Dist.* (S.Ct.1982). In the latter case a state initiative was passed after the Seattle school district adopted a plan for extensive use of mandatory busing. The initiative prohibited school boards from requiring any student to attend a school other than the one nearest or next nearest to his home, but it set out numerous exceptions which had the effect of permitting assignments to nonneighborhood schools for virtually all purposes except integration. The Court noted that the initiative had restructured the political process in such a way as to require statewide rather than local action to remedy de facto segregation and concluded that this placed a special burden on racial minorities in violation of the equal protection clause: the initiative "does 'not attempt to allocate governmental power on the basis of any general principle. . . .' Instead, it uses the racial nature of an issue to define the governmental decisionmaking structure, and thus imposes substantial and unique burdens on racial minorities."

It is not easy to reconcile the *Crawford* and *Seattle* cases. Indeed, a majority of the Court found the cases to be indistinguishable, although that majority was divided over the validity of the two provisions. Justice Marshall captured the essential problem in his dissent in *Crawford*. He observed that in both cases the state had curtailed "the use of mandatory student assignment or transportation as a remedy for *de facto* segregation" by restricting the power of some unit of government. Until the California constitution was amended, the minority community could ask a school board to take voluntary steps to alleviate racial imbalance and then could seek additional relief from a state court. The Washington initiative, as Justice Marshall said, "attempted to deny minority children the first step of that procedure [while the California provision] eliminated by fiat the second stage." The governmental process was thus "restructured" in both cases for essentially the same reason. Why the state should have less power under the fourteenth amendment to curtail the authority of school boards than that of courts was not adequately explained.

§ 21. NON-AREAWIDE SEGREGATION

In some regions, purposeful segregation has been imposed on certain parts of a community and not on others. Two patterns have emerged. In one, a single school district is found to have deliberately segregated some of its schools; in the other, certain school districts in a given area have operated unitary systems while an adjoining district has maintained a dual system. The Court has dealt quite differently with these two situations.

Partial Segregation of a Single District. *Keyes v. School Dist.* (S.Ct.1973) involved the purposeful segregation of part of the school district of Denver. The Court held that where "school authorities have carried out a systematic program of segregation affecting a substantial portion of the students, schools, teachers and facilities within the school system ... there exists a predicate for a finding of the existence of a dual school system." In such cases courts must at least fashion "a remedy commensurate to the ... specific violations." *Dayton Board of Educ. v. Brinkman* (S.Ct.1977). But in addition, a determination that a meaningful portion of the system was deliberately segregated shifts to the government "the burden of proving that other segregated schools within the system are not also the result of intentionally segregative actions." *Keyes.* Unless that burden is sustained, the entire system is deemed de jure segregated and must be dismantled, presumably in the manner dictated by *Swann*.

Partial Segregation of a Multi–District Area. In *Milliken v. Bradley* (S.Ct.1974), the issue was whether a multi-district remedy may be judicially imposed for de jure segregation in a single school district. The city of Detroit had purposefully segregated its schools, but because only about 30% of the students there were white, the trial judge found that remedies limited to the city would not achieve desegregation. He therefore ordered cross-busing of students between Detroit and a number of suburban districts which had not been shown to have deliberately segregated their schools. On review the Supreme Court, emphasizing the tradition of local control over public education, held that an interdistrict remedy under these circumstances exceeded the remedial powers of the federal judiciary. Such a remedy would be permissible "where the racially discriminatory acts of one or more school districts cause racial segregation in an adjacent district, or where district lines have been deliberately drawn on the basis of race." But when there is no interdistrict violation or effect, multi-district remedies cannot be judicially decreed. Indeed, at one point the Court said that an interdistrict violation *and* effect were required, and a later decision indicated that such an effect is a prerequisite to multi-district relief even in jurisdictions which enforced statewide segregation until 1954. *Evans v. Buchanan* (D.Del.1975).

There seems little doubt that if Detroit and its outlying areas had constituted a single school district, there would have been "a predicate for a finding" of a dual system. *Keyes.* No school system has been held to have achieved "the greatest possible degree of actual desegregation" when the racial disparity within its schools was as great as that among Detroit and its suburbs. The critical factor distinguishing *Keyes* was that the metropolitan Detroit area which was "partially" segregated encompassed many separate school districts. Since different boards of education governed the various districts, there was no basis for invoking *Keyes'* presumption that "where school authorities have effectuated an intentionally segregative policy in a meaningful portion of the school system, similar impermissible considerations may have motivated their action in other areas of the system." And although the state of Michigan was assumed to share responsibility for Detroit's school segregation, the Court found insufficient evidence that the state "engaged in activity that had a cross-district effect."

By limiting the availability of multi-district relief, *Milliken* sought to protect the autonomy of local government units that were "not implicated in any constitutional violation." *Hills v. Gautreaux* (S.Ct. 1976) (approving an interdistrict remedy for de jure segregated housing where "local rights and powers," such as those expressed through zoning laws, would not be displaced). It is clear nevertheless that in many cases the *Milliken* rule could make it virtually impossible for courts to desegregate urban schools. Of course, the legislative branches have power to consolidate school districts or develop other remedies of their own; and a court can order compensatory training to alleviate the consequences of segregation, *Milliken v. Bradley* (S.Ct.1977), but federal judicial relief in metropolitan areas will often be quite limited. See *Missouri v. Jenkins* (S.Ct. 1995), holding that a judicially mandated salary increase for teachers in a segregated school system exceeded the district court's remedial authority because it was designed to serve the "*inter*district goal" of attracting white students from surrounding districts, which was "beyond the scope of the *intra*district violation" before the court.

§ 22. DE FACTO SEGREGATION

One of the most controversial questions arising out of the school cases was whether de facto segregation, which the Court distinguishes from de jure segregation by the absence of an "intent to segregate," violates the equal protection clause. Several decisions have now indicated a negative answer. The first indication came at the conclusion of the opinion in *Swann v. Board of Education*. After attempting to define the duty to desegregate, *Swann* acknowledged that demographic changes would inevitably affect the racial composition of schools which had converted to a unitary system, and it proceeded to issue this critical ruling: "Neither school authorities nor district courts are constitutionally required to make year-by-year adjustments in the racial composition of student bodies once the affirmative duty to desegregate has been accomplished.... In the absence of a showing that either the school authorities or some other agency of the State has deliberately attempted to fix or alter demographic patterns to affect the racial composition of the schools, further intervention by a district court should not be necessary." Thus absent government efforts to control demographic patterns, federal courts were not to intervene with desegregation orders to counteract shifts in population. See *Pasadena City Board of Educ. v. Spangler* (S.Ct.1976) (same conclusion). The implications of that ruling are striking since it is apparent that, without post-conversion intervention, demographic changes will cause some formerly segregated school systems to fall back into racially isolated patterns after successful desegregation. If this is constitutionally tolerable, it would seem to follow that there is no constitutional requirement to remedy racial separation which is wholly adventitious. For if there were a federal duty to maintain racial dispersion, there would be no reason to exempt a previously de jure segregated school system from that duty.

This view of the obligation of school districts was reinforced by *Spencer v. Kugler* (S.Ct.1972), which affirmed without opinion the ruling of a three-judge court that there is no "affirmative duty to cure racial imbalance in the situation of de facto segregation...." Finally, further confirmation, albeit in dictum, was received from *Washington v. Davis* (S.Ct.1976), which said: "The school desegregation cases have ... adhered to the basic equal protection principle that the invidious quality of a law claimed to be racially discriminatory must ultimately be traced to a racially discriminatory purpose. That there are both predominantly black and predominantly white schools in a community is not alone violative of the Equal Protection Clause." See also *Dayton Board of Educ. v. Brinkman* (stating that the existence of predominantly white and black schools "without more ... does not offend the Constitution").

Judicial reluctance to invalidate de facto segregation may be explained in part by uncertainty over the effects of fortuitous racial isolation. There is substantial evidence that racial balance serves important interests by improving student performance, by insulating minorities against unfair allocation of resources and, as *Swann* noted, by helping to prepare students for life in a pluralistic society. Nevertheless, conflicting evidence can be found on each point. This conflict in data does not foreclose—indeed it liberates—legislative action: in light of our limited knowledge in this field, the political branches of government are entitled to considerable deference if they choose to attack racial isolation by nondiscriminatory measures. On the other hand conflicting evidence is a much less suitable predicate for judicially mandated action. Accordingly, *Swann* gave general approval to voluntary attempts to correct racial imbalance, but de facto segregation has not been held unconstitutional.

One should not, however, exaggerate the importance of judicial rulings which decline to invalidate adventitious segregation. To a large extent the significance of such rulings will depend upon the ease or difficulty of proving that racial separation is purposeful. If, for example, the adoption of attendance zones causing racial isolation were held to shift to the state the burden of proving an innocent purpose, the lawfulness of fortuitous segregation would assume less importance than has usually been attributed to it. Moreover the Court has explicitly reserved the question of the constitutionality of segregation caused by non-school officials. It is possible, therefore, that purposeful segregation in housing will provide a basis for finding unlawful segregation in the schools. Such a decision would again reduce the importance of holding adventitious racial imbalance to be constitutionally permissible.

§ 23. PREFERENTIAL TREATMENT OF RACIAL MINORITIES

One of the most controversial questions concerning racial classifications is whether they may be employed by government to create preferences for minorities which have been subjected to invidious discrimination in the past. The issue has arisen in a variety of contexts, including employment, housing and public schools. See Ely, The Constitutionality of Reverse Racial Discrimination, 41 U.Chi. L.Rev. 723 (1974). Since it is essential that the government respond conscientiously to the needs of those exposed to racial injustice, while still avoiding inappropriate discrimination against others, the significance of the issue can scarcely be exaggerated.

Early Decisions. The difficult problem of enforcing school desegregation has led the Court to approve, even to demand, the use of some racial classifications. On this issue, as on many others, the *Swann* case is now a leading authority and requires careful examination. In *Swann* the Court

(1) sustained the use of racial quotas "as a starting point in shaping a remedy" for school segregation, (2) upheld racial gerrymandering of attendance zones as an "interim corrective measure," (3) prescribed a majority-to-minority transfer plan, and (4) invalidated a North Carolina statute which prohibited student assignments based on race or for the purpose of achieving racial balance.

The first and last of these rulings can be easily understood and have rather limited application. North Carolina's ban on the consideration of race in student assignment plans was itself a racial classification requiring close judicial scrutiny, since it singled out race for special treatment. Often a prohibition against the use of racial criteria is constitutionally valid, *Heart of Atlanta Motel v. U.S.* (S.Ct. 1964), but in the context of racially isolated schools such a prohibition would perpetuate segregation and could not be sustained. See *Hunter v. Erickson* (S.Ct.1969) (restriction on municipal power to regulate racial discrimination in housing held to be unconstitutional classification by race.) Similarly, the approval of racial quotas "as a starting point in shaping a remedy" does not appear to authorize preferences based on color. The Court indicated that this starting point was to consist merely of "an awareness of the racial composition of the whole school system." Federal courts have themselves been using this type of racial "awareness" for many years as a means of testing compliance with the duty of nondiscrimination. E.g., *Norris v. Ala.* (S.Ct.1935) (utilizing population surveys to find unlawful exclusion of blacks from jury service). Admittedly, the authority to focus on racial composition in formulating a remedy carries the risk of being escalated in actual practice into an inflexible mandate or "voluntary" action designed to avert possible litigation. That risk, however, is also implicit in the use of racial data to detect constitutional violations. Yet invalidation of the practice of collecting such data, a course already rejected in *Tancil v. Woolls* (S.Ct.1964), might seriously impair the integrity of anti-discrimination laws; and once the data become available, a rule prohibiting judicial awareness of race could scarcely be enforced. Thus *Swann's* narrow authorization of racial quotas may well be as limited as the Court could reasonably hope to make it.

The most formidable issues of racial classification in *Swann* arose out of the prescription of specific remedies. In upholding the interim use of racially gerrymandered attendance zones, the Court said that " 'racially neutral' assignment plans ... may fail to counteract the continuing effects of past school segregation" and that in such circumstances "remedial altering of attendance zones is proper to achieve truly non-discriminatory assignments." The Court thereby found that racially differentiated treatment of groups is sometimes permissible as a remedy for official discrimination. The limits on this power to discriminate in the interest of nondiscrimination is, like much of *Swann's* teaching, not detailed. Its possible implications, however, are important. For *Swann* is saying much more than that the consequences of racial discrimination can be cancelled out, like a breach of contract, by compensating the victims of a wrong at the expense of its beneficiaries. Many of those who are disadvantaged by the racially differentiated treatment which the Court has upheld will have neither controlled nor profited from the past discriminatory policy. Indeed, in some cases it is the very victims of those policies who will be compelled, over their objection, to abandon the schools of their preference. If *Swann* approves the imposition of racial burdens notwithstanding the innocence of the group disadvantaged by them, the decision may provide support for corrective classification by race in many other areas.

However, racially gerrymandered school zones do not predicate official action upon the race of an individual. The zones are doubtless selected with a view to their overall racial composition and to that extent government benefits might be racially determined, but each individual within the zone is presumably treated alike. There is no need therefore to ascertain the race of a particular person or to deny him, because of his color, a benefit to which his next-door neighbor is entitled. For these reasons the classification is arguably less invidious than, and hence not precedent for, the racially differentiated treatment of individuals.

The Court's majority-to-minority transfer plan will differentiate among individual students on the basis of race, and where the receiving school offers a "better" education than the sending school, the government will be implicated in a conferral of racially predicated benefits. Nevertheless, there is a significant difference between the harm resulting from an assignment to a particular school and that resulting from preferential hiring or university admissions programs which completely exclude an individual on the basis of color. Since one of the questions raised by racial classifications is whether "the public interest involved outweighs the detriments that will be incurred by the affected private parties," the degree of harm imposed by the classification will be a critical factor in assessing its constitutionality. Note, 82 Harv.L.Rev. 1067, 1103 (1969). Moreover the reality of the school problem is that a racially neutral transfer policy would tend toward resegregation, and a denial of all transfers would leave many black children with no alternative to a segregated education. The attraction of a majority-to-minority transfer program—which the Court found to be "indispensable" for alleviating segregation and hence in compliance with the requirement that racial classifications be necessary to an overriding purpose—is that it avoids both of those defects; and yet transfers of this kind should not harm the children who are ineligible for them. The *Swann* case thus provided a measure of support for corrective classification by race but ultimately left the most difficult issues unresolved.

Early cases dealing with racial classifications in voting and employment were also inconclusive. *United Jewish Organizations of Williamsburgh v. Carey* (S.Ct.1977) upheld a reapportionment plan deliberately drawn to attain a non-white voting majority of 65% in certain legislative districts in New York. The 1965 Voting Rights Act, as construed by earlier cases, required the state to establish that redistricting would not have the purpose or effect of abridging the right to vote on account of race. (See pp. 226–28.) Four members of the Court, noting congressional concern that the voting strength of minorities could be diluted through reapportionment, said that the racial composition of an area can be considered in drawing district lines in order to prevent violations of the statute through such diluting effects. But a majority of the Justices concluded in two separate opinions that there had, in any event, been no cognizable discrimination against whites: since the reapportionment plan left white majorities in 70% of the districts in a county with a 65% white population, the plan could not be said to deprive whites of "fair representation" nor to have "the purpose or effect of discriminating against them on the basis of their race...." In short, the case was found not to involve any racially preferential treatment at all.

The employment cases—which present claims, not to fair political representation, but to individual opportunity—are more nearly on point. *Franks v. Bowman Transportation Co.* (S.Ct.1976) held that identifiable victims of job discrimination are entitled under the 1964 Civil Rights Act to constructive seniority retroactive to the date of the discriminatory treatment. The result may be to displace employees hired after that date so that such victims are restored to the position they would have occupied absent the unlawful discrimination. But awards of constructive seniority "do not present problems of racially preferential remedies. The beneficiaries receive a preference not because they are minorities, but because [they applied for jobs earlier than any displaced worker and] the employer discriminated against them; they are entitled to a priority not over whites alone but over all incumbents, including any minorities, hired during the relevant period." Brest, Forward: In Defense of the Antidiscrimination Principle, 90 Harv.L.Rev. 1, 39 (S.Ct.1976). *McDonald v. Santa Fe Trail Transportation Co.* (S.Ct.1976) did involve a minority preference, but the preference was held to be unlawful under federal statutes regulating employment discrimination. (See §§ 45–46.) In ruling that white employees cannot be subjected to more severe disciplinary measures than similarly situated blacks, the Court emphasized that white people are protected "upon the same standards" as non-whites against racial discrimination in employment. Although the opinion purported to reserve the issue of corrective classification by race, such classifications are not easily reconciled with the mandate to apply "the same standards" to whites and non-whites.

From Bakke to Adarand. In *Regents of the University of California v. Bakke* (S.Ct.1978), the Supreme Court addressed the question whether racial classifications may be employed by a state university to give special treatment to minorities previously subjected to invidious discrimination. At issue was the validity of a special admissions program designed to increase minority enrollment in the Medical School of the University of California at Davis. Under that program, 16 of 100 seats in each class were set aside for minority applicants. Allan Bakke, who had been denied admission to the medical school despite having higher grade and test scores than the average student admitted under the special admissions program, filed suit alleging that the program violated the equal protection clause and Title VI of the 1964 Civil Rights Act. Justice Powell, writing an opinion which announced the judgment of the Court, applied strict scrutiny to the admissions policy: "We have held that in 'order to justify the use of a suspect classification, a State must show that its purpose or interest is both constitutionally permissible and substantial, and that its use of the classification is necessary ... to the accomplishment of its purpose or the safeguarding of its interest.'" It did not matter that the disadvantaged group was the white majority since "The guarantee of equal protection cannot mean one thing when applied to one individual and something else when applied to a person of another color." Moreover the white majority is itself composed of numerous subgroups, many of which have themselves been subjected to discrimination in the past.

Justice Powell found the governmental interest in remedying societal discrimination to be insufficiently compelling to justify the use of racial classifications, noting that "We have never approved a classification that aids persons perceived as members of relatively victimized groups at the expense of other innocent individuals in the absence of judicial, legislative, or administrative findings of constitutional or statutory violations." Justice Powell believed that the University's interest in achieving a diverse student body was compelling, but he concluded that the special admissions program at Davis was not necessary to advance that interest because other admission policies would also serve the interest of diversity. Four members of the Court agreed that the special admissions program was invalid but relied on Title VI of the 1964 Civil Rights Act, which prohibits "discrimination under any program or activity receiving Federal financial assistance."

The critical point in the *Bakke* case was the availability of alternative means for achieving a diverse student body. Although Justice Powell mentioned the possibility of considering race as one of several factors in admissions, it would also be possible to achieve racial diversity through a racially neutral admissions policy. For example, a policy giving favorable treatment to disadvantaged applicants of every race could generate as much diversity as the Davis policy. The inclusion of whites in a special admissions program would increase the cost of the program, since disadvantaged students generally need financial aid and the addition of whites would enlarge the number of special admittees. But the Court has never accepted the claim that racial discrimination can be justified by a financial benefit to the discriminating party. Cf. *Missouri ex rel. Gaines v. Canada* (S.Ct.1938).

Eight years after *Bakke,* the Court reached a similar result when a racial classification was directed toward diversity in the faculty rather than in the student body. *Wygant v. Jackson Board of Educ.* (S.Ct.1986) involved a provision in a collective bargaining agreement which stated that, in the event of a layoff, "teachers with the most seniority ... shall be retained, except that at no time will there be a greater percentage of minority personnel laid off than the current percentage of minority personnel employed at the time of the layoff." Again a plurality of the Court, speaking through Justice Powell, said "the level of scrutiny does not change merely because the challenged classification operates against a group that historically has not been subject to government discrimination." The opinion stated that "any racial classification 'must be justified by a compelling governmental interest'" and "must be 'narrowly tailored to the achievement of that goal.'" Justice Powell rejected a suggestion that the layoff provision was needed to remedy past discrimination: "This Court never has held that societal discrimination alone is sufficient to justify a racial classification. Rather, the Court has insisted upon some showing of prior discrimination by the governmental unit involved before allowing limited use of racial classifications in order to remedy such discrimination." Justice Powell denied that the need to provide role models for minority students was compelling, since the role model theory would permit discriminatory practices "long past the point required by any legitimate remedial purpose," and he concluded that the layoff provision was "not sufficiently narrowly tailored."

The Court has, however, permitted some racial classifications to be used as a remedy for prior discrimination by the governmental unit employing the classification. *United States v. Paradise* (S.Ct. 1987) arose out of a long history of purposeful exclusion of blacks from employment as Alabama state troopers. Eleven years after a judicial finding of discrimination in hiring, there were still no black state troopers employed above the rank of corporal. A federal court then ordered the promotion of one black trooper for each white trooper elevated in rank, as long as qualified black candidates were available. In response to a contention that the state had been found guilty of discrimination in hiring rather than in promotional practices, a plurality of the Court ruled that "the race-conscious relief at issue here is justified by a compelling interest in remedying the discrimination that permeated entry-level hiring practices and the promotional process alike." See also *United Steelworkers of America v. Weber* (S.Ct.1979), ruling in a nonconstitutional case that the 1964 Civil Rights Act "does not condemn all private voluntary race-conscious affirmative action plans."

Nevertheless, *City of Richmond v. Croson Co.* (S.Ct.1989) struck down a municipality's use of racially based set-asides for minority business enterprises. The city of Richmond had established a plan requiring prime contractors on municipal construction projects to certify that at least 30% of the amount of each contract would be subcontracted to minority businesses, defined as an enterprise at least 51% of which was owned by black, spanish-speaking, oriental, Indian, Eskimo or Aleut citizens. In adopting this plan, the city council had apparently relied on the disparity between the city's 50% black population and the 0.67% of prime contracts awarded to minority businesses, and on testimony that there was widespread discrimination in the construction industry. The Supreme Court subjected the Richmond plan to exacting scrutiny and held that it violated the equal protection clause. *Fullilove v. Klutznick* (S.Ct.1980), which had upheld a congressionally required set-aside for minority businesses, was distinguished on the ground that Congress "has a specific constitutional mandate to enforce the dictates of the Fourteenth Amendment." (See §§ 41–42, discussing Congress' broad powers under the enforcement clause of the fourteenth amendment.)

As in *Wygant,* the Court asked whether the government had demonstrated a compelling interest in classifying by race and whether the racial classification was narrowly tailored to that interest. It found that Richmond's minority set-aside plan violated both prongs of the *Wygant* standard. Absent specific evidence of identified discrimination in the Richmond construction industry, the city did not have a compelling interest in racially based set-asides. Reliance on a comparison of the percentage of minorities in the general population to the percentage of prime contracts awarded to minority businesses was misplaced since statistical comparisons to the general population are inappropriate where special qualifications are required. Moreover, the minority set-asides were not narrowly tailored to a legitimate remedial purpose. The plan extended to minority groups, like Indians and Eskimoes, who were not shown to have been affected by any discrimination in Richmond, and to minority businesses anywhere in the country, notwithstanding that they had never done business in Richmond. Lastly, the city council appeared not to have considered racially neutral measures to increase minority participation in construction, such as city financing for small businesses without regard to race.

It would be difficult to exaggerate the importance of the *Croson* case. The Court clearly required substantial evidence of specific or "identified" discrimination as a precondition for minority set-asides. General societal discrimination is not enough, and the Court suggested at one point that the use of racially based set-asides must be limited to situations in which the state can put forward "a prima facie case of constitutional or statutory violation." Under this approach, the equal protection clause would permit racial classifications only as a remedy for specific acts of illegal discrimination. The scrutiny in the *Croson* case also focused on whether "remedial action was necessary" and on the availability of an alternative to classification by race. As Justice Marshall observed in his dissenting opinion, "for the first time a majority of [the] Court has adopted strict scrutiny as its standard of equal protection review of race-conscious remedial measures." This standard, if applied as it was in

§ 23　　　SUSPECT CLASSIFICATIONS　　　109

Croson, would plainly impose substantial restrictions on the use of racial classifications, even when they are designed to benefit the victims of past societal discrimination.

Finally, in *Adarand Constructors, Inc. v. Pena* (S.Ct.1995), the Court revisited the question of *congressional* power to give preferential treatment to racial minorities. *Adarand* arose out of a highway construction project funded by the U.S. Department of Transportation. The Department awarded the prime contract to Mountain Gravel & Construction Company under terms which promised additional compensation if Mountain Gravel hired subcontractors that were certified as small businesses controlled by "socially and economically disadvantaged individuals." In order to qualify for the additional payment, Mountain Gravel rejected Adarand's low bid and awarded a subcontract for guardrails to a certified company. Under federal law, African Americans, Hispanics and certain other minorities were presumed to be socially and economically disadvantaged, and Adarand argued that this presumption discriminated on the basis of race in violation of the due process clause of the fifth amendment.

On review, the Supreme Court ruled that all government classifications by race must be subjected to "the strictest judicial scrutiny." The Court rejected the suggestion that Congress has greater latitude than the states in adopting racial classifications, and it overruled *Metro Broadcasting, Inc. v. FCC* (S.Ct.1990), which had followed *Fullilove* in upholding federally mandated preferences for racial minorities. The *Adarand* case acknowledged that some racial classifications can survive strict scrutiny: "When race-based action is necessary to further a compelling interest, such action is within constitutional contraints" if the action has been narrowly tailored. See *United States v. Paradise* (discussed at page 106 above), which *Adarand* cited as an example of a valid racial classification. But cases applying strict scrutiny have shown that this test is extremely difficult to satisfy. E.g. *Shaw v. Hunt* (S.Ct.1996); *Bush v. Vera* (S.Ct.1996).

The Court has also applied strict scrutiny to the use of race in drawing election district lines for the purpose of increasing the likelihood that minority candidates will be elected. If the use of race can be inferred from the "bizarre" shape of the district, or if it is otherwise shown that race was a "predominant" factor in drawing district lines, courts must apply strict scrutiny. See *Shaw v. Reno* (S.Ct.1993) and *Miller v. Johnson* (S.Ct.1995).

General Policy Considerations. A number of arguments have been advanced in an effort to show that racial preferences are, or are not, necessary to an overriding governmental purpose. These arguments are treated elsewhere in great detail and can be sketched here only briefly. See e.g., DeFunis Symposium, 75 Colum.L.Rev. 483 (1975). In general, racial preferences have been put forth as a means of compensating for the continuing effects of official discrimination. A colorblind government, it is contended, cannot satisfy present needs, much less redress accumulated grievances; instead the government must give special treatment to those who were disadvantaged by more than a century of color-consciousness. In addition, it is often urged that minority preferences are needed to produce suitable role models for non-whites and to create diversity within an academic or professional community.

The argument on the other side has stressed the risks inherent in racially differentiated treatment, risks which are especially serious for black people and members of other minority groups. Such treatment, even though intended to neutralize discrimination and achieve equality, may actually generate more private prejudice. Blacks as well as whites might instinctively attribute the preferential treatment of a minority race to a low assessment of its capabilities. Racially predicated government action may thereby appear to confirm the folklore of racism, and it cannot be assumed that appearances will give way to underlying subtleties.

This danger of stigmatizing blacks and reinforcing racial stereotypes was at the heart of Justice Douglas's rejection of racial preferences in law school admissions. His opinion in *DeFunis v. Odegaard* (S.Ct.1974) addressed the problem directly: "A segregated admissions process creates suggestions of stigma and caste no less than a segregated classroom, and in the end it may produce that result despite its contrary intentions. One other assumption must be clearly disapproved, that blacks or browns cannot make it on their individual merit. That is a stamp of inferiority that a State is not permitted to place on any lawyer." Of course, the argument that blacks are able to "make it on their individual merit" suggests that the interest in diversity and role models can be served without racially based preferences, albeit by modifying traditional criteria for selection.

Racial preferences have also been criticized as "unjust to those [who are] excluded" without having themselves been implicated in the wrongdoing which preferences attempt to rectify. See Symposium, supra at 520. Although blacks will often have experiences and needs different from those of whites, in some cases a white applicant will have similar needs and analogous experiences. If he is nevertheless excluded from compensatory programs, it is because of factors which are common to his race, but neither uniquely nor universally applicable to it. Critics object that this kind of disability, imposed on the basis of racial generalizations, is at odds with the Court's repeated emphasis on the personal nature of equal protection rights and tends to legitimize the type of thinking which underlies the very bigotry we seek to combat. Beyond this, it is argued that the special treatment of a racial class, drawn to include individuals of diverse need and to exclude others of equal need, are highly devisive and tend to dilute the political strength of all disadvantaged peoples by placing their interests in sharp conflict.

Many observers believe that the risks inherent in racially differentiated treatment would nevertheless be justified if no other effective remedy could be found, for it is difficult to conceive of a more important goal than the achievement of racial equality. They point out, however, that Congress and the states have broad power to answer the needs of black people and of disadvantaged members of other groups through racially neutral corrective action. State universities, for example, can admit on a nonracial basis students who, because of previous disadvantage, do not qualify under existing admissions requirements. In addition to modifying admissions criteria, the states can undertake vigorous recruitment and other affirmative action which does not discriminate by race. Critics therefore assert that neutral measures may prove adequate to meet the needs of black people and others similarly situated, and that racial preferences have not been "shown to be necessary to the accomplishment of [the] state objective." *Loving v. Va.* (S.Ct.1967).

§ 24. SEX DISCRIMINATION

The Standard of Review. Unlike racial classifications which have long been subject to strict scrutiny, gender-based distinctions have never been held by a majority of the Court to be constitutionally suspect. Initially the Court applied an extremely deferential standard of review to classifications by sex. Thus *Goesaert v. Cleary* (S.Ct.1948) upheld as rational a statute that prohibited a woman from obtaining a bartender's license unless she was "the wife or daughter of the male owner" of a licensed establishment. And in *Hoyt v. Fla.* (S.Ct.1961), the Court rejected an equal protection challenge to a provision which limited jury service by women to volunteer registrants, stating that "woman is still regarded as the center of home and family life" and that jury duty might not be "consistent with her own special responsibilities." Compare *Taylor v. La.* (S.Ct.1975) which held 14 years later that such a provision violates the sixth amendment guarantee to trial by a jury drawn from a representative cross-section of the community.

Beginning in 1971 judicial review of sex classifications seemed to become more demanding in fact, if not always in name, than *Goesaert* and *Hoyt* had portended. The first of the modern cases was *Reed v. Reed* (S.Ct.1971), which purported to apply the rationality test to strike down a requirement that "of several persons claiming and equally entitled to administer [an estate], males must be preferred to females." The Court said that "the [statutory] objective of reducing the work load on probate courts by eliminating one class of contests is not without some legitimacy." It concluded, however, that giving a preference to members of one sex is "the very kind of arbitrary legislative choice forbidden by the Equal Protection Clause." Since an automatic preference served the state's interest in reducing administrative disputes, commentators have argued that reliance on the rationality test was misplaced and that only a special sensitivity to sex classifications can adequately explain the result in *Reed*. But despite this quite plausible analysis, *Reed* provided little security against deferential review in future cases since the Court explicitly relied on rationality alone. Conceivably, *Reed* might have reached the same conclusion if a preference had been given to people with blue eyes or brown hair rather than to males. Read this way, the thrust of the decision would be that it is irrational to create any "arbitrary" preferences, except presumably through random selection, as a means of establishing priorities among similarly situated individuals.

Frontiero v. Richardson (S.Ct.1973) came closer than any other case to endorsing a strict scrutiny standard for sex classifications. The Court there invalidated statutory provisions which allowed male members of the armed forces to claim their wives as dependents for the purpose of qualifying for certain benefits, but required female members to show that their husbands were actually dependent upon them in order to qualify. The government argued that this classification promoted interests in economy and administrative convenience because "wives in our society frequently are dependent upon their husbands, while husbands rarely are dependent upon their wives." However, that logic encounters at least two major difficulties. First, broad generalizations of this kind provide a wholly unacceptable predicate for sex discrimination, particularly when the underlying condition of presumed dependency may well be itself a product of other discrimination; second, the argument of economy and convenience assumes that "it is actually cheaper to grant increased benefits with respect to *all* male members, than it is to determine which male members are in fact entitled to such benefits...." (plurality opinion in *Frontiero*). Accordingly the Court had no difficulty striking down the classification, but only four Justices found gender-based distinctions to be suspect, while four others simply invoked the rationale of the *Reed* case. The standard of review for such distinctions thus remained as uncertain as the *Reed* case had made it.

This uncertainty was reinforced by *Stanton v. Stanton* (S.Ct.1975). At issue in *Stanton* was the constitutionality of a Utah statute setting the age of majority at 21 for males and at 18 for females. The Court held that in the context of child support a differential age of majority based on sex could not satisfy "any test" of equal protection—"compelling state interest, or rational basis, or something in between ..." It therefore rejected the Utah Supreme Court's reliance on "old notions" concerning the male's responsibilities to his family and the need "for him to get a good education ... before he undertakes those responsibilities." But the *Stanton* case also illustrates the limits of constitutional protection against sex discrimination. The Court can demand equal treatment in child support, but the level of support and its duration are matters of state law. The Utah legislature responded to *Stanton* by requiring child support until age 18, with a proviso that courts "may order support to age 21." Utah Code 15–2–1 (1975). Whether the state judges who invoked the "old notions" in *Stanton* will be less deferential to those notions in exercising their discretion under the new statute is open to serious question. Cf. *Stanton v. Stanton* (S.Ct. 1977).

Craig v. Boren (S.Ct.1976) marked the emergence of a new standard of review for gender classifications. That case brought a challenge to the constitutionality of an Oklahoma statute which prohibited liquor licensees from selling "nonintoxicating 3.2% beer" to males under the age of 21 or females under the age of 18. The attorney for the state argued that the statute was aimed at the enhancement of traffic safety, and he relied on statistics showing that 2% of the males between the ages of 18 and 20 were arrested for driving under the influence of alcohol, while only .18% of the females in that age group were arrested for the same offense. The Supreme Court said the equal protection clause requires "that classifications by gender must serve important governmental objectives and must be substantially related to achievement of those objectives." While not disputing the importance of traffic safety, the Court found that objective to be only tenuously related to the purchase by men of nonintoxicating beer since (a) no more than a 2% correlation between traffic safety and gender had been asserted and (b) the statute did not regulate the *consumption* of beer by males after its "purchase by their 18–20–year–old female companions." Given the latter fact and the skepticism it aroused as to the actual purpose of the statute, it is doubtful that the Court would have reached a different result under a meaningful application of the rationality test. (See pp. 171–77.)

Nevertheless *Craig v. Boren* broke significant new ground in the treatment of sex discrimination.

Exactly how significant the breakthrough will be depends largely on the manner in which the *Craig* rule is applied—specifically on what is required to make a governmental objective "important" rather than merely legitimate and to make a relationship to the objective "substantial" rather than rational. It was impossible to discern from *Craig* the probable impact of the new standard, since the justification offered for discriminating in that case was "far too tenuous" to test the stringency of the standard.

The uncertainty of *Craig's* impact became apparent in *Michael M. v. Sonoma County Superior Court* (S.Ct.1981). At issue in *Michael M.* was the validity of California's statutory rape law, which prohibited sexual intercourse "with a female not the wife of the perpetrator, where the female is under the age of 18 years." The statute, which was defended as an attempt to prevent illegitimate teenage pregnancies, clearly embodied a gender classification since only men were subject to prosecution under it. Justice Rehnquist's plurality opinion stated that "the traditional minimum rationality test takes on somewhat 'sharper focus' when gender-based classifications are challenged" but that such a classification will be upheld when it "realistically reflects the fact that the sexes are not similarly situated." Finding that women "suffer disproportionately the profound physical, emotional, and psychological consequences of sexual activity," the opinion concluded that California's statutory rape law was "*sufficiently* related to the State's objectives to pass constitutional muster." (Emphasis added.) Four dissenting Justices noted that a gender-neutral statute could have a deterrent effect on twice as many potential offenders and argued that California's statutory rape law violated the equal protection clause.

The important question raised in *Michael M.*, as observed in Justice Steven's dissenting opinion, was whether a state "may always punish the male and never the female when they are equally responsible or when the female is the more responsible of the two." Certainly a 13–year–old boy would not always be more culpable than a 16 or 17–year–old partner of his. Nor is it obvious that such a boy would necessarily suffer less than an older partner the "emotional and psychological consequences of sexual activity." In short, both the culpability of the parties and their exposure to harm are likely to vary from case to case rather than to fall consistently along gender-based lines. It is not surprising, therefore, that the Court made no claim that the *Craig* standard had been satisfied. Instead, the opinion said it was "hardly *unreasonable* for a legislature acting to protect minor females to exclude them from punishment" and that the statute was "sufficiently related to the State's objectives." *Michael M.* seemed therefore to suggest a willingness to retreat from the heightened scrutiny that was implicit in the substantial relationship test of *Craig v. Boren.*

The uncertainty aroused by *Michael M.* was compounded in *Rostker v. Goldberg* (S.Ct.1981). The *Rostker* case dealt with a provision in the Selective

Service Act which authorized the President to require men, but not women, to register for the draft. The Court, speaking through Justice Rehnquist, said the purpose of registration "was to prepare for a draft *of combat troops*" and that under restrictions not challenged in this case women were ineligible for combat. The Court concluded that the exemption of women from registration was "closely related" to the purpose for registration and was constitutionally valid: "Men and women, because of the combat restrictions on women, are simply not similarly situated for purposes of a draft or registration for a draft." But the standard of review in *Rostker* was obscured by the Court's pointed refusal to reaffirm *Craig v. Boren* and by the Court's deference to congressional authority on national defense and military matters.

However, the Court reaffirmed its support for a heightened standard of review in *U.S. v. Virginia* (S.Ct.1996). At issue in that case was the validity of a state admissions policy which excluded women from the Virginia Military Institute (VMI) without providing them with equivalent educational opportunities at another state institution. For many years, VMI pursued its mission of producing citizen-soldiers through an adversarial method of training designed to instill physical and mental discipline. In response to a federal court decision that effectively required either the admission of women at VMI or the establishment of a parallel institution, the state proposed a program for women at Mary Baldwin College, a private liberal arts school. The latter program would share VMI's mission of producing citizen-soldiers, but it would differ from VMI in its method of instruction, its academic offerings and its financial resources. The state tried to justify the differential treatment of women on two grounds: that single-sex instruction at VMI would contribute to diversity in education and that the adversative method of training would have to be significantly modified if women were admitted to VMI.

On review, the Supreme Court rejected both of those arguments. Writing for a 7–1 majority, Justice Ginsburg said the state had not shown that VMI "was established, or has been maintained, with a view to diversifying ... educational opportunities." The Court also rejected the suggestion that the admission of women would destroy the adversative system: "the expert testimony established [that some women] 'are capable of all of the individual activities required of VMI cadets,' and the parties agree that 'some women can meet the physical standards VMI now imposes on men.'" The Court said it was for these women that a remedy must be crafted. Since some women were capable of all the required activities, the state's goal of producing citizen-soldiers was not "substantially advanced by women's categorical exclusion, in total disregard of their individual merit."

But while the Court applied an intermediate standard of review, it also said that "Parties who seek to defend gender-based government action must demonstrate an 'exceedingly persuasive justification' for that action." This caused Chief Justice

Rehnquist to observe in a concurring opinion that the Court had introduced "an element of uncertainty respecting the appropriate test." Of course, this was the same kind of uncertainty that Rehnquist himself had introduced in the opinions he authored in *Rostker* and *Michael M*. The intermediate standard is obviously subject to some manipulation from either side. See also *J.E.B. v. Alabama ex rel. T.B.* (S.Ct.1994), applying the intermediate standard to prohibit the state's use of peremptory challenges based on gender.

Compensatory Treatment. Since sex classifications have not been held to be suspect, the Court has had relatively little difficulty approving compensatory treatment in this area. *Kahn v. Shevin* (S.Ct.1974) was the first case on the subject. It upheld a Florida law which granted widows, but not widowers, an annual property tax exemption. The Court cited evidence that "the job market is inhospitable" to women in justifying the exemption in their favor: "We deal here with a state tax law reasonably designed to further the state policy of cushioning the financial impact of spousal loss upon the sex for whom that loss imposes a disproportionately heavy burden."

But the generalities in the *Kahn* opinion ignore the fact that "the financial impact of spousal loss" will sometimes be greater for widowers than for widows. Some members of the Court asserted that a widower's financial distress does not result "from sex discrimination as in the case of widows." However this assumes that the widower was self-supporting during his wife's lifetime, for it would disregard reality to suggest that discrimination in employment will disadvantage women but not their dependents. A widower who had been financially dependent upon his wife would suffer from discrimination against her while she lived and from Florida's discrimination against himself after she died. Only by indulging the same assumptions of male self-sufficiency and female dependency, which the Court has elsewhere repudiated, could *Kahn* overlook the plight of dependent widowers. This of course, does not mean that the Florida tax exemption is irrational but simply that, as the majority and dissenting opinions make clear, relaxed scrutiny was needed to sustain it.

The Court was more sensitive to overgeneralization in *Weinberger v. Wiesenfeld* (S.Ct.1975). That case involved a section of the Social Security Act which provided for benefits to be paid to the wife, but not the husband, of a deceased wage earner with minor children. The Court found that since these benefits were conditioned upon responsibility for a minor they must have been intended to facilitate the care of children rather than to compensate for past discrimination. Given that purpose, it was "entirely irrational" to draw a gender-based distinction: "It is no less important for a child to be cared for by its sole surviving parent when that parent is male rather than female." The fact that men "are more likely than women to be the primary supporters" of the family and less likely to avail themselves of the opportunity to remain at home with their children could not justify "the denigration of the efforts of women ... whose earnings contribute significantly to their family's support." No doubt, dependent widowers who were denied tax exemptions under *Kahn* would have appreciated a similar respect for the efforts of working women in Florida.

A rationality test was again applied, though with different results, in *Schlesinger v. Ballard* (S.Ct.1975). An attack was there made against a federal policy under which male naval officers were discharged upon being twice passed over for promotion, while female officers were allowed to remain in the Navy for 13 years before being discharged for want of promotion. The Court ruled that in light of the Navy's restrictions on combat and sea duty by women, which were not challenged in the case, Congress could "quite rationally have believed that women line officers had less opportunity for promotion than did their male counterparts, and that a longer period of tenure for women officers would, therefore, be consistent with the goal to provide women officers with 'fair and equitable career advancement programs.'" Unlike the classification in *Frontiero* which served only administrative convenience, the provisions in *Ballard* were said to produce "a flow of promotions commensurate with the Navy's current needs." Why the Navy should be permitted to define its needs in terms of gender is a question the Court did not address. Nor did it rebut the dissenters' argument that a compensatory rationale is difficult to harmonize with the fact that men and women do not compete against one another for naval promotions but are subject to separate parallel systems. Perhaps the answer is that the separate systems are themselves discriminatory, but this is the very question the Court declined to examine.

Four post-*Craig* cases complete the record to date. In *Califano v. Webster* (S.Ct.1977), a statutory provision was sustained allowing women to eliminate three more years of low income than men could eliminate for the purpose of calculating retirement benefits. All members of the Court agreed that the statute "operated directly to compensate women for past economic discrimination." *Califano v. Goldfarb* (S.Ct.1977) sparked more controversy. That case set aside a section of the Social Security Act under which survivors' benefits were paid to a widower only upon proof that "he was receiving at least one-half of his support" from his deceased spouse, while the widows of covered wage earners were paid such benefits automatically. The plurality opinion, written for four members of the Court, said that the provision was based on "an intention to aid the dependent spouses of deceased wage earners, coupled with a presumption that wives are usually dependent." Given this interpretation, which ruled out a compensatory rationale, the case was held to be squarely controlled by *Frontiero* and *Wiesenfeld* where the Court had found unlawful discrimination against female employees. Mr. Justice Stevens, whose concurring vote was needed to overcome a four-member dissent, concluded that the relevant discrimination in *Goldfarb* fell upon surviving males, rather than upon deceased female wage earners, and was an unconstitutional product of legislative "habit," not of "analysis or actual reflection." His opinion recognized the contrary tenor of *Kahn v. Shevin,* but clearly indicated his dissatisfaction with that decision. See also *Wengler v. Druggists Mut. Co.* (S.Ct. 1980), invalidating a workmen's compensation law which granted death benefits to widows but not, in the absence of proof of dependency, to widowers: "there [may be] empirical support for the proposition that men are more likely [than women] to be the principal supporters of their spouses and families ... but the bare assertion of this argument falls far short of justifying gender-based discrimination...."

Finally, the Court struck down a state university's practice of denying men admission to nursing school in *Mississippi Univ. For Women v. Hogan* (S.Ct.1982). The state's primary justification for the single-sex admissions policy was that it compensated for discrimination against women. In an important ruling on compensatory treatment, the Court said that "a State can evoke a compensatory purpose to justify an otherwise discriminatory classification only if members of the gender benefited by the classification actually suffer a disadvantage related to the classification." Since no showing could be made that women, who earned more than 90% of baccalaureate degrees in nursing, lacked adequate opportunities in that field, the Court had no difficulty holding that the single-sex admissions policy violated the equal protection clause: "Rather than compensate for discriminatory barriers faced by women, [the] policy of excluding males from admission to the School of Nursing tends to perpetuate the stereotyped view of nursing as an exclusively woman's job."

Family Rights. Between 1979 and 1983 the Supreme Court decided a number of sex discrimination cases dealing with personal and property rights within the family. *Kirchberg v. Feenstra* (S.Ct. 1981) involved a Louisiana statute that gave a husband, as "head and master" of property jointly owned with his wife, the power to dispose of such property without his spouse's consent. Since the statute embodied the same kind of generalization as *Reed v. Reed,* the Court found it easy to hold the provision unconstitutional. The fact that a woman could avoid the discriminatory impact of the statute by making a "declaration of authentic act" to prohibit her husband from unilaterally mortgaging their home was not enough to save the statute: "As we have previously noted, the 'absence of an insurmountable barrier' will not redeem an otherwise unconstitutionally discriminatory law." And in *Orr v. Orr* (S.Ct.1979), the Court set aside a state law providing that husbands, but not wives, could be required to pay alimony upon the dissolution of marriage. Although husbands were arguably less likely to be in need of financial support, sex could not be used as a proxy for need because individualized hearings were already held to measure financial circumstances, and so gender-based generalizations were unnecessary.

However, *Parham v. Hughes* (S.Ct.1979) upheld a statute that allowed the mother of an illegitimate child to sue for the child's wrongful death but disallowed such a suit by the father unless he had formally legitimated the child. Both the plurality and concurring opinions emphasized that it was within the father's power to remove himself from the statutory disability by legitimating the child. But neither opinion addressed the Court's frequent admonition that the "absence of an insurmountable barrier" will not save an otherwise unconstitutional discriminatory law.

Two decisions on adoption complete the picture of family rights cases to date. In *Caban v. Mohammed* (S.Ct.1979), the Court invalidated a New York statute that required the consent of the birth mother, but not that of the father, for the adoption of a child born out of wedlock. The Court, making no mention of *Parham v. Hughes,* which was decided the same day, said that "no showing has been made that the different treatment afforded unmarried fathers and unmarried mothers ... bears a substantial relationship to the proclaimed interest of the State in promoting the adoption of illegitimate children." Four years later, *Lehr v. Robertson* (S.Ct.1983) upheld the application of a New York statute that gave the mother of an illegitimate child the right to receive notice and to veto a proposed adoption, but denied notice to the father unless he had entered his name in a "putative father registry" or had satisfied certain other statutory conditions. The Court distinguished *Caban* on the ground that the father in that case had participated in the rearing of the children: "If one parent has an established custodial relationship with the child and the other parent has either abandoned or never established a relationship, the Equal Protection Clause does not prevent a State from according the two parents different legal rights." Yet the *Lehr* opinion offered no explanation for permitting the state to give notice and veto rights to all mothers of illegitimates, while giving those rights to fathers only if they had "established a relationship" with the child.

The Equal Rights Amendment and Unique Physical Characteristics. The proposed equal rights amendment provided that "Equality of rights under the law shall not be denied or abridged by the United States or any State on account of sex" and that Congress shall have power to enforce the amendment by appropriate legislation. The amendment failed of passage but has been reintroduced in Congress. The standard of review of sex classifications was a central issue under the equal rights amendment, as it has been in the cases previously discussed. Although it was occasionally said that rational gender distinctions would be permissible under the amendment, this seems a wholly untenable interpretation. The equal protection clause already prohibits irrational classifications by gender, and it could scarcely have been the mission of the equal rights amendment merely to reiterate that prohibition. Others have read the proposed amendment to require strict scrutiny of sex-based distinctions, much as the Constitution now requires of racial ones. This was evidently the view of Justice Powell and two other members of the Court in the *Frontiero* case. A third interpretation of the amendment would forbid all official classifications by gender except to protect privacy or in dealing with physical characteristics unique to one sex. It has been widely assumed that this interpretation would maximize protection against gender-based discrimination. However, that assumption should be re-examined in light of the decision in *Geduldig v. Aiello* (S.Ct.1974).

The *Aiello* case raised the question whether a state insurance program which provided coverage against most disabling injuries and illnesses, but excluded disabilities arising out of normal pregnancy, ran afoul of the equal protection clause. Three Justices believed that "by singling out for less favorable treatment a gender-linked disability peculiar to women" the state had created an unconstitutional "double standard." However, the majority upheld the classification on the ground that it was reasonably related to legitimate interests in avoiding higher insurance rates, government subsidies or lower rates of benefits for insured disabilities. The Court reduced to a footnote its view that the classification was not "based upon gender as such" because it benefited nonpregnant members of both sexes and was not shown to be a pretext "designed to effect an invidious discrimination." Given the outcome in *Aiello,* the exception for unique physical characteristics which some commentators find in the equal rights amendment may prove to be far broader than they anticipate unless the exception itself is controlled by strict scrutiny.

§ 25. DIFFERENTIAL TREATMENT OF INDIANS

Morton v. Mancari (S.Ct.1974) upheld a federal statute granting employment preferences in the Bureau of Indian Affairs to qualified Native Americans. The Court ruled that the preferences were political, not racial, in nature since they applied only to those Indians who were members of federally recognized tribes. Because the classification was reasonably related to the "non-racially based goal" of Indian self-government and of making "the BIA more responsive to the needs of its constituent groups," the provision survived attack under the due process clause of the fifth amendment. See also *U.S. v. Antelope* (S.Ct.1977) (applying *Mancari* to sustain the exercise of federal criminal jurisdiction over certain acts by tribal Indians on a reservation, even though non-tribal members would be subject to state jurisdiction for the same acts). Most federal Indian law can be explained on a racially neutral basis though some statutes, classifying in terms of a person's "quantum of Indian blood," probably cannot. See *Simmons v. Eagle Seelatsee* (E.D.Wash.1965).

§ 26. WEALTH AND AGE CLASSIFICATIONS

Despite occasional dicta to the effect that "lines drawn on the basis of wealth [are] highly suspect and thereby demand a more exacting judicial scrutiny," *McDonald v. Board of Election Commissioners* (S.Ct.1969), the Court has sustained wealth classifications upon a showing of no more than rational justification. *James v. Valtierra* (S.Ct.1971) is the leading case. It upheld a state constitutional provision that no "low-cost housing project," defined as housing "for persons of low income," could be developed unless approved by a referendum in its proposed locality. The Court emphasized that "this procedure insures that all the people of a community will have a voice in a decision which may lead to large expenditures of local governmental funds for increased public services and to lower tax revenues." In spite of the majority's assertion that the poor had not been "singled out for mandatory referendums" because the same procedure was required for certain other government activities, it seems apparent that *Valtierra* involved an explicit wealth classification: low-cost, but not medium or high-cost, housing was subject to a veto at the polls. The fact that a referendum was required for other activities does not make the classification in *Valtierra* wealth-free any more than the exclusion of women from the jury, together with blacks, made the classification in the *Strauder* case racially neutral.

Valtierra makes it clear that wealth has not joined race as a suspect criterion. In a few areas of constitutionally heightened interest, such as access to instruments of criminal justice, wealth-related policies may be closely scrutinized. (See § 32.) But as some cases have noted, the Court "has never ... held that wealth discrimination alone provides an adequate basis for invoking strict scrutiny." *San Antonio Ind. School Dist. v. Rodriguez* (S.Ct. 1973).

Age has also been held not to be a suspect classification. In *Massachusetts Board of Retirement v. Murgia* (S.Ct.1976), the Supreme Court sustained a statute requiring uniformed state police officers to retire at age 50. The Court distinguished between age and racial classifications: while the aged have sometimes been subjected to discrimination, they "have not experienced a 'history of purposeful unequal treatment' or been subjected to unique disabilities on the basis of stereotyped characteristics not truly indicative of their abilities.... Old age does not define a 'discrete and insular' group ... in need of 'extraordinary protection from the majoritarian political process.' Instead, it marks a stage that each of us will reach if we live out our normal span." The Court then applied a reasonableness test to sustain the statute: "Since physical ability generally declines with age, mandatory retirement at 50 serves to remove from police service those whose fitness for uniformed work presumptively has diminished with age." See also *Vance v. Bradley* (S.Ct.1979) (upholding mandatory retirement at 60 for federal personnel of the Foreign Service). *Cleburne v. Cleburne Living Center* (S.Ct.1985) reaffirmed *Murgia's* suggestion that suspect classifications generally involve governmental use of factors which "are so seldom relevant to the achievement of any legitimate state interest that laws grounded in such considerations are deemed to reflect prejudice and antipathy...." (See § 34 for discussion of *Cleburne's* refusal to treat mental retardation as a suspect classification.)

§ 27. DISCRIMINATION AGAINST ALIENS

The Supreme Court has reviewed three major types of discrimination against aliens—restrictions on employment, prohibitions against owning real property, and limitations on access to natural or financial resources of the government. *Graham v. Richardson* (S.Ct.1971), dealing with the third category, held that state laws denying welfare benefits to all aliens, or to those who had resided in the United States for less than 15 years, violated the equal protection clause and encroached upon federal power over resident aliens. The Court ruled that "classifications based on alienage, like those based on nationality or race, are inherently suspect and subject to close judicial scrutiny. Aliens as a class are a prime example of a 'discrete and insular' minority ... for whom such heightened judicial solicitude is appropriate." Attempts to justify welfare restrictions on the basis of a special public interest in the distribution of limited funds were unsuccessful since "there can be no 'special public interest' in tax revenues to which aliens have contributed on an equal basis with the residents of the State." See also *Takahashi v. Fish & Game Comm.* (S.Ct.1948), holding a state's property interest in offshore fish inadequate to support the denial of fishing rights to persons ineligible for citizenship.

The Supreme Court has had no recent occasion to reconsider its early decision in *Terrace v. Thompson* (S.Ct.1923), which upheld state power to deny aliens the right to own land. However, the current vitality of *Terrace* is extremely doubtful in light of *Graham* and its progeny. Indeed, state courts had taken the initiative in striking down alien land laws even before *Graham* was decided. E.g. *Fujii v. State* (Cal.1952).

Occupational restrictions on aliens have also been closely scrutinized in some cases. *In re Griffiths* (S.Ct.1973) struck down the exclusion of resident aliens from eligibility to practice law. Elaborating on *Graham,* the Court wrote: "In order to justify the use of a suspect classification, a State must show that its purpose or interest is both constitutionally permissible and substantial, and that its use of the classification is 'necessary [to] the accomplishment' of its purpose or the safeguarding of its interest." Under that test the total exclusion of aliens could not be justified by the government's "undoubted interest in high professional standards." Similarly, a requirement of citizenship for notaries public was found unconstitutional in *Ber-*

nal v. Fainter (S.Ct.1984). The government's interest in assuring that notaries be familiar with state law was insufficient to satisfy the demands of strict scrutiny, since aliens as a class are not incapable of familiarizing themselves with the law. See also *Examining Bd. of Engineers v. Flores de Otero* (S.Ct.1976) (invalidating a requirement of citizenship for licensed engineers); *Sugarman v. Dougall* (S.Ct.1973) (invalidating a citizenship requirement for employment in the state's classified civil service).

However, the Court has carved out an exception of uncertain dimension for positions involving a "political function." For example, *Ambach v. Norwick* (S.Ct.1979) upheld a state law denying employment as public school teachers to aliens who were eligible for citizenship but declined to be naturalized. The Court said that the exclusion of aliens from positions that "go to the heart of representative government" need only bear a rational relationship to a legitimate state interest. For this reason, citizenship requirements have also been sustained for police officers and probation officers. *Foley v. Connelie* (S.Ct.1978); *Cabell v. Chavez–Salido* (S.Ct.1982). Nevertheless, the scope of the "political function" exception remains unclear. The Court has said that what distinguishes offices within the exception is "policy-making responsibility or broad discretion in the execution of public policy." *Bernal*. But only a gradual process of case-by-case determinations can reveal how great a discretionary or policymaking role will be needed to trigger a reduced level of scrutiny.

Because of the "paramount federal power" to regulate immigration and matters affecting foreign relations, it is possible that "overriding national interests may provide a justification for a citizenship requirement in the federal service even though an identical requirement may not be enforced by a State." *Hampton v. Mow Sun Wong* (S.Ct.1976). For much the same reasons, Congress has broader power than the states to restrict an alien's eligibility for government benefits. Compare *Mathews v. Diaz* (S.Ct.1976) (upholding congressional authority to limit participation by aliens in a medicare program to those continuously residing in the United States for five years and admitted for permanent residence) with *Nyquist v. Mauclet* (S.Ct.1977) (striking down a state statute that barred financial assistance in higher education to resident aliens unless they had applied for United States citizenship or planned to do so). But when aliens are excluded from federal employment, due process requires that "there be a legitimate basis for presuming that the [exclusion] was actually intended to serve" national interests and that the citizenship rule "be justified by reasons which are properly the concern of [the] agency" imposing it. *Hampton v. Mow Sun Wong* (regulation of the Civil Service Commission barring resident aliens from most federal jobs found invalid for failure to meet these standards).

§ 28. ILLEGITIMACY

Levy v. La. (S.Ct.1968) and *Glona v. Am. Guarantee & Liability Ins. Co.* (S.Ct.1968) invalidated on equal protection grounds the provisions of Louisiana's wrongful death statute which barred an unacknowledged illegitimate child from recovering for the death of his mother and a mother from recovering for the death of such a child. In each case the classification was found to be irrational, apparently on the theory that legitimate and illegitimate children are similarly situated in terms of their relationship to their mother. The state's contention that denial of recovery by mothers of illegitimates would deter conception out of wedlock was dismissed as "farfetched;" but the Court did not address the possibility, urged in dissent, that Louisiana law might encourage parents of illegitimates to acknowledge their children and did not discuss the problem of determining paternity since the cases involved only maternal relationships.

Three years after these decisions, *Labine v. Vincent* (S.Ct.1971) upheld a Louisiana statute which deprived an illegitimate child of the right to inherit from her father by intestate succession even though she had been formally acknowledged and had lived with her parents in a family unit. A closely divided Court observed that the state had created no "insurmountable barrier" to the child's recovery since the decedent had the option of preparing a will in order to pass property to his illegitimate offspring. A cryptic footnote implied that not even a showing of rationality was necessary to validate the statute but concluded that the provision "clearly has a rational basis in view of Louisiana's interest in promoting family life and of directing the disposition of property left within the state."

Faced with these opposing precedents in *Weber v. Aetna Cas. & Surety Co.* (S.Ct.1972), the Court found *Levy* more persuasive than *Labine*. The *Weber* case involved a state workmen's compensation statute which subordinated the claims of unacknowledged illegitimate dependents to those of legitimates upon the death of their natural father. The Court distinguished *Labine* as reflecting "traditional deference to a State's prerogative to regulate the disposition at death of property within its borders" and then put forward a twofold inquiry: "What legitimate state interest does the classification promote? What fundamental personal rights might the classification endanger?" Upon examination the statute failed to satisfy the equal protection clause because the distinction it drew bore "no significant relationship" to the purposes of workmen's compensation or to other legitimate state interests.

Weber appeared to adopt an intermediate standard of review, requiring something more than a rational explanation for differential treatment of illegitimates but less than a compelling justification. Although the opinion contains certain ambiguities, the demand for a "significant" relationship to legitimate state concerns clearly implied a closer scrutiny than is afforded under the traditional equal protection standard. This interpretation of *Weber* was reinforced by subsequent decisions striking down discrimination against illegitimates in entitlement to support. *Gomez v. Perez* (S.Ct.1973) set aside a statute limiting the right of paternal support to legitimate children, although a policy of avoiding the problem of determining paternity did not seem irrational before the onset of DNA testing. And a welfare provision which restricted the eligibility of illegitimate children to receive benefits was found unconstitutional. *N.J. Welfare Rights Organization v. Cahill* (S.Ct.1973). See also *Jimenez v. Weinberger* (S.Ct.1974) (ruling discrimination among afterborn illegitimate children to be impermissible).

But in *Mathews v. Lucas* (S.Ct.1976) the rationality test re-emerged as a measure of the constitutionality of discrimination against illegitimates. *Lucas* brought a challenge to the complex provisions of the Social Security Act which guarantee survivors' benefits to dependent children of a deceased wage earner, but in the case of illegitimate children require proof of one of the following: that the child would be entitled to inherit personal property from the decedent's estate under the applicable intestacy law or that the decedent (a) was living with the child or contributing support at the time of death, (b) had gone through a marriage ceremony with the other parent which was invalid because of a non-obvious defect, (c) had acknowledged the child, (d) had been found by a court to be the child's father, or (e) had been ordered by a court to support the child. Legitimate children, unless adopted by another individual, were entitled to benefits without evidence of dependency. The result under this statutory scheme was that a legitimate child was eligible for benefits even if the child was never in fact dependent upon the deceased parent. But an illegitimate might be ineligible despite years of support from the decedent if shortly before death occurred such support had been discontinued, possibly because of the burden of medical expenses, and the parents were separated—unless of course state intestacy law entitled the illegitimate to inherit property from the deceased, in which event actual dependency was again irrelevant.

In spite of the markedly unequal treatment afforded to children who were similarly situated in terms of their dependency on the deceased wage earner, the statute was upheld by a 6–3 vote. The Court first ruled that classification by illegitimacy is not constitutionally suspect. It noted that "illegitimacy does not carry an obvious badge"—an ameliorative feature which had not inhibited the Court from finding alienage to be a suspect classification—and that discrimination against illegitimates was historically less pervasive than discrimination against women and blacks. The Court then determined that "the statutory classifications are permissible ... because they are reasonably related to the likelihood of dependency" and "serve administrative convenience." But whatever might be said of the other statutory classifications, only under the most relaxed scrutiny can the likelihood of an illegitimate's actual dependency be deemed to vary with state intestacy laws.

Later cases have maintained the Court's ambivalent posture toward the standard of review for classifications based on legitimacy. *Trimble v. Gordon* (S.Ct.1977) dealt with an Illinois statute which allowed illegitimate children to inherit from their father by intestate succession only if the father had acknowledged the child and had married the child's mother. The Court said that "at a minimum ... a statutory classification must bear some rational relationship to a legitimate purpose." The opinion, noting that a support order had been entered after a judicial determination of paternity in an action involving the parties to this case and that the same determination could support a claim for inheritance, concluded that the statute did not reasonably promote any legitimate state objectives. The Court neither overruled the *Labine* case nor made any serious effort to distinguish it.

The opinion in *Lalli v. Lalli* (S.Ct.1978) managed to embrace *both* the rationality test and an intermediate standard of review. The *Lalli* case involved a New York statute which allowed an illegitimate child to inherit from his father by intestate succession only if, during the father's lifetime, a court of competent jurisdiction entered an order declaring paternity. At one point Justice Powell, who wrote for a plurality of the Court, said that classifications based on legitimacy must be "substantially related to permissible state interests." Yet, the opinion later stated that judicial inquiry should focus on "whether the statute's relation to the state interests is so tenuous that it lacks the rationality contemplated by the Fourteenth Amendment." In upholding the statute, Justice Powell argued that the provision served to discourage fraudulent claims "by placing paternity disputes in a judicial forum during the lifetime of the father." The *Trimble* case was distinguished on the ground that the statute there required the intermarriage of the parents.

Finally, *Clark v. Jeter* (S.Ct.1988) invalidated a state statute of limitations requiring that paternity proceedings be instituted within 6 years of the child's birth. An action had been brought for child support 10 years after the birth of an illegitimate child, and a blood test showed a 99.3% probability that the defendant was the child's father. The Supreme Court said that "intermediate scrutiny ... *generally* has been applied to discriminatory classifications based on ... illegitimacy." (Emphasis added.) The Court concluded that a 6–year period might not provide a reasonable opportunity to assert a claim on behalf of an illegitimate child and that a 6–year limitation was not substantially related to a state's interest in avoiding stale or fraudulent claims. See also *Mills v. Habluetzel* (S.Ct.1982) and *Pickett v. Brown* (S.Ct.1983), invalidating one and two year statutes of limitations on paternity actions.

Clark's characterization of legitimacy classifications as "generally" evoking intermediate review seems quite accurate. Certainly those classifications have not consistently been given heightened scrutiny. But there appears to be an increasing tendency to demand more than rationality for such classifications. Nevertheless, the inconsistent application of intermediate scrutiny raises a serious question as to whether the reasonableness test might resurface in illegitimacy cases or in other areas which have evoked intermediate scrutiny.

CHAPTER V

EQUAL PROTECTION: THE FOCUS ON SPECIFIC INTERESTS

§ 29. INTRODUCTION

The "new equal protection" analysis has required a compelling justification not only for suspect classifications but also for classifications which burden specially protected interests. The latter branch of equal protection doctrine appears to have originated in *Skinner v. Oklahoma* (S.Ct.1942). That case invalidated a statute which subjected to sterilization persons who were thrice convicted of larceny, but exempted those thrice convicted of embezzlement. The Court said that "if we had here only a question as to a State's classification of crimes, such as embezzlement or larceny, no substantial federal question would be raised." But because the statute involved "one of the basic civil rights of man," the majority concluded that "strict scrutiny ... is essential." Thus close scrutiny was thought to be justified, not by the nature of the classification, but by the nature of the interest it regulated. Years later, the Court applied the same reasoning to three major areas—voting, interstate travel and access to the courts.

§ 30. VOTING

Developing the Standard of Review. In *Harper v. Va. Board of Elections* (S.Ct.1966), the Court held that the right to vote cannot be conditioned upon the payment of a poll tax. Unlike a literacy requirement which had been sustained in *Lassiter v. Northampton County Board of Elections* (S.Ct.1959), tax payments were said to have "no relation" to voter qualifications, although three dissenters argued that such payments might rationally promote civic responsibility by "weeding out those who do not care enough about public affairs to pay $1.50 ... a year for the exercise of the franchise." Despite much debate as to whether *Harper* is a poverty case or a voting case, it seems clear that the decision rests on the special nature of the franchise. The Court expressly declined to invalidate the tax, choosing merely to prohibit disenfranchisement as a means of enforcing it; and the decision was made applicable to those "unable to pay a fee ... *or who fail to pay.*" (Emphasis added.) Consequently the poor could be induced, through sanctions other than disenfranchisement, to pay Virginia's $1.50 tax, and the rich no less than the indigent would be entitled to vote even if they refused to pay.

Kramer v. Union Free School Dist. (S.Ct.1969) elaborated on the standard of review in voting cases. *Kramer* involved a statute that limited the vote in school district elections to parents of public school children and persons owning or leasing property within the district. The Court ruled that provisions disenfranchising "some bona fide residents of requisite age and citizenship" must be shown to be "necessary to promote a compelling state interest." Assuming the state could legitimately limit the vote to those primarily interested in school affairs, the validity of the statute would depend "on whether all those excluded are in fact substantially less interested or affected than those the statute includes." Since the plaintiff was "interested" in the schools, while some eligible voters might not be, the exclusion was invalid. A stringent standard of review was deemed appropriate because "the presumption of constitutionality and the approval given 'rational' classifications in other types of enactments are based on an assumption that the institutions of state government are structured so as to represent fairly all the people. However, when the challenge of the statute is in effect a challenge of this basic assumption, the assumption can no longer serve as the basis for presuming constitutionality."

The force of the latter argument was blunted by the fact that the legislative body which had enacted the challenged statute was properly structured in all respects. But the Court insisted that strict scrutiny was appropriate because "any unjustified discrimination in determining who may participate in political affairs ... undermines the legitimacy of representative government." What the Court failed to explain is why the requirements of age, citizenship and residence need not be finely tailored to their objectives. Just as the plaintiff in *Kramer* might be more interested in school affairs than some parents, so might some non-residents and minors be better qualified and more interested than some eligible voters. Conversely, the dissenters argued, if inexact line drawing is permissible with regard to age, citizenship and residence, there is no reason why such precision should be required with reference to other standards of eligibility.

The rigorous scrutiny mandated by *Kramer* spawned the invalidation of many longstanding restrictions on the right to vote. These decisions can be set forth quite briefly. In general, they support "the basic principle ... that as long as [an] election ... is not one of special interest, any classification restricting the franchise on grounds other than residence, age, and citizenship cannot stand unless the ... State can demonstrate that the classification serves a compelling state interest." *Hill v. Stone* (S.Ct.1975).

Property Qualifications. Among the first electoral restrictions to fall were property qualifications for voting in general interest elections. *Cipriano v. City of Houma* (S.Ct.1969) struck down a statute limiting the franchise to property taxpayers in elections passing upon the issuance of revenue bonds by municipal utilities. Since the bonds were to be financed from the operations of the utilities rather than from property taxes, nonproperty owners were "as substantially affected and directly interested" in the election as those permitted to vote. A year later the Court reached the same result where general obligation bonds, to be paid from property tax revenues, were involved: nonproperty owners have a substantial interest in the services financed by the bonds and the burden of property taxes often is eventually borne by tenants and consumers. *City of Phoenix v. Kolodziejski* (S.Ct.1970). On the other hand, special purpose units of government can be elected by votes limited to members of disproportionately affected groups. Thus *Salyer Land Co. v. Tulare Lake Basin Water Storage Dist.* (S.Ct.1973) upheld a scheme that excluded nonlandowners and provided for weighted voting, based on assessed property values, in elections for water storage district directors whose main responsibility was to manage the acquisition, storage, and distribution of water for local farming: a water storage district was distinguishable from the subjects involved in earlier voting cases "by reason of its special limited purpose *and* of the disproportionate effect on landowners.... " (Emphasis added.) See also *Ball v. James* (S.Ct.1981).

Durational Residence Requirements. In *Dunn v. Blumstein* (S.Ct.1972), the Court invalidated a provision that conditioned eligibility to vote upon residence in a state for one year and in a county for three months. Although the state had a legitimate interest in preventing voter fraud, that interest could be satisfied by "less drastic means" and hence was not *necessary* to a compelling government objective. However, a 50–day requirement has been sustained as a means of assuring accurate voter eligibility lists. *Marston v. Lewis* (S.Ct.1973). Since extended residence cannot be required, a provision barring military personnel transferred into a jurisdiction from voting in state elections for as long as they remain in the service is clearly unconstitutional. See *Carrington v. Rash* (S.Ct.1965) (pre-*Dunn* ruling on other grounds).

Disqualification for Alleged Crimes. In *Richardson v. Ramirez* (S.Ct.1974), the Court upheld state power to disenfranchise convicted felons. It distinguished the *Harper–Kramer* line of cases by invoking § 2 of the fourteenth amendment which provides for reduced representation in Congress as a sanction for voter exclusions but exempts any exclusion based on participation in crime: the framers "could not have intended to prohibit outright in § 1 of that Amendment that which was expressly exempted from the lesser sanction of reduced representation imposed by § 2...." However, in the case of jail inmates awaiting trial or convicted of misdemeanors, states must provide absentee voting procedures if such procedures are available to other citizens and if no alternative means of voting is open to inmates. *O'Brien v. Skinner* (S.Ct.1974).

Ballot Access and Party Affiliation. The Court has entertained a variety of challenges to laws conditioning access to the ballot upon the payment of filing fees or the submission of burdensome nominating petitions. Absent reasonable alternatives for securing a place on the ballot, states may not require an indigent candidate to pay filing fees which he cannot afford. "Selection of candidates solely on the basis of ability to pay a fixed fee without providing any alternative means is not reasonably necessary to the accomplishment of the State's legitimate election interests." *Lubin v. Panish* (S.Ct.1974); see also *Bullock v. Carter* (S.Ct. 1972). Similarly, a law conditioning the access of new parties to the ballot upon the filing of nominating petitions totaling 15% of the voters in the last gubernatorial election violates the equal protection clause for want of any compelling justification. *Williams v. Rhodes* (S.Ct.1968). However, a lesser requirement of 5% of the registered voters has been upheld in the interest of limiting ballot placement to candidates showing significant community support. *Jenness v. Fortson* (S.Ct.1971). See also *Munro v. Socialist Workers Party* (S.Ct.1986); *American Party v. White* (1974) (requirement of 1% plus the holding of nominating conventions ruled valid).

The Court has been more tolerant of party affiliation requirements. In *Rosario v. Rockefeller* (S.Ct. 1973), it upheld a provision which required voters to enroll in a political party at least 30 days before a general election in order to be eligible to vote in the next party primary, thereby preventing a change in party affiliation for about 11 months. Such provisions, the Court said, do not "unduly burden" the right to vote and serve "to inhibit party 'raiding,' whereby voters in sympathy with one party designate themselves as voters of another party so as to influence or determine the results of the other party's primary." Because of its "compelling" interest in political stability, a state also may deny a place on a primary ballot to candidates who have had registered affiliations with a different political party within the previous year, *Storer v. Brown* (S.Ct.1974), or have voted in another party's primary within the previous four years. *Lippitt v. Cipollone* (S.Ct.1972). But a law prohibiting persons from voting, as distinguished from running, in a primary election if they voted in another party's primary within the preceding 23 months is unconstitutional because less drastic means are available to prevent party raiding, as the *Rosario* case demonstrates. *Kusper v. Pontikes* (S.Ct.1973).

Although the Court has purported to apply strict scrutiny in each of these cases, the precise articulation of the standard of review has varied widely. Several opinions demand proof that a restriction is "necessary to serve a compelling interest." *Illinois State Board of Elections v. Socialist Workers Party* (S.Ct.1979) (invalidating an Illinois system which required new parties and independent candidates to gather more voter signatures for access to the ballot in Chicago elections than for access in statewide elections). Other opinions ask merely whether the restriction imposes an "undue burden" or whether the burden is "reasonably necessary" to achieve "legitimate election interests." *Lubin*. See *Clements v. Fashing* (S.Ct.1982) (upholding statutory provisions which required certain officeholders to complete their current term before running for the state legislature or to resign before running for other offices). Finally, some cases seem to articulate varying standards within the same opinion: requirements whose validity "depends upon whether they are necessary to further compelling state interests" have been upheld because they were "*reasonably* undertaken in pursuit of vital state objectives that cannot be served equally well in significantly less burdensome ways." *American Party v. White*. See also *Anderson v. Celebrezze*

(S.Ct.1983) and *Tashjian v. Republican Party of Connecticut* (S.Ct.1986), applying a first amendment analysis to voting regulations without clearly articulating the standard of review. This variety of expression became important in determining the constitutionality of federal campaign financing, which addressed significant governmental concerns but created inequalities in political opportunity that could arguably have been avoided by a different response to those concerns.

Campaign Financing. The federal plan for public finance of Presidential election campaigns was brought before the Court in *Buckley v. Valeo* (S.Ct.1976). This plan provided that (1) "major parties", defined as those whose most recent Presidential candidates obtained at least 25% of the popular vote, may receive $2,000,000 for nominating convention expenses and $20,000,000 for general election expenses if they agree to limit expenditures to those amounts; (2) a "minor party", defined as one whose candidate secured at least 5% but less than 25% of the vote in the most recent election, may receive a portion of the major-party entitlement determined by its ratio of votes to the average obtained by the major parties, provided it agrees not to incur expenses in excess of the major-party entitlement; (3) all other parties are denied public financing for nominating conventions and are entitled to campaign funds for the general election only after the election is held and only if they receive at least 5% of the popular vote; (4) candidates are entitled to matching funds for support of primary campaigns if they privately raise at least $5,000 in each of 20 states in amounts not exceeding $250 from each contributor and if they agree to abide by statutory spending limits. It was argued that this arrangement for public finance invidiously discriminated in favor of established political parties.

Buckley rejected the equal protection challenge. The Court found public finance less restrictive of the electoral process than ballot access regulations because it did not limit the choice of the voters and because it entailed a concomitant acceptance of ceilings on expenditures. In any event, the varied formulations in the ballot access cases made available enough standards of review to accommodate almost any result. The Court's conclusory assessment was that Congress enacted public financing "in furtherance of sufficiently important governmental interests and has not unfairly or unnecessarily burdened the political opportunity of any party or candidate." By eliminating the improper influence of large private contributions, public funding furthered a "significant" interest; and the unequal treatment accorded to non-major parties was apparently justified by "policies against fostering frivolous candidacies, creating a system of splintered parties, and encouraging unrestrained factionalism."

§ 31. THE RIGHT TO TRAVEL

The Supreme Court stated at an early date that "all citizens of the United States ... have the right to pass and repass through every part of [the country] without interruption...." *Crandall v. Nev.* (S.Ct.1867). The right to travel free from state interference has been variously attributed to the privileges and immunities clause of the fourteenth amendment, the commerce clause or the interstate privileges and immunities clause of Article IV, which provides that "The citizens of each state shall be entitled to all privileges and immunities of citizens in the several states." Whatever the appropriate source, it is now settled that freedom to travel abroad and from state to state is constitutionally protected, *Aptheker v. Secretary of State* (S.Ct.1964), *U.S. v. Guest* (S.Ct.1966), although restrictions on travel have sometimes been upheld where national security or other important interests were thought to require them. See *Zemel v. Rusk* (S.Ct.1965) (denying a passport to Cuba); *Jones v. Helms* (S.Ct.1981) (upholding state power to increase the criminal sanction against parents who leave the state after abandoning dependent children).

The right to travel may be impermissibly abridged not only by outright prohibitions but also by more indirect government burdens. *Shapiro v. Thompson* (S.Ct.1969) was the seminal case in this field. It involved an equal protection challenge to statutory provisions which made welfare assistance available to persons who had resided in their respective jurisdictions for the preceding 12 months but not to needy residents of later arrival. The Court noted that the durational residence requirement denied access to the "necessities of life" because of recent interstate travel, and it rejected arguments that the requirement was rationally related to permissible budgetary and administrative objectives. But more important, the rationality test itself was rejected: "Since the classification here [penalizes] the fundamental right of interstate movement, its constitutionality must be judged by the stricter standard of whether it promotes a *compelling* state interest." The Court's emphasis on "fundamental" rights and the "necessities of life" bristled with far-reaching implications for the unequal allocation of other vital state services which, many commentators believed, might trigger strict scrutiny even in the absence of a mandatory waiting period. That result did not come to pass (see § 33), but *Shapiro's* limitation on durational residence requirements has endured.

As noted above, a one-year residence requirement for voting was set aside by *Dunn v. Blumstein* (S.Ct.1972). And in *Memorial Hospital v. Maricopa County* (S.Ct.1974), the Court struck down a similar requirement for non-emergency medical treatment of indigents at public expense. Finding that "medical care is as much 'a basic necessity of life' to an indigent as welfare assistance," the majority held the waiting provision to be an unconstitutional penalty on the right to travel. The Court did not question the validity of "a bona fide residence requirement," as distinguished from a requirement of durational residence. See *McCarthy v. Philadelphia Civil Serv. Comm.* (S.Ct.1976) (upholding "a condition placed on municipal employment that a person be a [city] resident *at the time* of his application" and service). Furthermore, it was noted in *Maricopa County* that the *Shapiro* case had involved not merely the right of movement but the right " 'to migrate [and] resettle....' "

It is apparent, however, that every durational residence requirement burdens the freedom of migration by according less favorable treatment to persons who have recently migrated than to other residents. Yet *Shapiro* had stated that some waiting periods might be valid because they did not constitute "penalties" on the right to travel. This prompted Mr. Justice Rehnquist to chide the majority in *Maricopa County:* "Since the Court concedes that 'some waiting periods ... may not be penalties,' one would expect to learn from the opinion how to distinguish a waiting period which is a penalty from one which is not." His criticism went unanswered, but a year later Justice Rehnquist wrote for the Court in *Sosna v. Iowa* (S.Ct.1975), sustaining a one-year residence requirement for filing a divorce action. He distinguished the earlier cases on the ground that they involved only "budgetary or record-keeping" interests of government. *Sosna* on the other hand implicated, most importantly, the state's interest "in both avoiding officious intermeddling in matters in which another State has a paramount interest, and in minimizing the susceptibility of its own divorce decrees to collateral attack."

But the Court has also upheld a one-year residence requirement for reduced tuition rates at state universities. *Starns v. Malkerson* (S.Ct.1971). The latter requirement seems plainly to find its support in "budgetary" considerations like those rejected by *Shapiro* and *Maricopa County* and to have nothing in common with the type of interests which prevailed in *Sosna*. It is apparent, therefore, that the scope of the penalty doctrine has yet to be defined and that, until it is, no one can adequately "distinguish a waiting period which is a penalty from one which is not." Compare *Suffling v. Bondurant* (D.N.M.1972) (waiting period for admission to the bar upheld) with *King v. New Rochelle Munic. Hous. Auth.* (2d Cir.1971) (waiting period for eligibility to rent public housing invalidated). Since *Dunn* can be understood as a voting case, "penalties" on the right to travel could be limited to cases in which the "necessities of life" are withheld. However, *Sosna* chose not to distinguish the *Shapiro* and *Maricopa County* cases on this basis. Moreover if the theory is that denying life necessities will discourage travel, the argument may be flawed by the lack of evidence that the availability of non-emergency health care will have a greater impact on decisions to travel than the availability of divorce and reduced tuition.

Finally, some states have attempted to allocate benefits on the basis of past residence in the jurisdiction. Although these laws impose no durational residence requirement, they create fixed distinctions based on length of residence in the state. In *Zobel v. Williams* (S.Ct.1982), the Court found such a distinction, awarding Alaska residents $50 for each year they lived in the state since 1959, not to be rationally related to any legitimate state interest. Similar results have been reached in more recent cases. See *Hooper v. Bernalillo County Assessor* (S.Ct.1985) (property tax exemption for Vietnam veterans who resided in New Mexico before 1976 held invalid); *Attorney General v. Soto–Lopez* (S.Ct. 1986) (special credit on civil service exam for veterans who lived in New York when they joined the military ruled invalid).

§ 32. ACCESS TO CRIMINAL AND CIVIL JUSTICE

Criminal Appeals. Beginning with *Griffin v. Illinois* (S.Ct.1956), the Court has closely reviewed certain financial restraints upon access to criminal justice. *Griffin* involved a state requirement that defendants provide an appellate court with a bill of exceptions or certified report of trial proceedings, which often could not be furnished without a transcript of the record. The plurality opinion, relying on both the equal protection and due process clauses, found unconstitutional discrimination in the government's failure to supply indigents with a free transcript or its functional equivalent: "In criminal trials a State can no more discriminate on account of poverty than on account of religion, race, or color. Plainly the ability to pay costs in advance bears no rational relationship to a defendant's guilt or innocence."

The *Griffin* rule has been applied "even [to] petty offenses" punishable only by fine, *Mayer v. City of*

Chicago (S.Ct.1971), and to state proceedings before and after trial. *Roberts v. LaVallee* (S.Ct.1967) (requiring free transcripts of a preliminary hearing); *Long v. District Court* (S.Ct.1966) (transcript of state habeas corpus proceeding). It has also been held to preclude filing fee requirements for appeals or state post-conviction procedures. *Burns v. Ohio* (S.Ct.1959); *Smith v. Bennett* (S.Ct.1961). But the most controversial use of the "*Griffin* principle" came in *Douglas v. Calif.* (S.Ct.1963), which held that counsel must be provided to an indigent defendant on his first appeal as of right. The Court said: "There is lacking that equality demanded by the Fourteenth Amendment where the rich man, who appeals as of right, enjoys the benefit of counsel's examination into the record, research of the law, and marshalling of arguments on his behalf, while the indigent ... is forced to shift for himself." See also *Tate v. Short* (S.Ct.1971) and *Williams v. Illinois* (S.Ct.1970) (extending the *Griffin* analysis to prohibit automatic imprisonment of indigents for default in payment of fines).

Unlike the voting and travel cases, the *Griffin–Douglas* line of decisions did not explicitly endorse strict scrutiny. Instead, the Court argued that there is "no rational relationship" between ability to pay and guilt or innocence. But user fees may serve other legitimate interests, such as discouraging overutilization of scarce resources. Since the Court could not have been unaware that some criminal appeals are frivolous, its rulings in this area must rest on a belief that the pricing mechanism, although rational, does not promote interests sufficiently important to justify the denial of access to certain instruments of criminal justice.

Yet the parameters of this strict scrutiny have never been made clear. Some economic barriers to a successful appeal are constitutionally permissible. For example, *Ross v. Moffitt* (S.Ct.1974) held that indigents need not be provided with counsel on discretionary state appeals or applications for U.S. Supreme Court review: "The duty of the State ... is not to duplicate the legal arsenal that may be privately retained by a criminal defendant in a continuing effort to reverse his conviction, but only to assure the indigent defendant an adequate opportunity to present his claims fairly in the context of the State's appellate process." See also *U.S. v. MacCollom* (S.Ct.1976). In that light, perhaps *Griffin–Douglas* will be read as involving a constitutional right to effective participation in whatever criminal appellate process a state makes available, and cases like *Tate v. Short* may be viewed as implicitly grounded in the eighth amendment. Such an approach would provide constitutional underpinnings for close scrutiny in this field. Of course, there is no constitutional right to appeal, *McKane v. Durston* (S.Ct.1894), but there might nevertheless be a constitutional right of effective access when appeals are available—just as there is "a constitutionally protected right to participate in elections on an equal basis" even though there is no constitutional right to vote as such. *Rodriguez.* See *Bounds v. Smith* (S.Ct.1977), holding that the "constitutional

Civil Justice. *Boddie v. Conn.* (S.Ct.1971) raised the question whether access to divorce courts could be conditioned upon the payment of fees amounting to about $60. In answering that question in the negative, the Court relied on the due process guarantee of "a meaningful opportunity to be heard" rather than upon equal protection: "Given the basic position of the marriage relationship in this society's hierarchy of values and the concomitant state monopolization of the means for legally dissolving this relationship, due process [prohibits] the State from denying, solely because of inability to pay, access to its courts to individuals who seek judicial dissolution of their marriage."

Despite the emphasis on the state monopolization of power to dissolve marriages, *Boddie* was susceptible to extremely broad application since the government always has a monopoly over the judicial process, and many legal disputes are impossible to settle without a credible threat of ultimate resort to the courts. Mr. Justice Black, after dissenting in *Boddie,* argued that the result reached there was applicable to all civil actions, *Meltzer & Stine v. Buck LeCraw* (S.Ct.1971), and lower courts seemed to agree. But when the issue reached the Supreme Court in *U.S. v. Kras* (S.Ct.1973), which challenged a $50 fee in bankruptcy proceedings, *Boddie* was narrowly construed and the fee upheld: the marriage relationship was not involved, and "in contrast with divorce, bankruptcy is not the only method available to a debtor for the adjustment of his legal relationship with his creditor." Under these circumstances the rationality test was controlling, and a rational basis for requiring fees was "readily apparent" in the congressional intent to "make the [bankruptcy] system self-sustaining and paid for by those who use it rather than by tax revenues drawn from the public at large." See also *Ortwein v. Schwab* (S.Ct.1973), upholding a $25 filing fee for judicial review of administrative rulings on welfare benefits.

In view of *Kras* and *Ortwein,* the ban on court fees in actions brought by indigents may be limited to cases like child adoption, in which judicial approval is required by state law to formalize specially protected relationships. Furthermore, since access to the courts is often vital to the protection of other important interests, the narrow construction of *Boddie* may well portend a narrow application of the restriction on payment requirements in general. See *Maher v. Roe* (S.Ct.1977), noting that the *Griffin–Douglas* rules "are grounded in the criminal justice system, a governmental monopoly in which participation is compelled," and "do not extend to legislative classifications generally." However, it will be possible in some cases to attack payment requirements in the legal system through the case law governing procedural due process. See *Little v. Streater* (S.Ct.1981) (due process requires the state to pay for the blood test of an indigent defendant in a government-sponsored paternity action); *Lassiter v. Dept. of Social Services* (S.Ct.1981) (in some cases procedural due process may require an appointment of counsel in legal actions to terminate parental rights).

§ 33. DEFINING "FUNDAMENTAL" INTERESTS

In *Shapiro v. Thompson,* Mr. Justice Harlan detected a "cryptic suggestion that the 'compelling interest' test is applicable merely because the result of the classification may be to deny ... 'food, shelter, and other necessities of life.'" He argued that "when a statute affects only matters not mentioned in the Federal Constitution and is not arbitrary or irrational ... I know of nothing which entitles this Court to pick out particular human activities, characterize them as 'fundamental,' and give them added protection under an unusually stringent equal protection test." Such a use of the fundamental rights doctrine could reach a host of public services ranging from education to waste disposal, and thereby convert the new equal protection into a functional equivalent of the old substantive due process. Within a few years, however, it became clear that the Court would largely reject the cryptic suggestion and confine the scope of "fundamental rights."

The retrenchment began with *Dandridge v. Williams* (S.Ct.1970). At issue there was a program for aid to families with dependent children which limited monthly grants to a maximum of $250, regardless of a family's size or estimated need. The result of the maximum grant regulation was that some large families would receive less assistance for each child than other families. The Court, noting that the disputed classification did not intrude upon constitutionally protected freedoms, said it was enough to satisfy equal protection demands that the regulation was rationally related to the state's legitimate interests in encouraging gainful employment and maintaining an equitable balance between welfare families and the working poor.

Dandridge was applied in quick succession to a series of social welfare cases. First, a provision of the Social Security Act reducing disability benefits for recipients of state workmen's compensation, but not for recipients of private insurance benefits, was upheld as "rationally based." *Richardson v. Belcher* (S.Ct.1971). Then the reasonableness standard was employed to sustain a statutory scheme under which aid to families with dependent children was maintained at a lower level in relation to need than other forms of welfare assistance. *Jefferson v. Hackney* (S.Ct.1972). And in *Lindsey v. Normet* (S.Ct.1972), the Court upheld summary eviction procedures that limited the triable issue to a tenant's alleged default in payment of rent, thereby precluding defenses based on the landlord's failure to maintain the premises. The claim that "a more stringent standard than mere rationality should be applied" because housing qualified as a fundamental interest was expressly rejected: "The Constitution does not provide judicial remedies for every social and economic ill. We are unable to perceive in that document any constitutional guarantee of access to dwellings of a particular quality or any recognition of the right of a tenant to occupy the real property of his landlord beyond the terms of his lease...."

This sequence of cases set the stage for a more definitive ruling on the scope of the fundamental rights doctrine. That ruling came in *San Antonio Ind. School Dist. v. Rodriguez* (S.Ct.1973), which raised the question whether local finance of public education that produced large disparities in spending by the various school districts violated the equal protection clause. In response to the contention that education is a fundamental interest requiring a compelling justification for its unequal allocation, the majority said: "It is not the province of this Court to create substantive constitutional rights in the name of guaranteeing equal protection of the laws. Thus the key to discovering whether education is 'fundamental' is not to be found in comparisons of the relative societal significance of education as opposed to subsistence or housing.... Rather, the answer lies in assessing whether there is a right to education explicitly or implicitly guaranteed by the Constitution." Education was found not to be constitutionally guaranteed, and so *Rodriguez* applied "the traditional standard of review, which requires only that the State's system ... bear some rational relationship to legitimate state purposes." Because local funding of education was thought to be reasonably related to the goal of encouraging "a large measure of participation in the control of each district's schools at the local level," the Court found no denial of equal protection. *Rodriguez* also rejected the claim that strict scrutiny was warranted by the wealth discrimination implicit in basing educational expenditures on local property values: lack of funds had not occasioned a total deprivation of schooling, and there was insufficient evidence of a general correlation between individual and district wealth to show discrimination against an identifiable class of poor people. These features sufficed to distinguish the *Griffin–Douglas* line of cases, while *Shapiro, Skinner* and *Kramer* were treated as involving respectively the constitutional right to travel, to privacy and to vote "on an equal basis with other citizens."

The *Rodriguez* case has crucial significance for the fundamental rights doctrine. It holds in essence that the doctrine applies, not to matters of high importance generally, but only to matters of constitutional right. The difference between these two measures of fundamental interest is dramatic. Public health care, for instance, might well be "fundamental" in terms of its social importance but courts have not found it to be constitutionally protected, as required under the *Rodriguez* standard. And what holds true for health care applies also to a wide variety of other government services. Indeed, it is precisely because of the potentially broad reach of *Shapiro* that the Court repudiated its "cryptic suggestion," as being "too reminiscent" of the heavy-handed judicial intervention during the *Lochner* era. See *Dandridge v. Williams*. The upshot is that the compelling justification test can now be invoked only for suspect classifications and constitutionally protected rights, while a less stringent test applies in other equal protection cases.

Of course, the fundamental rights concept retains some elasticity since it extends to matters "implicitly" guaranteed by the Constitution as well as to those specifically enumerated in the Bill of Rights. Cf. *Zablocki v. Redhail* (S.Ct.1978) (invalidating after "critical examination" a statute which prohibited the marriage of any person under court order to support minor children, absent proof that the order had been and would continue to be met). But the Court, in applying *Rodriguez,* has not taken an expansive view of the notion of implicit constitutional guarantees. Post–*Rodriguez* cases have turned aside several new pleas for enforcement of the compelling justification standard. For example, in *Village of Belle Terre v. Boraas* (S.Ct.1974), an equal protection challenge was made to the constitutionality of a zoning ordinance which generally limited the occupancy of one-family dwellings to persons who were married or related by blood, or to groups no larger than two. The Court upheld the ordinance under a rationality standard, despite claims that the regulation touched upon rights of privacy and association. And in *Marshall v. U.S.* (S.Ct.1974), it employed the same standard to sustain the exclusion of twice convicted felons from rehabilitative treatment for narcotics addiction. Finally, *Johnson v. Robison* (S.Ct.1974) upheld the government's power to deny educational benefits to conscientious objectors who performed alternate service, while providing such benefits to veterans who served on active duty in the Armed Forces: the statutory classification was reasonably related to the congressional purpose of facilitating readjustment to civilian life and to the objective of "enhancing and making more attractive service in the Armed Forces of the United States."

Nevertheless, the rationality test has been applied with unusual vigor when state law calls for a total deprivation of public education. *Plyler v. Doe* (S.Ct. 1982) dealt with a Texas statute which withheld from local school districts any state funds for the education of children who were not legally admitted into the United States, and which authorized school districts to deny enrollment to such children. The Court emphasized the importance of education to individual achievement and said the statute would impose a lifetime of hardship on a discrete class of children not responsible for their disabling status. The Court concluded that "in determining the rationality of [the Texas statute] we may appropriately take into account its costs to the Nation and to the innocent children who are its victims. In light of these countervailing costs, the discrimination contained in [the statute] can hardly be considered rational unless it furthers some substantial goal of the State." No such goal was found to be served by excluding undocumented alien children from the public schools. Four dissenting Justices noted that the majority "rejects any suggestion that illegal aliens are a suspect class ... or that education is a fundamental right.... Yet by patching together bits and pieces of what might be termed quasi-suspect-class and quasi-fundamental-rights analysis, the Court spins out a theory custom-tailored to the facts of [this case].... If ever a court was guilty of an unabashedly result-oriented approach, this case is a prime example."

But it is clear that the *Plyler* decision did not alter *Rodriguez's* restrictions on the fundamental rights doctrine. Cf. *DeShaney v. Winnebago County Dept. of Social Services* (S.Ct.1989) (ruling that the fourteenth amendment imposes no duty on a state to provide members of the general public with adequate protective services). And even in the specific area of public education, *Plyler* has had a limited impact. See *Martinez v. Bynum* (S.Ct.1983), which upheld a Texas statute that authorized local school districts to deny tuition-free education to children residing apart from their guardians and living in the district for the primary purpose of attending the public schools: "A bona fide residence requirement ... furthers the substantial state interest in assuring that services provided for its residents are enjoyed only by residents." See also *Kadrmas v. Dickinson Public Schools* (S.Ct.1988) (sustaining the validity of a user fee for school bus transportation, despite its impact on the educational opportunity of the poor).

§ 34. THE REQUIREMENT OF RATIONALITY

The Traditional Standard.. As was briefly noted above, the equal protection clause requires at least that a classification be rationally related to a permissible purpose. See *Railway Express Agency v. New York* (S.Ct.1949). *Rodriguez* and its progeny clearly give added importance to the meaning of that requirement.

In ascertaining the legislative purpose and measuring the reasonableness of its relationship to the classification, courts have traditionally been quite deferential to the political branches of government. Instead of asking what the legislative purpose is, they often ask what legitimate objective might be served by the government's action and attribute the action to that objective. This approach virtually assures a finding of a permissible purpose. Thus in *McGowan v. Md.* (S.Ct.1961), Sunday closing laws which evidently were originally intended to promote religious observance—a constitutionally prohibited objective—were found to serve the legitimate goal of providing a uniform day of rest. In addition, some courts assume the existence of any state of facts which can reasonably be conceived to sustain a classification: "Legislatures are presumed to have acted constitutionally even if source materials normally resorted to for ascertaining their grounds for action are otherwise silent, and their statutory classifications will be set aside only if no grounds can be conceived to justify them." *McDonald v. Board of Election* (S.Ct.1969). This application of the reasonableness requirement reduces judicial scrutiny to such a minimal level as to make a constitutional challenge extremely difficult to sustain. See *New York City Transit Authority v. Beazer* (S.Ct.1979), upholding as rational the refusal of the Transit Authority to hire any methadone users even though it was "clear that substantial numbers of methadone users are capable of performing many of the [available] jobs."

Nevertheless the rationality test is a far more flexible tool than has generally been supposed. The deferential gloss placed on that test by cases like *McGowan* has not been uniformly followed. As a result the demand for reasonableness has sometimes brought significant scrutiny to state and federal activity.

Variations on the Traditional Rule. *U.S. Dept. of Agriculture v. Moreno* (S.Ct.1973) provides a good example of meaningful review under the rationality standard. That case involved a section of the Food Stamp Act which denied coverage to "any household containing an individual who is unrelated to any other member of the household." This classification was "clearly irrelevant to the stated purposes of the Act"—satisfying nutritional needs and aiding the agricultural economy—but the government argued that Congress might have expected the exclusion to help minimize fraud. The Court replied that the exclusion did not rationally protect against fraud since unrelated persons could avoid its impact by simply moving into separate households. Of course, the greater cost of maintaining a separate household might well offset the benefit of food stamps and thereby discourage such a response. However, the Court never addressed that possibility. The critical point was that many persons who share a household for reasons of economic necessity, rather than for the purpose of contriving eligibility for food stamps, would be penalized by the exclusion; and the impact on innocent needy people would undermine the very objectives stated in the Act. Thus the exclusion fell, not because no facts could be conceived to support it, but because it was not "rational" to employ a device which was so grossly overinclusive in relation to the aim of controlling fraud. See also *Logan v. Zimmerman Brush Co.* (S.Ct.1982), in which a majority of the Court found it irrational for a state agency to dismiss as untimely an employment discrimination complaint that the agency itself had inadvertently scheduled for hearing at a date after the statutory time period had expired: "Terminating a claim that the State itself has misscheduled is [not] a rational way of expediting the resolution of disputes." (plurality opinion)

In *Cleburne v. Cleburne Living Center* (S.Ct. 1985), the Court again applied the rationality test with some vigor. The *Cleburne* case arose out of a city's decision to require a special permit for the operation of a group home for the mentally retarded and to refuse to issue such a permit. The Court rejected the suggestion that mental retardation be treated as a quasi-suspect classification, noting that "retardation is a characteristic that the government may legitimately take into account in a wide range of decisions" and that "lawmakers have been addressing [this problem] in a manner that belies a continuing antipathy or ... need for more intrusive oversight by the judiciary." It then applied the rationality test to Cleburne's ordinance, which required that a special use permit be obtained for homes for the mentally retarded but not for boarding houses, hospitals, sanitariums, private clubs or nursing homes for other than mentally or drug impaired persons. Because a home for the mentally retarded did not "threaten legitimate interests of the city in a way that other permitted uses ... would not," the Court concluded that "requiring the permit in this case appears ... to rest on an irrational prejudice against the mentally retarded." But cf. *Heller v. Doe* (S.Ct.1993), applying less stringent review to uphold a statutory scheme that set a lower burden of proof for involuntary commitment of the mentally retarded than for involuntary commitment of the mentally ill.

Most recently, *Romer v. Evans* (S.Ct.1996) used the rationality test to invalidate a voter-approved initiative in Colorado, which barred the enforcement of state or local laws prohibiting discrimination on the basis of "homosexual, lesbian or bisexual orientation, conduct, practices or relationships." The Court said that the initiative was "born of animus toward the class of persons affected" and did not "bear a rational relationship to a legitimate governmental purpose." A classification based on homosexual conduct would presumably advance the state interests articulated in *Bowers v. Hardwick* (1986). But the Colorado initiative clearly reached homosexual orientation as well as conduct, and it was therefore found to be a "status-based enactment divorced from any ... legitimate state interests." Justice Scalia argued that, because homosexual conduct can be regulated, it is reasonable to deny protection "to those with a self-avowed tendency or desire to engage in [that] conduct." However, Colorado did not penalize those with a "self-avowed tendency or desire" to engage in illicit heterosexual conduct, and it is not clear why sexual orientation in itself is a matter of state concern when homosexuals are involved but not when heterosexuals are involved.

The "Newer Equal Protection." A more fully reasoned proposal for intensified rational scrutiny has been advanced by Professor Gerald Gunther. He urges the Court to "take seriously a constitutional requirement that has never been formally abandoned: that legislative means must substantially further legislative ends." He suggests that the Court "assess the means in terms of legislative purposes that have substantial basis in actuality, not merely in conjecture" and that reasonableness be measured "on the basis of materials that are offered to Court, rather than ... rationalizations created by perfunctory judicial hypothesizing." See Forward, 86 Harv.L.Rev. 1 (1972).

Some support can be found for this approach. For example, *McGinnis v. Royster* (S.Ct.1973), involving a state scheme of "good time" credit for prison inmates but not for presentence inmates of a county jail, said the equal protection test was "whether the challenged distinction rationally furthers some legitimate, *articulated* state purpose." (Emphasis added.) The good time credit plan was held to be reasonably related to the state's rehabilitative goals because programs of rehabilitation were not offered in county jails, but the Court expressly refused to supply any "imaginary basis or purpose for this statutory scheme." Similarly, in *Mass. Board of Retirement v. Murgia* (S.Ct.1976), a provision requiring uniformed police officers to retire at age 50 was sustained because it rationally furthered the purpose "identified by the State" of assuring the officers' physical readiness: "Since physical ability generally declines with age, mandatory retirement at 50 serves to remove from police service those whose fitness for uniformed work presumptively has diminished...." See also *Eisenstadt v. Baird* (S.Ct.1972), rejecting the claim that a ban on distribution of contraceptives, except by physicians treating married patients, was intended to protect public health or discourage premarital sex, and holding the ban unconstitutional.

Nevertheless, use of the newer equal protection has been sporadic and uncertain. *United States R.R. Retirement Board v. Fritz* (S.Ct.1980) flatly rejected the suggestion that courts should determine the actual purpose for legislative action: "Where, as here, there are plausible reasons for Congress' action, our inquiry is at an end. It is, of course, 'constitutionally irrelevant whether this reasoning in fact underlay the legislative decision,' because this Court has never insisted that a legislative body articulate its reasons for enacting a statute." Yet, *Minnesota v. Clover Leaf Creamery Co.* (S.Ct.1981), which was decided the same Term as the *Fritz* case, appeared to call for an examination of the actual legislative purpose: "the Court will assume that the objectives articulated by the legislature are actual purposes of the statute, *unless* an examination of the circumstances forces us to conclude that they 'could not have been the goal of the legislation.'" Recent cases have been similarly ambivalent. Compare *FCC v. Beach Communications, Inc.* (S.Ct.1993) ("it is entirely irrelevant for constitutional purposes whether the conceived reason for the challenged distinction actually motivated the legislature") with *Nordlinger v. Hahn* (S.Ct.1992) ("this Court's review does require that a purpose may conceivably or 'may reasonably have been the purpose and policy' of the relevant governmental decisionmaker").

§ 35. REAPPORTIONMENT

The Rule of Reynolds v. Sims. For many years the equal protection clause was thought not to address the problem of malapportioned legislatures, and consequently reapportionment was left to state control. But since any attack on the problem would inevitably risk a loss of political power, legislators were not inclined to overactivity in this field. The result was that district lines which were drawn before the massive shift in population from rural to urban areas often remained unaltered long after that shift had taken place. It was in the face of this history of legislative inaction that *Reynolds v. Sims* (S.Ct.1964) read the equal protection clause to require seats in both houses of a bicameral state legislature to be apportioned on a population basis. The Court said that "in a society ostensibly grounded on representative government, it would seem reasonable that a majority of the people of the state could elect a majority of that State's legislators.... The fact that an individual lives here or there is not a legitimate reason for overweighting or diluting the efficacy of his vote." This rationale was controlling even when an alternative apportionment system was approved in a referendum by a majority of the voters in every county of the state. *Lucas v. Forty–Fourth General Assembly* (S.Ct.1964). In determining the population of a district for the purpose of applying *Reynolds v. Sims,* states are permitted to exclude certain groups—such as aliens, transients, and disenfranchised felons—from their computations; but representation based on actual or registered voters is "susceptible to improper influences" and has been approved only where the outcome was not substantially different from that secured by employing a broader base. *Burns v. Richardson* (S.Ct.1966).

Applicability of the Equal–Vote Principle. The rule of *Reynolds v. Sims* applies not only to state legislatures but also to "units of local government having general governmental powers over the entire geographic area served by the body." *Avery v. Midland County* (S.Ct.1968). Accordingly, equal protection is denied "when the members of a city council, school board, or county governing board are elected from districts of substantially unequal population." *Avery*. See also *Hadley v. Jr. College Dist.* (S.Ct.1970) (college trustees). On the other hand, special purpose units of government which disproportionately affect certain groups need not be apportioned on a population basis. *Salyer Land Co. v. Tulare Lake Basin Water Storage Dist.* (§ 30 supra); *Town of Lockport v. Citizens for Community Action* (S.Ct.1977) (sustaining state power to insist that changes in a county charter be ratified by separate majorities of city and noncity dwellers in order to safeguard "the differing interests" of the two groups, even though this rule had thwarted the will of the majority within the county as a whole). And a requirement that 60% of the voters approve the issuance of local government bonds was upheld in *Gordon v. Lance* (S.Ct.1971), despite its anti-majoritarian implications. The Court, noting that the provision was not concerned with election of public officers and that the Federal Constitution itself requires a supermajority on some issues, said: "so long as such provisions do not discriminate against or authorize discrimination against any identifiable class they do not violate the Equal Protection Clause." Finally, *Reynolds v. Sims* is inapplicable to the election of state-court judges, *Wells v. Edwards* (S.Ct.1973), and to the appointment of certain administrative or other non-legislative officers. *Sailors v. Board of Educ.* (S.Ct.1967). See also *Dusch v. Davis* (S.Ct.1967), permitting a city "to choose its legislative body by a scheme that included at-large voting for candidates, some of whom had to be residents of particular districts" of unequal population.

Permissible Departures From Mathematical Equality. In congressional elections the constitutional provision for selection of members of the House "by the People of the several states" requires that districts be as nearly equal in population as practicable. *Wesberry v. Sanders* (S.Ct. 1964). The Court has disapproved a plan in which the maximum deviation from mathematical exactness was less than 5%, *White v. Weiser* (S.Ct.1973), and has rejected attempts to justify even minimal variations on the basis of a policy of deterring the use of gerrymanders or avoiding the fragmentation of political subdivisions. *Kirkpatrick v. Preisler* (S.Ct.1969). See also *Karcher v. Daggett* (S.Ct. 1983) (no *de minimus* population variations which could be practicably avoided are permissible without justification).

However, a much greater tolerance for departures from ideal equality has emerged in cases involving state legislative districts. A deviation of 9.9% has been upheld without any showing of justification: "It is now time to recognize ... that minor deviations from mathematical equality among state legislative districts are insufficient to make out a prima facie case ... so as to require justification by the State." *Gaffney v. Cummings* (S.Ct.1973); *White v. Regester* (S.Ct.1973). And where some justification is offered, such as a desire to maintain the integrity of political subdivision lines, deviations can be even larger. *Mahan v. Howell* (S.Ct.1973) (16.4% approaches but does not exceed constitutional limits); *Abate v. Mundt* (S.Ct.1971). "One can reasonably surmise that a line has been drawn at 10%—deviations in excess of that amount are apparently acceptable only on a showing of justification by the

State; deviations less than that amount require no justification whatsoever." *White v. Regester* (Brennan, J., dissenting). Cf. *Brown v. Thomson* (S.Ct. 1983) (upholding a state plan granting each county one representative, even though the maximum deviation under the plan was 89%). Only in the case of *judicially-devised* reapportionment plans has the Court strictly adhered to the rule that state legislative districts "must be 'as nearly of equal population as is practicable.'" *Connor v. Finch* (S.Ct. 1977). See also *Chapman v. Meier* (S.Ct.1975).

Gerrymandering. The extraordinary difficulty of scrutinizing political gerrymanders imposes an even more important limitation on the efficacy of *Reynolds v. Sims* than the retreat from the standard of mathematical equality. *Gaffney v. Cummings* (S.Ct.1973), a leading case in this area, reviewed a reapportionment plan which had drawn "virtually every Senate and House district line ... with the conscious intent to ... achieve a rough approximation of the statewide political strengths of the Democratic and Republican Parties...." The Court did not controvert the challengers' characterization of the plan as "a gigantic political gerrymander" but instead made clear that gerrymandering is rarely subject to judicial scrutiny: "Politics and political considerations are inseparable from districting and apportionment. The political profile of a State, its party registration and voting records are available precinct by precinct, ward by ward.... It requires no special genius to recognize the political consequences of drawing a district line along one street rather than another.... The reality is that districting inevitably has and is intended to have substantial political consequences." Although political gerrymandering through "multimember districts may be vulnerable if racial or political groups have been fenced out," the Court said that "Beyond this, we have not ventured far nor attempted the impossible task of extirpating politics from what are the essentially political processes of the sovereign States."

Neither has the Court "ventured far" in examining multimember districting. Such districting has been upheld, *Whitcomb v. Chavis* (S.Ct.1971), even though "bloc voting by delegates from a multimember district may result in undue representation of residents of these districts relative to the voters in single-member districts." *Chapman v. Meier* (S.Ct.1975) (holding that court-ordered reapportionment plans should ordinarily avoid multimember districting). Where multimember districts are "operated as purposeful devices to further racial or economic discrimination," they are constitutionally impermissible. *Whitcomb.* Cf. *United Jewish Organizations of Williamsburgh v. Carey* (pp. 100–01.) However, the plaintiff's burden in such cases "is to produce evidence to support findings that the political processes leading to nomination and election were not equally open to participation by the group in question." *White v. Regester* (S.Ct.1973). In cases of political gerrymandering, "unconstitutional discrimination occurs only when the electoral system is arranged in a manner that will consistently degrade a voter's or a group of voters' influence on the political process as a whole." *Davis v. Bandemer* (S.Ct.1986) (plurality opinion).

The issue raised by the Court's inability to deal effectively with gerrymandering is whether anything of substance can be accomplished by requiring districts of equal population if nothing can be done to prevent districts from being drawn in such a way as to dilute the impact of some votes and magnify the impact of other votes. Dean Phil Neal commented that "The districting problem ... suggests how relatively little control over the adequacy of a representation plan is provided by a constitutional principle that all votes must have approximately equal weight.... An asserted constitutional principle that may not be much more useful than one half of a pair of pliers ought to be viewed with some skepticism." Neal, Baker v. Carr: Politics in Search of Law, 1962 Sup.Ct.Rev. 252, 277–78. *Reynolds v. Sims* has succeeded in forcing state legislatures to engage the apportionment problem. Whether it has assured that "a majority of the people [can] elect a majority of ... legislators" is another question indeed.

CHAPTER VI
STATE ACTION
§ 36. INTRODUCTION

It was established at an early date that the fourteenth and fifteenth amendments, like the provisions in the Bill of Rights, apply only to action by government. The *Civil Rights Cases* (S.Ct.1883) held that under the fourteenth amendment "it is state action of a particular character that is prohibited. Individual invasion of individual rights is not the subject-matter of the amendment." In so holding, the Court relied on the language of the amendment, which provides that "no state" shall engage in certain specified conduct. It is sometimes suggested that the framers intended to require the enforcement of racial equality through state law and that governmental failure to redress private discrimination might "constitute responsible 'state action' within the meaning of the Fourteenth Amendment." *Bell v. Md.* (S.Ct.1964) (Goldberg, J., concurring). However, a majority of the Court has not accepted the view that a finding of state action is warranted whenever the government fails to prevent private discrimination or other wrongdoing. See *DeShaney v. Winnebago County Dept. of Social Services* (S.Ct.1989), holding that a state's failure to protect a small child from severe physical abuse by his father did not violate the fourteenth amendment, which was designed to shelter "people from the State, not to ensure that the State protected them from each other."

The state action requirement reflects a concern for values of pluralism and personal freedom, which are considered important even when that freedom is exercised along arbitrary or irrational lines. As stated by Justices Douglas and Marshall, "The associational rights which our system honors permit all white, all black, all brown, and all yellow clubs to be formed." *Moose Lodge No. 107 v. Irvis* (S.Ct.1972) (dissenting because of "special circumstances"). On the other hand the government cannot be allowed to use private agents to promote discrimination while escaping constitutional restraints; and private parties who receive substantial governmental assistance may be prohibited from using such assistance for discriminatory purposes, since otherwise the state itself might be implicated in the discriminatory treatment. Accordingly, the Court has found state action in a variety of cases dealing with "public functions," judicial enforcement of private discrimination, or other "significant state involvement." (See §§ 37–39.) But when it is clearly the government itself that has acted, no additional inquiry is needed. See *Lebron v. National R.R. Passenger Corp.* (S.Ct.1995) (Amtrak held to be a governmental actor, since the United States created Amtrak for the furtherance of governmental objectives and retained permanent authority to appoint a majority of its board of directors). Because most of the cases concern racial discrimination, the discussion which follows refers generally to discriminatory treatment, but of course a finding of government action can trigger constitutional safeguards other than the equal protection clause.

§ 37. THE PERFORMANCE OF "PUBLIC FUNCTIONS"

The theory that private performance of governmental functions constitutes state action has been applied by the Supreme Court in two principal areas of activity: (1) pre-general elections in which candidates for public office are selected and (2) the use of private property such as parks, shopping centers and company-owned towns for alleged municipal purposes. Decisions finding state action in the election cases have survived intact, but efforts to apply constitutional restrictions to the use of private property have had only limited success.

The White Primary Cases. *Nixon v. Herndon* (S.Ct.1927) struck down a Texas statute excluding blacks from participation in a state primary. There was, of course, no difficulty finding state action in a legislative mandate to discriminate. Later, when black people were barred from the primaries by decision of the Democratic Party of Texas, the Court ruled that "delegation to a [political] party of the power to fix the qualifications of primary elections is delegation of a state function that may make the party's action the action of the state." *Smith v. Allwright* (S.Ct.1944). Such a delegation was found in statutes which prescribed primary procedures and controlled access to the general election ballot. Finally, in *Terry v. Adams* (S.Ct. 1953), the exclusion of blacks from pre-primary elections of the Jaybird Democratic Association, an organization of voters in a Texas county whose candidates since 1889 had nearly always won the Democratic primary and general election without opposition, was held to be unconstitutional state action. Three members of the Court said that "it violates the Fifteenth Amendment for a state ... to permit within its borders the use of any device that produces an equivalent of the prohibited election." Four other members concurred on the ground that the Jaybirds were "part and parcel of the Democratic Party" and hence subject to the rule of *Smith v. Allwright*. Although the *Terry* and *Allwright* cases were decided under the fifteenth amendment's ban on racial discrimination in voting, it is likely that the same result would be reached under the fourteenth amendment if an ethnic group—Italian–Americans, for instance—were excluded from primary elections. So understood, the cases arguably prohibit "party organization upon [arbitrary] lines, at least where the party has achieved political hegemony." Wechsler, Toward Neutral Principles of Constitutional Law, 73 Harv.L.Rev. 1, 29 (1959). Such a prohibition would presumably rest on the proposition that management of the electoral process is an inalienable governmental function. (See pp. 192–93.)

Access to Private Property. In *Marsh v. Ala.* (S.Ct.1946), the Court held that a state may not impose criminal punishment for the distribution of literature on the streets of a company-owned town contrary to the wishes of the town's management. The predicate for finding state action was not the enforcement of trespass laws (see § 38), but the fact that the property in question had "all the characteristics of any other American town" except for its private ownership. In concluding that property rights were outweighed in this context by interests in speech and religion, the Court explicitly endorsed a public function analysis: "The more an owner, for his advantage, opens up his property for use by the public in general, the more do his rights become circumscribed by the statutory and constitutional rights of those who use it. Thus, the owners of privately held bridges, ferries, turnpikes and railroads may not operate them as freely as a farmer does his farm. Since these facilities are built and operated primarily to benefit the public and since their operation is essentially a public function, it is subject to state regulation."

Inevitably, the advent of suburban shopping centers led to the question whether *Marsh* would be extended to the "functional equivalent" of a downtown business district. At first the Court gave a strong affirmative answer, holding in *Amalgamated Food Employees Union v. Logan Valley Plaza* (S.Ct. 1968) that a labor union must be permitted to picket a store in a privately owned shopping center in protest against the store's non-union status since the picketing was "directly related in its purpose to the use to which the ... property was being put." But four years later the Court began to shift direction. In *Lloyd Corp. v. Tanner* (S.Ct.1972), it sustained a shopping center ban on the distribution of handbills protesting the draft and the war in Viet Nam. The opinion noted that the handbilling "had no relation to any purpose for which the center was ... being used" and that the case was significantly different from *Marsh,* which involved "all of the attributes of a state-created municipality." Although the shopping center was open to the public, the implied invitation was "to come to the center to do business with the tenants," not to use the property "for any and all purposes, however incompatible with the interests of both the stores and the shoppers whom they serve." This philosophy, which was attentive to "the Fifth ... Amendment rights of private property owners," eventually ripened into a decision that there is no right to engage in speech activity at a private shopping center over the owner's objection even if the activity is directly related to the center's operations. *Hudgens v. NLRB* (S.Ct.1976), overruling *Logan Valley.* The Court, invoking the rule that prohibits states from discriminating in the regulation of speech on the basis of content, concluded that if the parties in *Lloyd* could be forbidden "to enter [a] shopping center to distribute handbills concerning Vietnam, then" a labor union can be forbidden "to enter [a] shopping center for the purpose of advertising" its dispute with one of the tenants.

A shift in direction can also be detected in the application of public function analysis to privately owned parks. *Evans v. Newton* (S.Ct.1966), which invalidated a racial restriction on the use of land devised in trust to a city for development of a park for white people, stated that "mass recreation through the use of parks is ... a public function" "regardless of who ... has title" to the property. A few years later, however, *Evans v. Abney* (S.Ct. 1970) affirmed a ruling that, because the park could not be operated on a racially exclusive basis, the trust had failed and the land reverted to the heirs of the testator. The majority in *Abney* assumed arguendo that the state could not constitutionally close its own parks for reasons of racial animus but held that a contrary result was warranted when it is "a private party which is injecting the racially discriminatory motivation." In so holding, the Court rejected a public function analysis under which state action could be found "regardless of who ... has title," and it apparently limited *Evans v. Newton* to an alternative rationale that predicated a finding of state action on official maintenance and control of the park.

The Rationale and Vitality of Public Function Analysis. The early public function cases purported to rely upon, and some actually involved, an official delegation of power. E.g. *Nixon v. Condon* (S.Ct.1932) (statute authorizing the executive committee of the Democratic Party of Texas to prescribe qualifications for voting in primary elections). However, public function analysis was soon extended to situations in which there was apparently no governmental activity whatever, but merely an assumption of "sovereign-like" authority. See *Marsh*. It was this aspect of the analysis—finding state action on the basis of the magnitude of power being exercised, rather than on grounds of any involvement with government—that seemed to offer the greatest potential for expanding the limits of state action. If private institutions became subject to constitutional restrictions because of the scope of their influence or because their conduct paralleled some government operations, it would be possible to find state action in corporate activity, or in the undertakings of labor unions and other groups which exert vast power even in the absence of official involvement. See Berle, Constitutional Limits on Corporate Activity—Protection of Personal Rights from Invasion through Economic Power, 100 U.Pa.L.Rev. 933 (1952) (urging that corporations be governed by the Federal Constitution when they are state-chartered and have sufficient economic power to invade individual rights to a significant degree).

This potential was never realized. Instead, the public function doctrine came under heavy criticism from both judicial and non-judicial quarters. In his lecture on state action, Judge Friendly said: "The argument that any institution performing an 'essentially public function' is necessarily subject to Fourteenth Amendment sanctions is ... unconvincing. Here the inarticulate premise must be that the state can constitutionally allow private persons to offer services parallel to those it offers or could offer only if it requires them to conform to the same standards the Fourteenth Amendment imposes upon it. One is permitted to ask why.... Particularly in these days when the state's activities embrace not only the fields traditional when the Amendment was adopted but higher education, health, transportation, power production, housing and many others, a principle that all Fourteenth Amendment guarantees apply to all institutions serving 'public purposes' is much too expansive." H. Friendly, The Dartmouth College Case and the Public–Private Penumbra 24 (1968). Education provided an apt example. Since parochial schools are permitted under the Constitution to engage in religious exercises and instruction which would be prohibited in public schools, it is difficult to sustain the broad proposition that private duplication of government activity is necessarily state action. See *School Dist. v. Schempp* (S.Ct.1963); *Pierce v. Society of Sisters* (S.Ct.1925).

Criticism of public function analysis did not pass unheeded. As the sequence of shopping center cases illustrates, the governmental function doctrine has not been significantly expanded beyond voting and the management of company towns. Moreover, the decision in *Jackson v. Metropolitan Edison Co.* (S.Ct.1974) indicates that the doctrine will remain relatively narrow. The *Jackson* case involved a privately owned utility which terminated electrical service to a consumer without a hearing upon alleged nonpayment of fees. The Court rejected a claim that the utility's performance of an essential public function constituted state action which required compliance with the demands of procedural due process. The opinion appears to confine the public function theory to the exercise of powers, like those in *Marsh* and the *White Primary Cases,* which are "traditionally associated with" or even traditionally reserved "exclusively" to the sovereign. Although the second description is especially restrictive, both characterizations reject the notion that private assumption of governmental functions is per se state action. *Jackson* also impliedly repudiated the power theory, noted above, by finding no government action despite the monopolization of electrical services by a large state-licensed utility.

The restrictive view taken in the *Jackson* case was reinforced by *Flagg Bros. v. Brooks* (S.Ct.1978). In *Flagg Bros.*, the Court held that a warehouseman's sale of stored goods, pursuant to express statutory authorization, did not constitute state action. The Court rejected a suggestion that state action should be found on the basis of a delegation of sovereign monopoly power over binding conflict resolution. The majority emphasized that while many functions, including dispute resolution, "have been traditionally performed by governments, very few have been 'exclusively reserved to the State.'" The Court withheld judgment on whether such functions as tax collection or police and fire protection, which are administered with a greater degree of exclusivity than dispute resolution, might trigger a finding of state action under public function analysis. Later cases have continued to suggest that a history of exclusive governmental activity is necessary for a finding of state action on the basis of the performance of public functions. See *Rendell-Baker v. Kohn* (S.Ct.1982) and *Blum v. Yaretsky* (S.Ct. 1982), finding no state action in the dismissal of teachers by a privately-owned school or the discharge of patients by a private nursing home.

§ 38. JUDICIAL ENFORCEMENT OF PRIVATE DISCRIMINATION

Shelley v. Kraemer (S.Ct.1948) was a landmark decision on the enforcement of racially restrictive covenants. State courts had there enjoined black buyers of homes that were subject to such covenants from taking possession of the property. On review the Supreme Court found unconstitutional state action in the issuance of injunctive relief although the covenants themselves, as private agreements, were said to be outside the purview of the fourteenth amendment: the injunctions "made available ... the full coercive power of government to deny petitioners, on the ground of race or color, the enjoyment of property rights in premises which petitioners are willing and financially able to acquire and which the grantors are willing to sell." An attempt to enforce a similar covenant by suit for damages was equally unsuccessful. See *Barrows v. Jackson* (S.Ct.1953), noting that an award of damages would discourage sale to blacks or stimulate an increase in the selling price.

The Court appeared in the *Shelley* case to have embraced the principle that state enforcement of the private right to discriminate is impermissible under the fourteenth amendment. A serious commitment to that principle would leave very little opportunity to discriminate privately since property rights, and personal liberty as well, are ultimately dependent upon government protection in most instances. Critics argued that if trespass laws could not be enforced against persons excluded by a club or home owner because of race, and a will establishing scholarships for black or Jewish students could not be admitted to probate, the right to discriminate privately in those areas would be largely illusory. Professor Herbert Wechsler, attacking the logic that might require such results, asked: "[W]hy is the enforcement of the private covenant a state discrimination rather than a legal recognition of the freedom of the individual? That the action of the state court is action of the state ... is, of course, entirely obvious. What is not obvious, and is the crucial step, is that the state may properly be charged with the discrimination when it does no more than give effect to an agreement that the individual involved is, by hypothesis, entirely free to make." Wechsler, Toward Neutral Principles of Constitutional Law, 73 Harv.L.Rev. 1, 29 (1959).

In fact, the broad implications of *Shelley v. Kraemer* have never come to fruition. Trespass cases which raised the question of state power to enforce discrimination at the demand of private citizens were consistently decided on grounds that studiously avoided any reliance on *Shelley*. E.g. *Peterson v. City of Greenville* (S.Ct.1963). (See § 39.) Even more significant, the *Shelley* case was held not to inhibit a state court from ruling that property devised in trust for use by "white people only" reverted to the heirs of the grantor upon invalidation of the racial restriction. In an opinion which adopted much of Professor Wechsler's reasoning, the Supreme Court found dispositive the fact that it was not the state but "a private party which is injecting the racially discriminatory motivation." *Evans v. Abney* (S.Ct.1970).

The meaning of *Shelley v. Kraemer,* therefore, remains open to dispute some 40 years after the case was decided. A few writers have suggested that the decision rests on the application of a balancing test under which the interest in equal access to the housing market was found to outweigh the interest in associational freedom of the complaining covenantees. However, this interpretation encounters at least two major difficulties. First, neither the *Shelley* opinion nor Supreme Court cases construing it made any mention of the balancing test. The omission of such an important point is unlikely to have been inadvertent, given the Court's familiarity with and frequent use of that test in other areas. Second, it has been said that courts simply "lack the time, the empirical knowledge, and the wisdom to handle every claim of unequal or arbitrary treatment by individuals enforced or not prevented by the states." H. Friendly, The Dartmouth College Case and the Public–Private Penumbra 17 (1968). Since, as previously noted, liberty and property rights are typically dependent upon government enforceability, almost every private act of discrimination or arbitrariness would present an occasion for possible constitutional litigation if a balancing test controlled the state action issue.

An alternative interpretation of *Shelley* is that it prohibits a state from compelling parties to adhere to an agreement to discriminate but does not preclude official enforcement of *voluntary* private discrimination. There is important, if somewhat tentative, support for this view. Thus state courts are permitted to enforce, at the behest of private parties, contractual provisions which the government itself could not constitutionally impose. See *Black v. Cutter Laboratories* (S.Ct.1956) (sustaining the discharge of an employee under a collective bargaining agreement which made membership in the Communist party "just cause" for dismissal). At the same time *Moose Lodge No. 107 v. Irvis* (S.Ct. 1972) has held that the *Shelley* case bars the states from ordering a fraternal organization to comply with its own bylaws when those bylaws mandate racial discrimination. A state may permit such organizations to discriminate, but it cannot require them to do so.

The voluntariness rationale has been criticized on the ground that it fails to identify which decision-making unit must act voluntarily: "Is the 'willing' seller who can not be interfered with ... through court orders, the corporation or merely its authorized personnel? In the case of a trust, is the willing donor [the settlor or the] trustee?" Haber, Notes on the Limits of Shelley v. Kraemer, 18 Rutg.L.Rev. 811, 817 (1964). The probable answer is that *no* private party can be compelled by government to discriminate racially in a manner which would be constitutionally proscribed to the state itself. *Moose Lodge* is again in point. It enjoined all official enforcement of an organization's discriminatory bylaws without distinguishing among the potential targets of enforcement. Similarly, in *Shelley v. Kraemer* it was immaterial that some covenantees wished to adhere to the racial restrictions; those who felt otherwise must be free from state compulsion to discriminate. In short, the focus of a voluntariness rule would not be on determining which parties favor discrimination but on maintaining freedom from state coercion for any party that chooses not to discriminate.

§ 39. SIGNIFICANT STATE INVOLVEMENT

The Burton Case. If *Shelley v. Kraemer* had arisen at a later date, the opinion might have invoked the rule prohibiting significant state involvement in private discrimination. But that rule did not mature until *Burton v. Wilmington Parking Authority* (S.Ct.1961) was decided. *Burton* arose out of the denial of service to blacks by a coffee shop located within a parking facility owned by a government agency. Space in the facility had been leased to private tenants for commercial use in order to make practicable the financing of the building. The Court said that the arrangement between the coffee shop and the parking authority yielded mutual benefits and economic profits which, taken together with the government's failure to insert a nondiscrimination clause in the lease, brought the state "into a position of interdependence" with the restaurant and made it a "joint participant in the challenged activity...." Because of this "significant state involvement," the lessee was bound by the fourteenth amendment's proscription of racial discrimination.

However, the *Burton* case does not control all government leases. *Burton* called for a process of "sifting facts and weighing circumstances" to determine the extent of official involvement, and the outcome in the case was based on a composite of factors. The Court held only that the fourteenth amendment applies "when a state leases public property in the manner and for the purpose shown to have been the case here...." This limited holding made it possible for subsequent cases to view *Burton* narrowly as involving an effective partnership or "symbiotic relationship" between the state and a private party. See e.g. *Moose Lodge.*

Encouraging or Aiding Private Action. When private discrimination does not stem from a close relationship with government, state action may be found on the basis of official encouragement to discriminate. *Reitman v. Mulkey* (S.Ct.1967) was evidently decided on this ground. The *Reitman* case involved a California constitutional amendment, enacted directly by the voters, which forbade the state to abridge the right of an individual to sell or lease residential property or refuse to do so "in his absolute discretion." The amendment had the effect of displacing state anti-discrimination statutes, and the California Supreme Court found that in the "milieu" of its operation it would encourage racial discrimination. The United States Supreme Court purported to rely on that finding to invalidate the amendment. While noting that official authorization to discriminate is sometimes said to be unconstitutional, the Court did not rule that states may never put in statutory form a policy of neutrality with respect to private discrimination. Instead it stressed that the effect of the amendment was, not merely to authorize discrimination by repealing statutory restraints, but to "encourage ... discrimination" by embodying the right to discriminate "in the State's basic charter, immune from legislative, executive, or judicial regulation at any level of state government." A number of commentators have expressed doubt that a constitutional provision gives substantially greater encouragement to racial discrimination than a statutory one, particularly where, as in *Reitman,* the provision does not classify explicitly in terms of race. But this analysis could lead to either of two opposite conclusions: some writers believed the state action requirement was passing into oblivion, while others insisted that *Reitman* was wrongly decided.

Many of those who were critical of *Reitman* agreed, however, that a finding of unconstitutional state action would be justified where the government is "actively fostering" racial discrimination. (Harlan, J., dissenting.) For example, if the government mandates discrimination, private acts conforming to that mandate may be charged to the state even though it is possible that the actor would have chosen to discriminate in any event. Thus, *Peterson v. City of Greenville* (S.Ct.1963) held that sit-in demonstrators at a segregated lunch counter could not be prosecuted for trespass where an ordinance made integrated service unlawful: "When the State has commanded a particular result, it has saved to itself the power to determine that result and thereby 'to a significant extent' has 'become involved' in it, and in fact, has removed that decision from the sphere of private choice."

There is a good deal of irony in the *Peterson* decision. It announces that by ordering discrimination the state makes it impermissible for private parties to discriminate. The irony seems even greater when one takes account of the state's utter inability to enforce its unconstitutional order. Furthermore any effort to revoke the order would raise a whole new set of state action problems. If the purpose and effect of revocation is to facilitate private discrimination by making *Peterson* inapplicable, the state might be found to have fostered and encouraged discriminatory treatment. Whether this final irony—restricting state power to withdraw an unconstitutional order—will materialize is open to question; but *Peterson* itself is firmly grounded on a legitimate concern for the public perception and practical effect of an official mandate, however invalid the mandate might be.

Governmental involvement with discrimination has sometimes consisted of aiding parties engaged in discriminatory treatment rather than of mandating such treatment. In *Norwood v. Harrison* (S.Ct. 1973), the Court held it unconstitutional for a state to lend textbooks to students in private segregated schools pursuant to a long-established policy of supplying free books to all students within the jurisdiction. Although the state "might provide to schools in common with others" such "generalized services" as police and fire protection, a program for lending textbooks or reimbursing parents for tuition expenditures at segregated academies is impermissible because it "has a significant tendency to facilitate, reinforce, and support private discrimination." Even tax deductions and exemptions that benefit fraternal orders or charitable foundations practicing racial discrimination have been declared invalid by lower courts. E.g. *McGlotten v. Connally* (D.D.C.1972). See also *Gilmore v. City of Montgomery* (S.Ct.1974) (enjoining exclusive access to public facilities by segregated private schools). However, the Supreme Court has not ruled that government aid converts private activity into state action, requiring the actor to adhere to constitutional restrictions, but only that the aid itself must be terminated when it "subsidizes" discriminatory practices.

The principle that bars government subsidies for racial discrimination is easy to understand. Taxpayers should not be compelled to support such discrimination, and the state should not become implicated in it. The difficulty, as in the case of aid to parochial schools, is in determining which government benefits constitute unlawful assistance and which do not. Tax allowances, for instance, are available to nearly everyone. And it has been suggested that if such allowances are equated with illegal subsidies in the case of charitable foundations or fraternal societies, there may be "no really tenable basis for distinguishing the tax deductions allowed individuals or corporations." *Jackson v.*

Statler Foundation (2d Cir.1973) (Friendly, J., dissenting).

The Court has made it clear that a finding of state action is not justified merely on the basis of substantial government funding, so long as there is no "subsidy" for the challenged action. *Rendell–Baker v. Kohn* (S.Ct.1982), for example, found no state action involved in the dismissal of teachers by a privately-owned school even though public funds accounted for 90% of the school's operating budget. The Court concluded that "The school ... is not fundamentally different from many private corporations whose business depends primarily on contracts to build roads, bridges, dams, ships, or submarines for the government. Acts of such private contractors do not become acts of the government by reason of their significant or even total engagement in performing public contracts." Similarly, *Blum v. Yaretsky* (S.Ct.1982) found no state action in the discharge of patients by a privately-owned nursing home that received substantial government funding. Although state regulations penalized services that were found to exceed a beneficiary's needs, the Court stressed that "those regulations ... do not dictate the decision to discharge or transfer *in a particular case.*" (Emphasis added.) Since particular decisions depended on the medical judgment of private parties, they were found to implicate no state action. See also *Polk County v. Dodson* (S.Ct.1981) (public defender's employment relationship with the state is insufficient to establish action "under color of law" in the representation of the criminally accused, since the state does not control the attorney's professional judgments).

The Court's treatment of other types of governmental involvement—mandating, authorizing, or participating in private action—requires some elaboration. A state mandate for invidious discrimination is clearly unconstitutional. The only serious question is whether the invalid command should defeat an otherwise recognized right to discriminate privately. But the right to practice racial discrimination has never been accorded constitutional status, and the loss of that right through a state order to discriminate affects individuals in essentially the same way as an order to cease discrimination.

More substantial problems would be raised by finding state action on the basis of "authorization" to discriminate. Virtually all unregulated activity is in some way authorized by state law. The authorization is often implicit in common law rules rather than expressed in a statute, but common law rules usually become explicit when the subject is litigated. It is difficult therefore to distinguish between permitting an activity, which several cases find insufficient to trigger fourteenth amendment restraints (see pp. 206–09), and authorizing the activity. In light of that difficulty, the Court has held officially authorized action such as self-help seizures of property under the Uniform Commercial Code not to be state action. See *Flagg Bros. v. Brooks*. However, if instead of merely giving private parties a free choice, the government attempts to influence that choice, state action can be found—

as in *Reitman*—on the basis of encouragement. Unfortunately none of the Court's opinions makes clear what types of inducement, short of outright command, might constitute encouragement. Apparently the "milieu" in which the state scheme operates may be critical in determining whether an official statement or other involvement is tantamount to encouragement. See *Reitman.*

The Court has also ruled that a private party's "joint participation" with government officials in the seizure of disputed property may support a finding of state action. In *Lugar v. Edmondson Oil Co.* (S.Ct.1982), a 5–4 majority relied on cases from *Snaidach* to *Di–Chem,* which had implicitly found state action as a necessary predicate for applying due process standards, to conclude that the use of public officials in attachment proceedings was sufficient to satisfy the state action requirement. *Flagg Bros.* was distinguished on the ground that the private warehouseman in that case had resorted to self-help, and hence there was no "overt, official involvement in the property deprivation." Compare *Edmonson v. Leesville Concrete Co.* (S.Ct.1991) (a private litigant's use of peremptory challenges to exclude jurors on the basis of race constituted state action in light of the trial court's overt involvement in jury selection). Nevertheless, *Lugar's* reliance on joint participation as a basis for finding state action was narrowly drawn. The Court emphasized that its holding "is limited to the particular context of prejudgment attachment," and it explicitly rejected any suggestion that a private party's mere invokation of legal procedures would constitute joint participation with state officials and thereby satisfy the state action requirement. See *NCAA v. Tarkanian* (S.Ct.1988) (state university's imposition of disciplinary sanctions against a basketball coach in compliance with NCAA demands did not justify a finding of state action on the part of the NCAA).

Regulation and Licensing. Official involvement with private activity often takes the form of licensing, regulating or approving the activity. *Moose Lodge v. Irvis* and the *Jackson* case are now the principal decisions on those subjects. The *Moose Lodge* case rejected a claim that racial discrimination by a heavily regulated private club holding a state liquor license violates the fourteenth amendment. The Court said it would "utterly emasculate" the distinction between private and state action to hold that "state regulation in any degree" or acceptance of "any sort of [government] service" subjects a party to constitutional restraints. Neither the fact that the regulation in *Moose Lodge* was detailed nor the fact that it could have included a ban on discriminatory treatment proved to be critical: "However detailed this type of regulation may be in some particulars, it cannot be said to in any way foster or encourage racial discrimination." And while the state limited the number of available liquor licenses, this fell "far short of conferring upon club licensees a monopoly in the dispensing of liquor in any given municipality...." Finally, *Burton* was deemed readily distinguishable since it involved a "symbiotic relationship between lessor and lessee" in a public building, rather than the licensing of "a private social club in a private building."

Jackson v. Metropolitan Edison Co. is as important for its treatment of the involvement concept as for its interpretation of the public function doctrine. (See § 37.) In holding that a utility company's termination of electrical service to a customer was not state action, the Court again discounted the element of regulation and gave limited scope to the notion that conduct approved by government constitutes state action. The Court agreed that the acts of a regulated utility with a *governmentally-protected* monopoly might be more easily attributed to the state than the acts of other entities, but said "the inquiry must be whether there is a sufficiently close nexus between the State and the challenged action of the regulated entity so that the action of the latter may fairly be treated as that of the State itself." Like *Moose Lodge,* the *Jackson* case revealed no "symbiotic relationship" with the state. Evidence of official approval of a tariff submitted by the utility, which provided for termination of service upon nonpayment, was also unavailing: "Approval by a state utility commission of such a request from a regulated utility, where the Commission has not put its own weight on the side of the proposed practice by ordering it, does not transmute a practice initiated by the utility and approved by the Commission into 'state action.'" This ruling weakens the thrust of *Public Utilities Comm'n v. Pollak* (S.Ct.1952), which seemed to find official action on the basis of government approval of the challenged activity. Approval that throws the government's weight behind private action must now be distinguished from approval that does not. However, government approval in any form would seem to constitute at least authorization for the activity, and so *Jackson* appears to confirm the view expressed above that authorization alone is deemed insufficient to convert otherwise private activity into state action. See also *Columbia Broadcasting System v. Democratic Nat'l Comm.* (S.Ct.1973) for a discussion by some Justices of the question whether a television broadcaster's policy of refusing paid editorial advertisements constitutes governmental action.

The *Jackson* and *Moose Lodge* cases have plainly limited the impact of official regulation, licensing and approval on the state action issue. Regulation is pertinent if it can be said to "foster or encourage racial discrimination;" but since encouragement to discriminate is unconstitutional independent of any regulation, the latter element may now add relatively little. The cases also demonstrate that the issuance of a government license does not itself impute responsibility to the state for acts of the licensee. Licensing might still assume some importance where it allocates a scarce resource or makes the licensee a "partner" of the state, cf. *Columbia Broadcasting System v. Democratic Nat'l Comm.;* and approval continues to be relevant in a small category of cases. But the overriding question is whether the state's involvement is "significant," and the implication of the *Moose Lodge* and *Jackson* opinions is that *Burton* will not be broadly construed. See *San Francisco Arts & Athletics, Inc. v. United States Olympic Committee* (S.Ct.1987) (neither the issuance of a federal charter nor the grant of exclusive use of "olympic" words and symbols warrants a finding that the U.S. Olympic Committee is a governmental actor).

The Elasticity of the Involvement Concept. The *Burton* case provided a highly flexible tool for measuring state action. But since the facts and circumstances which that case "sifted" and "weighed" will probably never be duplicated, and little guidance was offered for evaluating the significance of any particular involvement, the rule which emerged was essentially open-ended. As a result *Burton* can carry as much freight—or as little—as the Court desires. At the moment it seems to apply mainly to symbiotic relationships arising out of the use of government-owned property.

The reasons for restricting the involvement concept should not be sought simplistically in the changing composition of the Court, though that development is obviously not irrelevant. State action boundaries were expanded primarily in cases of racial discrimination during a period of history in which the judiciary seemed to be the only organ of government capable of assuring equal treatment to racial minorities. Some writers in fact urged that a lesser degree of state involvement be required in the context of racial discrimination than in other contexts, a position arguably supported by the central purpose of the fourteenth amendment to eradicate certain invidious distinctions based on race. But two recent developments have reduced the national dependency on courts for protection against racial discrimination. First, the scope of congressional power to regulate private action in this field has been greatly expanded (see § 43), and second, the stranglehold of the Senate filibuster on civil rights legislation has been broken. (See § 44.) Under these circumstances the Court has perceived less need for judicial intervention, and it is correspondingly less probable—though still conceivable— that state action will be measured by a special standard in race-related cases or, as some commentators propose, by an ad hoc balancing of interests in all cases. The result may be a reinvigoration of the state action requirement but, as the following chapter suggests, not necessarily a lack of effective vigilance against racial injustice. (See pp. 246–47, discussing alternative means for attacking racial discrimination after the finding of no state action in *Jackson* and *Moose Lodge*.)

CHAPTER VII

CONGRESSIONAL ENFORCEMENT OF CIVIL RIGHTS

§ 40. INTRODUCTION

Although the state action requirement limits the reach of constitutional prohibitions, it has not prevented Congress from enacting important statutory controls on discriminatory treatment. The enforcement clauses of the Civil War Amendments authorize appropriate legislation to implement the substantive sections of the amendments. Congress also has broad powers under the commerce clause, and its authority to protect rights of national citizenship against private or official interference is well settled. *U.S. v. Classic* (S.Ct.1941). Legislative activity in the field of civil rights was particularly intense in the Reconstruction era and during the period following *Brown v. Board of Education*. (See §§ 44–46.) As a result, discrimination is now regulated not only when imposed under color of law but also in many private contexts, especially those involving conspiratorial action or racially motivated refusals to do business.

§ 41. CONGRESSIONAL IMPLEMENTATION OF JUDICIALLY–DECLARED CONSTITUTIONAL RIGHTS

The enforcement provisions of the thirteenth, fourteenth and fifteenth amendments state that "Congress shall have power to enforce" the amendments "by appropriate legislation." At the core of these provisions is the power to protect rights which courts have found to be conferred in the body of the amendments. Thus Congress can undoubtedly impose both criminal and civil sanctions for the violation of judicially-declared constitutional rights. (See § 46.) However, the recent case law has also recognized congressional authority under the enforcement clauses to prohibit some acts which are not themselves unconstitutional.

An initial step in that direction was taken by *South Carolina v. Katzenbach* (S.Ct.1966). That case involved a challenge to provisions of the Voting Rights Act of 1965, which in certain geographical areas (a) suspended literacy tests and similar devices, (b) prohibited new voting regulations without prior federal approval and (c) authorized the replacement of state voting examiners with federal officials upon certification by the Attorney General. The Court found the record in the case replete with evidence of racially discriminatory uses of voting tests in states governed by the Act. It observed that "case-by-case litigation against voting discrimination" under prior statutes had "done little to cure the problem," and concluded: "As against the reserved powers of the States, Congress may use any rational means to effectuate the constitutional prohibition of racial discrimination in voting." Under this test the legislation was found to be a proper exercise of congressional power to enforce the fifteenth amendment, notwithstanding *Lassiter v. Northhampton Board of Elections* (S.Ct.1959), which had upheld the validity of a literacy requirement.

It seems clear, given *Lassiter,* that the Voting Rights Act did more than regulate unconstitutional activity. *South Carolina v. Katzenbach* attempted to relate the testing ban to unconstitutional applications of the tests and to the fact that continued testing "would freeze the effect of past discrimination in favor of unqualified white registrants" even if literacy requirements were fairly administered in the future. But the Court also sustained other sections of the Act without tying them to any freezing effects, and it later upheld a nationwide extension of the test ban, *Oregon v. Mitchell* (S.Ct.1970), despite the lack of evidence that literacy tests were everywhere used for discriminatory purposes. It was enough that the displaced state procedures would "unduly *lend* themselves to discriminatory application." *Oregon v. Mitchell* (Harlan, J., concurring) (emphasis added). It is apparent, therefore, that under the enforcement clauses Congress may prohibit some acts which are not themselves unconstitutional if the prohibition is a rational means to effectuate the guarantees of the amendments. This power, as the Court has noted, is analogous to that conferred by the necessary and proper clause of the Constitution, which enables Congress to deal with matters outside the area of enumerated federal concerns as a means of effectuating policies within that area: "Let the end be legitimate, let it be within the scope of the constitution, and all means which are appropriate, which are plainly adapted to that end, which are not prohibited, but consist with the letter and spirit of the constitution, are constitutional." *McCulloch v. Maryland* (S.Ct.1819) (creation of a national bank ruled permissible, despite lack of enumerated authority, as a reasonable way to facilitate the exercise of power to collect taxes, borrow money and support the army and navy).

City of Rome v. U.S. (S.Ct.1980) reaffirmed the power of Congress to regulate acts which are not themselves unconstitutional but which create a significant risk of constitutional violations. In that case a city challenged the Attorney General's refusal under the 1965 Voting Rights Act to approve certain electoral changes, including provisions for the at-large election of public officials by majority vote in an area where voters were predominantly white and racial bloc voting was prevalent. A federal district court found that the proposed electoral changes were not animated by a discriminatory purpose but would have a discriminatory effect. The city argued that § 1 of the fifteenth amendment prohibits only purposeful racial discrimination in voting and that congressional enforcement of the amendment pursuant to § 2 could not reach voting

§ 41　　*CONGRESSIONAL ENFORCEMENT*　　215

practices which had a discriminatory impact but lacked a discriminatory intent. In rejecting that argument, the Court relied on *South Carolina v. Katzenbach* and *Oregon v. Mitchell* to hold that even if § 1 of the fifteenth amendment prohibits only purposeful discrimination, Congress might regulate under § 2 voting practices having only a discriminatory effect: "Congress could rationally have concluded that, because electoral changes by jurisdictions with a demonstrable history of intentional racial discrimination in voting create the risk of purposeful discrimination, it was proper to prohibit changes that have a discriminatory impact." See also *Thornburg v. Gingles* (S.Ct.1986) (enforcing an amendment to the 1965 Voting Rights Act under which proof of a discriminatory effect, without a showing of discriminatory purpose, was enough to establish a statutory violation).

Congress thus has broad power to implement judicially-declared constitutional rights. However, it is not clear how the Court will determine whether Congress intends to enforce the fourteenth or fifteenth amendment when legislation does not specifically invoke the enforcement authority. In *Pennhurst State School v. Halderman* (S.Ct.1981), the majority said that because enforcing legislation "often intrudes on traditional state authority, we should not quickly attribute to Congress an unstated intent to act under its authority to enforce the Fourteenth Amendment." Yet two years later, the Court disclaimed any need for Congress to invoke its enforcement powers explicitly: "It is in the nature of our review of congressional legislation defended on the basis of Congress' powers under § 5 of the Fourteenth Amendment that we be able to discern some legislative purpose or factual predicate that supports the exercise of that power. That does not mean, however, that Congress need anywhere recite the words 'section 5' or 'Fourteenth Amendment' or 'equal protection.'" *EEOC v. Wyoming* (1983).

§ 42. CONGRESSIONAL MODIFICATION OF JUDICIALLY–DECLARED CONSTITUTIONAL RIGHTS

While *South Carolina v. Katzenbach* might be read to authorize only "remedial" congressional action under the Civil War Amendments, the decision in *Katzenbach v. Morgan* (S.Ct.1966) seemed to empower Congress to modify the substantive content of constitutional rights. *Morgan* upheld a provision of the Voting Rights Act which declared that persons who had completed the sixth grade in schools accredited by the Commonwealth of Puerto Rico, in which the language of instruction was other than English, could not be disenfranchised by any jurisdiction because of illiteracy in English. Although the Court was not prepared to invalidate the application of an English literacy requirement to a prospective voter who was literate in another language, *Cardona v. Power* (S.Ct.1966), it nevertheless found the legislation "appropriate ... to enforce the Equal Protection Clause." Alternative theories were offered in support of this result: (1) the federal statute would help to secure nondiscriminatory treatment of Puerto Rican people in the provision of government services; (2) Congress could find the disenfranchisement of persons covered by the statute to be itself unconstitutional. Under either theory the Court said it need only be able "to perceive a basis" upon which Congress might resolve the issue as it did. But *Morgan* insisted in an important footnote that the enforcement clause "does not grant Congress power to exercise discretion ... to enact 'statutes so as in effect to dilute equal protection and due process decisions of this Court....' Thus, for example, an enactment authorizing the States to establish racially segregated systems of education would not be ... a measure 'to enforce' the Equal Protection Clause since that clause of its own force prohibits such state laws." See also *Mississippi University for Women v. Hogan* (S.Ct.1982) ("neither Congress nor a State can validate a law that denies the rights guaranteed by the Fourteenth Amendment").

Under the first *Morgan* theory, Congress did no more than implement judicial interpretations of the fourteenth amendment barring discrimination against arbitrarily drawn classes, although the extraordinary deference accorded to any "perceived basis" for implementing the amendment through the franchise could admittedly result in a severe impairment of state control over voter qualifications. The second *Morgan* theory went beyond congressional enforcement of the Constitution to congressional interpretation: it appeared to allow Congress to make an independent judgment, contrary to *Lassiter* and notwithstanding *Cardona,* that an English literacy requirement "constituted an invidious discrimination in violation of the Equal Protection Clause." Understandably the latter theory was subjected to sharp criticism. Congressional power to interpret the Civil War Amendments was perceived as endangering the principle of judicial supremacy in constitutional adjudication. Many observers found no satisfactory explanation for allowing congressional expansions but not contractions of fourteenth amendment rights. Yet without an adequate predicate for that distinction, *Morgan* posed a significant threat to constitutionally protected freedoms, a threat which in fact ripened quickly into a number of bills designed to modify judicial decisions on school desegregation or criminal procedure. See also the "human life" bill, introduced by Senator Helms and Congressman Hyde, which found "a significant likelihood that actual human life exists from conception" and declared that "for the purpose of enforcing the obligation of the States under the fourteenth amendment not to deprive persons of life without due process of law, human life shall be deemed to exist from conception." S. 158, H.R. 900, 97th Cong., 1st Sess. Moreover even if the *Morgan* footnote were taken at face value, it would be difficult in many situations to determine whether rights were being expanded or diluted. Often constitutional liberties are in sharp tension: a restriction on publications relating to a pending criminal case may "enforce" the right to a fair trial, but it dilutes the right to a free press. In view of the far-reaching implications of the second *Morgan* rationale, students of the Court were not surprised that efforts were soon made to contain it.

Oregon v. Mitchell (S.Ct.1970) provided an opportunity to reconsider the meaning of the *Morgan* case. At issue was the validity of a federal statute which, in relevant part, effectively lowered the voting age to 18 in reliance upon the enforcement clauses of the fourteenth and fifteenth amendments. A closely divided Court, without agreeing on a majority opinion, ruled the statute unconstitutional as applied to state elections. Mr. Justice Stewart, writing for himself and two other members of the Court, interpreted the second *Morgan* theory to hold, not that Congress could displace a judicial determination as to what the Constitution means, but only that in protecting a "discrete and insular minority," Congress could "override state laws on the ground that they were in fact used as instruments of invidious discrimination even though a court in an individual lawsuit might not have reached that factual conclusion." Separate opinions by Justices Black and Harlan put forth similar arguments. Even the dissenters felt compelled to restate the second rationale of the *Morgan* case. Mr. Justice Brennan, who had authored *Morgan,* now argued that the superior fact-finding capacity of Congress enabled it to "determine whether the factual basis necessary to support a state legislative discrimination actually exists." Thus the theory was that while courts must ordinarily defer to a debatable state determination, Congress can override such a determination by finding that an adequate basis for it does not exist. However, judicial deference to state legislative policy rests, not only on relative fact-finding capabilities, but also on principles of federalism and political accountability. The Court acknowledged this point in a later case, which revisited the issue raised by *Morgan*.

City of Boerne v. Flores (S.Ct.1997) addressed the validity of the Religious Freedom Restoration Act of 1993 (RFRA). That Act prohibited the state and federal governments from "substantially burden[ing]" the free exercise of religion, even if the burden resulted from a rule of general applicability, unless the government demonstrated that the burden "(1) is in furtherance of a compelling governmental interest; and (2) is the least restrictive means of furthering that ... interest." The statutory right conferred in RFRA was clearly intended to be broader than the rights protected by the free exercise clause of the first amendment. See *Employment Division, Dept. of Human Resources v. Smith* (S.Ct.1990). Because zoning authorities in the city of Boerne had denied an application for a permit to enlarge a church in an officially-designated historic district, a suit was brought based largely on RFRA.

The Supreme Court held that, by enacting RFRA, Congress had exceeded its enforcement powers under section 5 of the fourteenth amendment. The majority rejected any suggestion that Congress could "decree the substance" of the fourteenth amendment; and Justice O'Connor agreed that "Congress lacks the ability independently to define *or expand* the scope of constitutional rights by statute," although she dissented on other grounds. (Emphasis added.) The power, recognized in earlier cases, to regulate acts not themselves unconstitutional was now confined to situations in which "many of the laws affected by the congressional enactment have a significant likelihood of being unconstitutional." The Religious Freedom Restoration Act was invalid because it was not narrowly designed to counteract state laws likely to be unconstitutional, and it involved "a considerable congressional intrusion into the States' traditional ... authority to regulate for the health and welfare of their citizens."

§ 43. CONGRESSIONAL POWER OVER PRIVATE DISCRIMINATION

Despite the limitations imposed by the state action concept, Congress has broad power to legislate against private discrimination. As illustrated by the first rationale of *Morgan* and by *South Carolina v. Katzenbach,* the Congress can prohibit some acts which are not unconstitutional if the prohibition tends reasonably to effectuate constitutional guarantees. Of course, the legislation in those cases was directed at state rather than private action, but the means-to-end rationale may be no less applicable to private activity which is unregulated by the fourteenth amendment than to official activity which is similarly unregulated. Accordingly, if Congress finds that a ban on private discrimination is an appropriate means of preventing unconstitutional state action—as, for instance, by attacking a condition like segregated housing which facilitates such action—and its finding is rationally based, the ban could be upheld under the Civil War Amendments.

Congressional power under the amendments may reach even further. In *U.S. v. Guest* (S.Ct.1966), six Justices stated in two concurring opinions that Congress can punish "all conspiracies—with or without state action—that interfere with fourteenth amendment rights." The *Guest* opinions have been interpreted to authorize federal protection against private interference with the private exercise of constitutional rights. E.g. *Action v. Gannon* (8th Cir.1971). This interpretation, unless qualified by a requirement of specific intent to intrude upon constitutional freedoms, has wide implications: an act of murder abridges the victim's right to vote but has not for that reason been considered a matter generally of federal concern. However, since "fourteenth amendment rights" run only against the state, it is possible that the application of *Guest* will be limited to cases in which a public official is inhibited by other parties from performing duties imposed by the Constitution. See e.g. *Brewer v. Hoxie School District No. 46* (8th Cir.1956) (enjoining private parties from intimidating school officials who were attempting to dismantle a de jure segregated school system).

Even if the power to enforce the fourteenth amendment is more narrowly circumscribed than a spacious reading of *Morgan* and *Guest* would suggest, Congress will have broad authority to regulate private discrimination under the commerce clause and the thirteenth amendment. The federal commerce power extends to all activity which substantially affects interstate commerce or which falls within a class of activities affecting commerce. See *Perez v. U.S.* (S.Ct.1971) (since "extortionate credit transactions, though purely intrastate, may in the judgment of Congress affect interstate commerce," the entire class of activities can be regulated without proof that the transaction under litigation itself affects commerce); see also *Wickard v. Filburn* (S.Ct.1942) (small farmer's production of 239 bushels of wheat for home consumption held subject to federal control because of the cumulative impact of such consumption on demand for interstate wheat). The commerce clause was the source of authority utilized in the Civil Rights Act of 1964, and decisions upholding the Act demonstrate the ample breadth of that authority. In *Katzenbach v. McClung* (S.Ct.1964), the Court wrote: "Of course, the mere fact that Congress has said when particular activity shall be deemed to affect commerce does not preclude further examination by this Court. But where we find that the legislators, in light of the facts and testimony before them, have a rational basis for finding a chosen regulatory scheme necessary to the protection of commerce, our investigation is at an end." Applying this modest requirement, the Court easily sustained the federal ban on racial discrimination in motels, restaurants and other places of public accommodation: Congress had a rational basis for believing that discrimination would have the effect of discouraging interstate commerce. *Heart of Atlanta Motel v. U.S.* (S.Ct. 1964); *Katzenbach v. McClung.*

Finally the thirteenth amendment, which states that "Neither slavery nor involuntary servitude ... shall exist within the United States," provides still another source of federal power over private discrimination. That amendment contains no state action requirement, and its enforcement clause was given an expansive interpretation in *Jones v. Alfred H. Mayer Co.* (S.Ct.1968). The Court there held that under this clause Congress has power "rationally to determine what are the badges and incidents of slavery, and the authority to translate that determination into effective legislation." It is difficult to conceive of substantial acts of racial discrimination which could not be regulated under this sweeping authority. Thus *Jones* sustained a prohibition against racial discrimination in the sale of housing; and subsequent decisions have applied the same rationale to discrimination in community recreational facilities, *Sullivan v. Little Hunting Park* (S.Ct.1969), and to "conspiratorial, racially discriminatory private action aimed at depriving [blacks] of the basic rights that the law secures to all free men." *Griffin v. Breckenridge* (S.Ct.1971) (interference with first amendment liberties and the right to travel). Some writers have suggested that the thirteenth amendment is entirely self-executing and so, by its own force, prohibits private action constituting a badge of slavery. But assuming arguendo that the amendment itself proscribes only involuntary servitude—an issue left open in the *Jones* case—the enforcement clause will permit Congress to reach private discrimination which is rationally found to be a residue of slavery. It is also possible that the thirteenth amendment, unlike the fourteenth, will reach nonpurposeful racial discrimination. See *Memphis v. Greene* (S.Ct.1981) (the "inconvenience" caused to black residents by the closure of a street at the border between black and white neighborhoods did not involve the kind of discriminatory impact which would violate the thirteenth amendment even if the amendment does not require a discriminatory purpose). An expansive interpretation of the thirteenth amendment is less far-reaching than a broad construction of the fourteenth amendment would be, since the latter amendment is in no way confined to badges of involuntary servitude. Indeed, the attractiveness of the thirteenth amendment lies precisely in its vast potential for regulating slavery-related discrimination without opening to federal control all matters touched by the fourteenth amendment. Compare *Griffin v. Breckenridge* with *Action v. Gannon*.

§ 44. CIVIL RIGHTS LEGISLATION IN THE POST-BROWN ERA

Three comprehensive civil rights laws were enacted by Congress in the post-*Brown* period: the Civil Rights Act of 1964, the Voting Rights Act of 1965, and the Civil Rights Act of 1968. 42 U.S.C.A. § 2000; 42 U.S.C.A. § 1973; 42 U.S.C.A. § 3601. The third of those statutes prohibits discrimination on grounds of race, color, religion or national origin in the sale or rental of housing; exceptions are drawn for private clubs, single-family dwellings, and boarding houses occupied by the owner but containing no more than three other family units. Actions designed to impede or discourage the demand for equal housing, as by "steering" clients to specific neighborhoods on the basis of race or subjecting them to discriminatory application procedures, are also unlawful. *U.S. v. West Peachtree Tenth Corp.* (5th Cir.1971); *Zuch v. Hussey* (E.D.Mich.1973). Lower courts have held that proof of discrimination can be established in housing cases in the same way as in employment cases. (See pp. 235–36.) A separate provision in the statute imposes criminal penalties upon the willful use of force or threats by any person to interfere with federally protected activities, such as participation in an election or in a government-administered program. 18 U.S.C.A. § 245(b).

The Voting Rights Act forbids the states and their political subdivisions to use any "voting qualification ..., standard, practice, or procedure ... in a manner which results in a denial or abridgement of the right of any citizen of the United States to vote on account of race or color" or because of membership in a "language minority group." Upon suit by the Attorney General or an aggrieved person, the court may appoint federal examiners who are empowered to place qualified individuals on the list of eligible voters. The statute further provides that failure to comply with any "test or device" shall not deny the right to vote and that bilingual election materials shall be available in areas where more than 5% of the citizens are members of a single language minority having an illiteracy rate higher than the national average. Finally, an important section of the Act prohibits a state or political subdivision which has employed literacy tests and which has less than a 50% voter participation rate from altering its voting qualifications or practices unless it first obtains approval from the Attorney General or secures a declaratory judgment from the federal court for the District of Columbia that the alteration "does not have the purpose or effect of denying the right to vote on account of race or color." The Supreme Court has ruled broadly that approval is required under this provision for "any state enactment which [changes] the election law of a covered state *in even a minor way.*" *Allen v. State Board of Elections* (S.Ct.1969) (emphasis added.) Election matters thereby subjected to federal supervision include (1) reapportionment of election districts, (2) municipal annexations, (3) relocation of polling places, (4) modifications in ballot form, and (5) revision of rules governing the qualification of candidates and the appointive or elective nature of the office. See *Georgia v. U.S.* (S.Ct.1973); *Perkins v. Matthews* (S.Ct.1971); *Allen v. State Board of Elections.* See also *Gaston County v. U.S.* (S.Ct. 1969) (finding that a literacy test, though impartially administered, would have the effect of perpetuating the inequities of a dual school system). If a change in the election law has the purpose *or* effect of denying or diluting the right to vote on the basis of race, it may be held to violate the statute. (See pp. 100–01.) Since some election law changes, such as legislative reapportionment, are constitutionally mandated and other changes of at least a "minor" nature will be a practical necessity from time to time, federal oversight in this field takes on major significance.

The Civil Rights Act of 1964 has been called "the most important civil rights legislation of this century." Schlei & Grossman, Employment Discrimination Law, vii (1976). The statute prohibits discrimination based on race, color, religion or national origin in various places of public accommodation, including lodging for transients and dining and entertainment facilities affecting interstate commerce. (See § 43.) The prohibition is inapplicable, however, to "private clubs or other establishments not in fact open to the public." *Daniel v. Paul* (S.Ct.1969) (club is exempt only if it has a nonpublic character, its members control finances and policy, and its admissions are genuinely selective). The Act also bans discrimination by race or national origin in any federally assisted program and authorizes the termination of federal funding when recipients violate the ban. See *Lau v. Nichols* (S.Ct. 1974) (ruling that the statute is violated by actions having a discriminatory purpose or effect and that public schools which require students to be proficient in English must therefore provide a remedy, such as bilingual instruction or compensatory training, to non-English speaking students of Chinese ancestry). Finally, the Act prohibits discrimination by employers, employment agencies and labor unions on the basis of race, color, religion, sex or national origin. Exemptions from coverage are provided for employers of fewer than 15 employees, as well as for cases "where religion, sex, or national origin is a bona fide occupational qualification reasonably necessary to the normal operation of [a] particular business or enterprise." The controls on discrimination in employment are the most heavily litigated of the post-*Brown* provisions and require a somewhat more detailed overview. (See § 45.) Additional statutory controls have been placed on discrimination in employment based on age or handicap and on sex discrimination in pay or in federally assisted educational programs. See Player, Employment Discrimination Law (1988).

§ 45. REGULATING DISCRIMINATION IN EMPLOYMENT

Purposeful Discrimination. Title VII of the 1964 Civil Rights Act was aimed most specifically at employment decisions predicated on race, color, religion, sex or national origin. A refusal to hire or retain employees on those grounds is obviously forbidden. See *McDonald v. Santa Fe Trail Transportation Co.* (S.Ct.1976) (protecting majority and minority persons under the same standards). However, the statute also extends to other forms of overt discrimination, such as addressing minority employees in derogatory terms or failing to maintain a working atmosphere free of racial intimidation. E.g. *Anderson v. Methodist–Evangelical Hospital* (6th Cir.1972). See *Meritor Savings Bank v. Vinson* (S.Ct.1986) (Title VII violation established by proof of sexual harassment in the workplace which creates a "hostile environment"); *Harris v. Forklift Systems* (S.Ct.1993) (a hostile environment is one which, considering all the circumstances, "would reasonably be perceived, and is perceived, as hostile or abusive"). Title VII likewise prohibits the racial segregation of employment facilities, including recreation areas and restrooms as well as places of work. *U.S. v. Jacksonville Terminal Co.* (5th Cir.1971). And claims for sex-based wage discrimination may be brought under Title VII, whether or not a co-worker of the opposite sex receives higher pay for equal work. *County of Washington v. Gunther* (S.Ct.1981) (violation found where an employer's own job evaluations showed female jail-guard positions to be worth 95% as much as male guard positions, but the employer proceeded to pay women guards only 70% as much as men).

Questions have arisen concerning the lawfulness of discrimination directed against a sub-class within a regulated classification. *Phillips v. Martin Marietta Corp.* (S.Ct.1971) provides an illustration. In that case an employer refused to accept job applications from women with pre-school age children although it employed fathers of pre-school children. The lower courts, noting that only 20 to 25% of those hired for the job in question were men, concluded that the facts did not establish discrimination against women but only discrimination between classes of women. However, the employer's classification, though denominated "sex plus" because it was not based solely on gender, was unmistakably sex-discriminatory since men with small children were treated more favorably than women with small children. The Supreme Court therefore reversed the judgment: because the statute "requires that persons of like qualifications be given employment opportunities irrespective of their sex," it is unlawful to establish "one hiring policy for women and another for men—each having pre-school age children." For the same reason, a corporation cannot restrict the job opportunities of married women if it employs men without regard to their marital status. *Sprogis v. United Air Lines* (7th Cir.1971).

Despite *Phillips'* ruling against disparate employment policies for men and women, lower courts have upheld the use of differential grooming standards based on sex. Thus it is deemed permissible for an employer to regulate the hair style of male employees while allowing females to wear their hair as they see fit. *Willingham v. Macon Telegraph Publishing Co.* (5th Cir.1975) (shoulder-length hair). Rules of this kind are explicitly discriminatory, and so the upshot of such decisions is that some sex discrimination will be permitted under Title VII even if no bona fide occupational qualification is involved. The usual explanation for these decisions is that grooming standards do not "relate to immutable characteristics or legally protected rights" like marriage and procreation. *Willingham.* But the statute prohibits sex discrimination as such, not merely discriminatory practices fitting into those two categories. Accordingly, a rule that female employees must wear contact lenses rather than glasses, while male employees may wear either, has been held to violate Title VII even though the regulation does not fall into the aforementioned categories. *Laffey v. Northwest Airlines, Inc.* (D.D.C.1973). Perhaps when the issue reaches the Supreme Court, differential grooming standards will be sustained on more narrow grounds permitting their use only when they serve a legitimate employer interest and have no significant impact on job opportunities. Unless restricted in some such way, the legitimation of differential standards threatens to undermine not only the ban on sex discrimination but possibly the regulation of discriminatory treatment based on religion or national origin, which can also be subjected to a "classification plus" analysis.

Another exception to the prohibition against employment discrimination is provided by the statutory exemption for bona fide occupational qualifications "reasonably necessary" to a business enterprise. The BFOQ exemption does not apply to racial discrimination but only to hiring on the basis of religion, sex or national origin. The theory was that classifications focusing on the latter characteristics are sometimes justifiable. However, the scope of the exemption is a matter of continuing debate. The legislative history furnishes three examples of bona fide occupational qualifications, as viewed by Senate floor leaders: (1) "the preference of a French restaurant for a French cook," (2) the selection of "male players for a professional baseball team," and (3) the preference of a merchant selling religious articles for salespersons who are adherents of the faith. These examples are suggestive of a surprisingly loose exemption—only faintly tied to an employee's ability to perform—since it is apparent that (1) a person need not be French to master the art of French cooking, (2) some women play baseball better than some men, and (3) religious articles can be sold by individuals who understand the tenets of the religion even though they do not practice it. In the *Phillips* case the Supreme Court seemed to take a similarly broad view of the exemption, stating that family obligations toward pre-school age children could arguably constitute a bona fide occupational qualification if such obligations are "demonstrably more relevant to job performance for a woman than for a man...." Later, the Court stated that the exemption is a narrow one, but it proceeded, without articulating any specific rule, to uphold the disqualification of women for employment as guards in certain prison facilities. *Dothard v. Rawlinson* (S.Ct.1977). Finally, in *UAW v. Johnson Controls, Inc.* (S.Ct.1991), the Court again said that the BFOQ exception is narrow, and it rejected an employer's claim that concern for the safety of the future children of its female employees could justify the exclusion of fertile women from employment opportunities.

Most of the lower courts have given limited scope to the BFOQ exemption. Some have taken the position that only cases involving unique physical characteristics or a need for authenticity—as in an acting role—can give rise to a bona fide occupational qualification. See *Rosenfeld v. Southern Pacific Co.* (9th Cir.1971) (demanding "a showing of individual incapacity" in other cases). This approach is attentive to the principal objectives of Title VII but is not easily reconciled with either the BFOQ exemption for national origin and religious classifications or the examples of bona fide occupational qualifications contained in the legislative history. Other courts have resisted demands for individual testing but require proof that "all or substantially all" members of an excluded class would be unable to perform the job safely and efficiently. *Weeks v. Southern Bell Tel. & Tel. Co.* (5th Cir.1969). Thus women cannot be excluded from every arduous or dangerous job, *Cheatwood v. South Central Bell Tel. & Tel. Co.* (M.D.Ala.1969), and "protective" state laws restricting women's working conditions are held to be preempted by Title VII. E.g. *Rosenfeld v. Southern Pacific Co.* (weight-lifting and maximum hours limitations). Nor can discrimination be justified by customer preferences, at least in the absence of important privacy interests. Compare *Diaz v. Pan American World Airways* (5th Cir.1971) (airline passengers' preference for cabin service by female attendants does not give rise to a bona fide occupational qualification) with *City of Philadelphia v. Pa. Human Relations Com'n.* (Pa.Cmwlth.1973) (supervisors in youth centers who conduct body searches and observe daily showers may be selected on the basis of sex). Finally, even when an employer can demonstrate a high degree of correlation between gender and ability to perform, courts have refused to find a bona fide occupational qualification unless "the *essence* of the business operation would be undermined by not hiring members of one sex exclusively." *Diaz v. Pan American World Airways* (better performance of female flight attendants in reassuring anxious passengers is tangential to an airline's primary function of providing safe transportation).

Proof, Remedies and Procedures. In *McDonnell Douglas Corp. v. Green* (S.Ct.1973), the Supreme Court set forth rules to govern the burden of proving that an employment decision has been based on a regulated classification. The Court said the black complainant in that litigation could establish a prima facie case of racial discrimination "by showing (i) that he belongs to a racial minority; (ii) that he applied and was qualified for a job for which the employer was seeking applicants; (iii) that despite his qualifications, he was rejected; and (iv) that, after his rejection, the position remained open and the employer continued to seek applicants from persons of complainant's qualifications." When a prima facie case is established, the burden shifts to the employer "to articulate some legitimate, nondiscriminatory reason" for denying employment opportunities, such as that other applicants were better qualified. If a legitimate reason is offered, the plaintiff will still prevail if he or she can "show that [the] stated reason ... was in fact pretextual." The latter burden can be discharged by proving, for instance, that similarly situated non-minority persons have not been similarly treated.

Texas Department of Community Affairs v. Burdine (S.Ct.1981) elaborated on the burden of proof in Title VII cases. In *Burdine,* the Court made clear that while the burden of production shifts to the employer upon establishment of a prima facie case, the burden of persuasion remains with the plaintiff at all times: "The burden that shifts to the defendant ... is to rebut the presumption of discrimination by producing evidence that the plaintiff was rejected ... for a legitimate, nondiscriminatory reason." If the trier of fact finds that an employer's asserted reasons are unpersuasive or contrived, that finding will permit, but does not require, an inference of unlawful discrimination. *St. Mary's Honor Center v. Hicks* (S.Ct.1993) (the fact that an employer's articulated reason was contrived did not prove that the employer discriminated on the basis of race, rather than on the basis of personal animosity or other grounds not regulated by Title VII).

A prima facie case may also be established by showing a general pattern of discrimination rather than individual acts of illegality. "Statistics can be an important source of proof in [such] cases since 'absent explanation, it is ordinarily to be expected that non-discriminatory hiring practices will in time result in a work force more or less representative of the racial and ethnic composition of the population in the community from which employees are hired,'" even though Title VII "'imposes no requirement that a work force mirror the general population.'" *Hazelwood School Dist. v. U.S.* (S.Ct.1977). Proof of a discriminatory hiring pattern creates a rebuttable presumption that individual job applicants were denied employment, not for neutral reasons, but because of their membership in the disfavored class. Moreover, non-applicants in these cases must be given an opportunity to show that they would have filed employment applications but for their knowledge of the employer's discriminatory policies, and hence should be granted the same relief as applicants. *International Brotherhood of Teamsters v. U.S.* (S.Ct.1977).

When a court finds an employment practice to be unlawful, it may enjoin the practice "and order such affirmative action as may be appropriate," including the reinstatement or hiring of employees. Damages have been held to be unavailable under Title VII, which was modeled on the remedial provisions of the National Labor Relations Act, denying such relief. E.g. *Loo v. Gerarge* (D.Hawaii 1974). But in light of the "make whole" objective of Title

VII, a remedy must ordinarily include an award of back pay, not to exceed two years, even if the illegal action was undertaken in good faith. *Albemarle Paper Co. v. Moody* (S.Ct.1975) (this remedy may be denied "only for reasons which, if applied generally, would not frustrate the central ... purposes" of the statute). Some lower courts have also awarded "front" pay to compensate for future benefits which an employee would receive absent the discriminatory act, but which he or she is denied while awaiting a vacancy in the position that is "due." *Bush v. Lone Star Steel Co.* (E.D.Tex.1974); contra, *EEOC v. Detroit Edison Co.* (6th Cir.1975).

Non-monetary relief, too, is available under Title VII. For example, the Supreme Court has approved the award of constructive seniority, retroactive to the date of unlawful action, in order to make whole the identifiable victims of discrimination. *Franks v. Bowman Transportation Co.* (S.Ct.1976). Lower courts granted constructive seniority even to employees who had failed to mount a timely challenge to discriminatory action, holding that an employer's denial of such seniority constituted a continuing violation of Title VII. But this position was repudiated in *United Air Lines v. Evans* (S.Ct.1977), which ruled that an otherwise neutral seniority system could not be attacked under these circumstances because an employer is entitled to treat past discrimination as lawful when the victim fails to file a timely charge. "A contrary view," the Supreme Court said, "would substitute a claim of seniority credit for almost every claim which is barred by [the statute of] limitations."

Procedures for bringing suit under Title VII require deference to state and federal administrative agencies. In states having fair employment laws and commissions, a charge of discrimination must first be filed with the local agency within the time prescribed by state law. That agency has exclusive jurisdiction for 60 days, after which the complainant is free to file a charge with the federal Equal Employment Opportunity Commission or to await action by the state agency. However, a charge must be filed with the EEOC within 300 days of the discriminatory act or within 30 days of notification that the local agency has disposed of the case, whichever occurs earlier. If a state has no agency for enforcing fair employment laws, a charge must be filed initially with the EEOC within 180 days of the discriminatory act.

After the EEOC has had jurisdiction over a case for 30 days, it may file suit in federal district court. An independent private action is then precluded, although the complaining party has a right to intervene. Alternatively, the EEOC may issue a right-to-sue letter notifying the complainant that he or she may bring a private action in federal court within 90 days. This letter is routinely issued (a) whenever the Commission completes its investigation or (b) upon request of the complainant if the Commission has had jurisdiction for at least 180 days. The filing of a private action following receipt of a right-to-sue letter forecloses suit by the

EEOC, which is then limited to a right of intervention. But although the jurisdiction of the EEOC is exclusive for only 180 days, there is no statutory time limit on its investigations and subsequent legal actions in the absence of a request for a right-to-sue letter. *Occidental Life Insur. Co. v. EEOC* (S.Ct. 1977). In sum, a private suit is permissible only for 90 days after receipt of a right-to-sue letter, which will be issued upon completion of an EEOC investigation or upon demand following the 180–day period of exclusive EEOC jurisdiction; and a complaint to the EEOC must be filed within 180 days of the discriminatory act, or in states having analogous agencies, within 30 days of notice of disposition by the agency or within 300 days of the illegal act.

Discriminatory Impact. Although purposeful discrimination was a central focus of Title VII, the statute also prohibits the use of certain facially neutral standards that have a discriminatory effect. *Griggs v. Duke Power Co.* (S.Ct.1971) was a seminal case in this area. The issue there was whether Title VII had been violated when a high school diploma and success on standardized intelligence tests were made conditions of employment. The lower courts had found that these requirements were not racially motivated but that they operated to disqualify black applicants at a substantially higher rate than white applicants. On review the Supreme Court rejected the proposition that an illicit motive is necessary to a violation of the statute: "The Act proscribes not only overt discrimination but also practices that are fair in form, but discriminatory in operation.... Congress directed the thrust of the Act to the *consequences* of employment practices, not simply the motivation." This, of course, does not mean that all practices having an unequal impact on job opportunities are forbidden. "The touchstone is business necessity." Employment standards may be valid despite a discriminatory effect, but the employer has "the burden of showing that any given requirement [has] a manifest relationship to the employment in question." In the *Griggs* case, the demand for a high school diploma and success on standardized tests impacted more heavily on blacks than on whites and had no demonstrable relationship to job performance. Accordingly, the provision in Title VII authorizing tests which are not "designed, intended, *or used* to discriminate" was inapplicable, and the requirements were invalid.

But Title VII "does not impose a duty to adopt a hiring procedure that maximizes hiring of minority employees." *Furnco Construction Corp. v. Waters* (S.Ct.1978). Conversely, the fact that a workforce is racially balanced does not immunize an employer from liability for acts of discrimination. See *Connecticut v. Teal* (S.Ct.1982) (use of tests which were not job-related and which had a disparate impact on black applicants violated Title VII even though the employer promoted a higher percentage of black candidates than of white candidates).

The Civil Rights Act of 1991 codified the ruling in *Griggs,* which required the plaintiff to prove that a facially neutral employment practice has discriminatory effects. However, the Act also provides that, after a showing of discriminatory impact, the burden of proof shifts to the employer to demonstrate that the challenged practice is job-related and consistent with business necessity. See 42 U.S.C.A. § 2000e–2(k), which rejects the contrary holding in *Wards Cove Packing Co. v. Atonio* (S.Ct.1989). Furthermore, even if the employer shows a business necessity, "it remains open to the complaining party to show that other [practices], without a similarly undesirable racial effect, would also serve the employer's legitimate interest in 'efficient and trustworthy workmanship.'" *Albemarle Paper Co. v. Moody*.

Applying these principles, the Supreme Court invalidated a height and weight requirement for prison guards which would disqualify about 40% of the female population, but less than 1% of the male population, and which was not shown to be job-related. *Dothard v. Rawlinson*. However, statistical evidence showing a high percentage of nonwhite workers in unskilled jobs and a low percentage of such workers in skilled jobs does not establish a prima facie case of disparate impact in violation of Title VII. The proper statistical comparison is "between the racial composition of the qualified persons in the labor market and the persons holding at-issue jobs." *Wards Cove*. Furthermore, some employment practices have been upheld, despite their apparent discriminatory effects, without regard to business necessity. In *Espinoza v. Farah Mfg. Co.* (S.Ct.1973), for example, a requirement that employees be United States citizens was sustained even though the requirement seems clearly to have the effect of discriminating against persons of foreign origin, since those born in the United States become citizens automatically. The Court, unable to discern a congressional intent to regulate alienage classifications, ruled that the statutory ban against discrimination based on national origin had not been violated.

The Court has also approved the enforcement of seniority provisions of collective bargaining agreements, which allocate various benefits on the basis of an employee's years of service for the employer. The discriminatory effect of such provisions can be easily demonstrated. In companies which refused to hire women or blacks until Title VII took effect, members of those groups will have had no opportunity to accumulate as much seniority as the white males who were hired years earlier. Consequently, if benefits are predicated on seniority, the effect will be to disfavor the victims of past discrimination. Nevertheless the Supreme Court, while conceding the discriminatory impact of seniority systems, held that an otherwise neutral seniority plan is not unlawful merely because it perpetuates pre-Title VII discrimination. *International Brotherhood of Teamsters v. U.S.* The Court said that Congress had "considered this very effect of many seniority systems and extended a measure of immunity to them" by enacting § 703(h) of Title VII which states: "It shall not be an unlawful employment practice for an employer to apply ... different terms, conditions, or privileges of employment pursuant to a bona fide seniority ... system ... provided that such differences are not the result of an intention to discriminate...." The opinion relied heavily on statements in the legislative history that "Title VII would have no effect on seniority rights existing at the time it takes effect.... This would be true even in the case where owing to discrimination prior to the effective date of the title, white workers had more seniority than Negroes." Similar considerations have led the Court to conclude that an employer's statutory duty reasonably to accommodate the religious practices of employees does not require a departure from a seniority system for the benefit of an individual whose religious beliefs prevented him from working on Saturday: "Absent a discriminatory purpose, the operation of a seniority system cannot be an unlawful employment practice even if the system has some discriminatory consequences." *Trans World Airlines, Inc. v. Hardison* (S.Ct.1977).

§ 46. THE RECONSTRUCTION STATUTES

The post-*Brown* controls on discrimination are complemented by a series of statutes which Congress enacted during the Reconstruction era for the protection of civil rights. Those statutes can be described quite briefly, though their implications, as noted below, are very far-reaching. The most pervasive of the Reconstruction statutes provides that any person who under color of law subjects another individual to the deprivation of any federal right shall be liable to the injured party in an action at law or in equity. 42 U.S.C.A. § 1983. A similar provision in the federal criminal code imposes penal sanctions against persons who wilfully engage in such conduct. 18 U.S.C.A. § 242. The latter provision requires proof of a specific intent to interfere with the right in question, *Screws v. U.S.* (S.Ct. 1945), but the corresponding civil statute does not. *Monroe v. Pape* (S.Ct.1961). Section 1983 provides an offensive weapon of great importance to the protection of constitutional rights and is the subject of a separate chapter (see § 47–51).

The Reconstruction statutes also provide that all persons "shall have the same right ... as is enjoyed by white citizens" to inherit, purchase, lease or sell real or personal property, 42 U.S.C.A. § 1982, and "to make and enforce contracts ... and to the ... equal benefit of all laws...." 42 U.S.C.A. § 1981. Finally, conspiracies designed (a) to interfere with the exercise of any federal right or (b) to deprive any person "of the equal protection of the laws or of equal privileges and immunities under the laws" are subject respectively to penal and civil sanctions. 18 U.S.C.A. § 241; 42 U.S.C.A. § 1985(3). The criminal sanction has been applied by the Supreme Court only to cases involving state action, *U.S. v. Price* (S.Ct.1966), or private interference with rights—such as interstate travel or voting in congressional elections—"which arise from the relationship of the individual and the federal government." *U.S. v. Williams* (S.Ct.1951). However six Justices, speaking through two concurring opinions in *U.S. v. Guest* (S.Ct.1966), stated that Congress may punish "all conspiracies—with or without state action—that interfere with Fourteenth Amendment rights." (See § 43.)

For many years the civil provisions of the Reconstruction statutes were almost wholly unenforced. This left much discretion to the states and led to congressional enactment of the post-*Brown* statutes. Ironically, when the Reconstruction laws were eventually revived, they received a far more generous interpretation than would have been likely if enforcement had not been long delayed.

With the exception of § 1983, which is limited to activity under color of law, *Adickes v. S.H. Kress & Co.* (S.Ct.1970), the civil provisions have been held to apply to private action. These provisions serve two important functions. First, the statutes protect against discriminatory conduct not reached by the Constitution because of the absence of state action. For example, it has been suggested that in light of *Jackson v. Metropolitan Edison Co.* (see pp. 192–93) a utility company would be constitutionally free to deny service to black customers. However, a racially motivated refusal to do business in this context would clearly abridge the § 1981 guarantee of "the same right ... to make and enforce contracts ... as is enjoyed by white citizens." This guarantee has already been found to bar racial discrimination in hiring by private employers. *Johnson v. Railway Express Agency* (S.Ct.1975). See the Civil Rights Act of 1991, which effectively overruled *Patterson v. McLean Credit Union* (S.Ct.1989) by amending

§ 1981 to provide that the "performance," as well as the formation, of a contract is governed by the statute. In addition, *Runyon v. McCrary* (S.Ct.1976) declared broadly that § 1981 rights are violated when a "private offeror refuses to extend to a Negro solely because he is a Negro, the same opportunity to enter contracts as he extends to white offerees." The Court specifically held that the statute prohibits private nonsectarian schools which offer their services to members of the general public from denying admission to prospective students because they are black. Although Mr. Justice Powell suggested in a concurring opinion that a different result might be reached where a contract is the foundation for a close "personal relationship," the *Runyon* decision is susceptible to application against social clubs like the Moose Lodge, which are not governed by the fourteenth amendment. (See pp. 206–07.)

Second, the Reconstruction statutes supplement the post-*Brown* legislation against racial discrimination by providing alternative procedures and regulating additional activities. Thus it is now apparent, despite early conflicting decisions in the lower courts, that § 1981 suits are not subject to the procedural requirements of Title VII. The Supreme Court, stressing the independent nature of the two statutes has said: "Congress did not expect that § 1981 actions usually would be resorted to only upon completion of Title VII procedures and ... efforts to obtain voluntary compliance." *Johnson.* Similarly, claims under § 1982 need not conform to the enforcement procedures of the 1968 fair housing law. Those procedures mandate the initial filing of complaints with the Secretary of Housing and Urban Development for conciliation or referral to a state agency when local housing laws provide "substantially equivalent" rights and remedies. Section 1982 on the other hand authorizes direct actions and has been widely held to function independently of such administrative prerequisites. E.g. *McLaurin v. Brusturis* (E.D.Wis.1970).

Sections 1981 and 1982 not only give injured parties an alternative source of relief but will also reach discriminatory practices that were untouched by the Civil Rights Acts of 1964 and 1968. The fair housing law, for instance, contains exceptions for single-family dwellings, private clubs and small boarding houses, none of which is explicitly exempted under § 1982. Since Congress was aware of the latter provision and yet chose to insert a broad "savings" clause into the 1968 statute to preserve any other law prohibiting discrimination in housing, it will be difficult to maintain that the exceptions in the new statute were intended to displace the apparently broader coverage of § 1982. See *Morris v. Cizek* (7th Cir.1974) (exemption for boarding houses ruled inapplicable to suits under § 1982). Similarly, the ban on job discrimination in § 1981 may apply to employers not covered by the 1964 Civil Rights Act and will make available not only the same remedies but other relief as well. See *Johnson v. Railway Express Agency,* noting that damages may be awarded under § 1981 and that back pay is not limited to the two-year period specified in the 1964 Act. Of course, the broader coverage of the Reconstruction laws undermines interests in associational privacy. But congressional concern for privacy in the post-*Brown* statutes was attenuated at best. Both the fair housing law of 1968 and the Civil Rights Act of 1964, while exempting certain parties from coverage in privacy-related contexts, specifically disavowed any intention to preempt state law and thereby made clear that the exemptions were not intended to confer immunity from regulation, even assuming that such immunity would be permissible under *Reitman v. Mulkey*.

More far-reaching issues of associational freedom are raised, however, by the potential applicability of § 1981 to every racially motivated decision not to enter a contract. See *Cornelius v. Benevolent Protective Order of Elks* (D.Conn.1974) (suggesting that the statute could be construed to permit a suit upon the refusal of an offer of marriage). While Mr. Justice Powell voiced support in *Runyon* for exempting close personal relationships from § 1981, he was unable to point to any language in the statute which would support that position; and the Constitution itself provides little, if any, guarantee of freedom to discriminate racially in contractual relations. Others have suggested that § 1981 does not apply "when an invitation to contract is extended only to ... a preselected group of individuals." Note, 90 Harv.L.Rev. 412, 426 (1976). But surely a private school could not avoid the impact of *Runyon v. McCrary* merely by sending invitations to all white students in the community. Preselection of offerees will often increase the difficulty of proving that refusals to contract are racially motivated, but it is a doubtful defense for cases in which selection is shown to have been based solely on race.

Other aspects of the Reconstruction laws raise equally serious questions of breadth. Section 1982 addresses not only the conveyance of property but also its inheritance. If that section prohibits private racial discrimination in the sale of property, as the *Jones* case held, it is unclear why the statute would not also prohibit a racially discriminatory bequest, thereby rendering the issue of state action academic in this context. (See § 38 supra.) In addition, § 1985(3) reaches private conspiracies where there is "some racial or perhaps otherwise class-based invidious discriminatory animus behind the conspirators' action" and the victim is injured or deprived of "any right or privilege of a citizen of the United States." *Griffin v. Breckenridge* (S.Ct. 1971). Unless the latter phrase is read to require *official* action where the Constitution itself does not operate directly on private parties (see pp. 220–21), the result could be a federal law of torts whenever a conspiratorial injury is racially motivated. Arguably a broad federal intrusion into tort, contract, and inheritance law would erode principles of federalism without a clear-cut contemporary mandate from Congress. Perhaps for this reason, the Court eventually held that a conspiracy to infringe fourteenth amendment rights "is not a violation of § 1985(3) unless it is proved that the state is involved in the conspiracy or that the aim of the conspiracy is to influence the activity of the state." *United Brotherhood of Carpenters & Joiners v. Scott* (S.Ct.1983) (finding *Griffin* inapplicable to a conspiracy "aimed at a right that is by definition a right only against state interference"). See also *Bray v. Alexandria Women's Health Clinic* (S.Ct. 1993) (opposition to abortion does not constitute a class-based animus under the statute).

CHAPTER VIII

ACTIONS UNDER 42 U.S.C.A. § 1983

§ 47. PERSONAL LIABILITY

The Monroe Case. A remarkable number of constitutional claims are now litigated under 42 U.S.C.A. § 1983 which provides that "Every person who, under color of any statute, ordinance, regulation, custom or usage, of any state or territory or the District of Columbia, subjects [any] other person ... to the deprivation of any rights, privileges, or immunities secured by the Constitution and laws, shall be liable to the party injured...." Section 1983 was enacted by Congress as part of the Ku Klux Klan Act of 1871. However, the provision remained obscure and underutilized for nearly a century because it was assumed to reach only misconduct that was officially authorized, and hence "under color of law," or was so widely tolerated as to involve "custom or usage."

That assumption was rejected by the Supreme Court in *Monroe v. Pape* (S.Ct.1961). The plaintiffs in the *Monroe* case brought an action under § 1983, alleging that their fourth amendment rights had been violated when Chicago police officers broke into their home in the early morning, "routed them from bed, made them stand naked in the living room, and ransacked every room, emptying drawers and ripping mattress covers." The Supreme Court framed the basic issue as "whether Congress in enacting Section 1983, meant to give a remedy to parties deprived of constitutional rights, privileges and immunities by an official's abuse of his position." In answering that question affirmatively, the Court said that officers are subject to suit even when their actions are not authorized by the state, but are in fact prohibited by local law, and state remedies are available for violations of the prohibition. Section 1983 was held to be "supplementary to [any] state remedy...." Accordingly, there is no requirement that plaintiffs must first exhaust their state remedies. *Patsy v. Board of Regents* (S.Ct.1982). Finally, the *Monroe* case also held that a municipality was immune from suit under § 1983, but that holding was later overruled (see § 48, infra) by *Monell v. Department of Social Services* (S.Ct.1978).

Individual defendants under § 1983 are liable not only for compensatory damages but, upon a showing of recklessness or callous indifference to personal rights, for punitive damages as well. The standard for compensatory and punitive damages need not be different, since compensatory damages are awarded as a matter of right, while punitive damages are awarded at the discretion of the jury. *Smith v. Wade* (S.Ct.1983). In addition to damages, a prevailing party in a § 1983 action is generally entitled to an award of reasonable attorney's fees. (§ 51, infra.) Such fees are intended to guarantee legal services to victims of civil rights violations and are sometimes more substantial than the judgment for damages. See *City of Riverside v. Rivera* (S.Ct. 1986) (approving attorney's fees of $245,456 in a case involving a verdict for $33,350 in damages).

Official Immunities. In many cases public officials are protected by either a qualified or an absolute immunity from suits under § 1983. Although Congress included no immunity provision in § 1983, the Court reasoned that some immunities were so firmly established at common law that Congress would have explicitly abolished them if it had intended to change the existing law. See *Tenney v. Brandhove* (S.Ct.1951) (legislative activity held absolutely immune from liability for damages under § 1983). The Court has given two basic reasons for official immunity: "(1) the injustice, particularly in the absence of bad faith, of subjecting to liability an officer who is required, by the legal obligations of his position, to exercise discretion; (2) the danger that the threat of such liability would deter his willingness to execute his office with the decisiveness and the judgment required by the public good...." *Scheuer v. Rhodes* (S.Ct. 1974).

Judges and legislators enjoy absolute immunity from damages for actions taken within the scope of judicial and legislative functions. See *Pierson v. Ray* (S.Ct.1967). Prosecutors also have absolute immunity for actions "intimately associated with the judicial phase of the criminal process," but their immunity does not extend to investigative activities. *Imbler v. Pachtman* (S.Ct.1976).

Police and executive officials have a qualified rather than an absolute immunity. For police officers, "the defense of good faith and probable cause, which [was available to officers] in the commonlaw action for false arrest and imprisonment, is also available [in an] action under § 1983." *Pierson v. Ray* (S.Ct.1967); see also Anderson v. Creighton (S.Ct.1987) (asking whether "a reasonable officer could have believed [his action] to be lawful, in light of clearly established law"). For higher level executives, the immunity problem is more complicated. *Scheuer v. Rhodes* (S.Ct.1974), involving the Governor of Ohio and other high ranking state officials, stated that "in varying scope, a qualified immunity is available to officers of the executive branch of government, the variation being dependent upon the scope of discretion and responsibilities of the office and all the circumstances as they reasonably appeared at the time of the action on which liability is sought to be based." Thus, the extent of executive immunity seems to depend upon the level of discretion and responsibility of the office in question.

Actions for prospective relief, such as an injunction or declaratory judgment, are distinguishable for immunity purposes from an action for damages. The rationales for protecting officials from liability for damages—that such liability would be unjust and would deter proper execution of official duties—are generally inapplicable to prospective relief. Accordingly, police officers and prosecutors are clearly subject to suit for prospective relief under § 1983;

and judges are also subject to such suits, at least in the absence of alternative remedies for unconstitutional judicial action. *Pulliam v. Allen* (S.Ct.1984) (state judge enjoined from requiring bond for nonjailable offenses and jailing those who could not pay). Legislators, on the other hand, are immune from both prospective relief and claims for damages. See *Supreme Court of Virginia v. Consumers Union* (S.Ct.1980).

Federal Officials. Although federal officers have no liability under § 1983 because color of state law is required, such officers may be liable in an action brought directly under the Constitution. *Bivens v. Six Unknown Named Agents of the Federal Bureau of Narcotics* (S.Ct.1971) (inferring a remedy in damages for violations of the the fourth amendment). Generally, the same immunity applies to comparable federal and state officials. *See Butz v. Economou* (S.Ct.1978), stating that it would be "untenable to draw a distinction for purposes of immunity law between suits brought against state officials under § 1983 and suits brought directly under the Constitution against federal officers." However, exceptions have been created for members of Congress and for the President. The speech or debate clause of the Constitution affords members of Congress and their aides an absolute privilege for official acts; and the President has an absolute immunity from the award of damages for official conduct extending to the "outer perimeter" of presidential responsibility. *Nixon v. Fitzgerald* (S.Ct. 1982).

Sifting Out Insubstantial Claims. Because the litigation process itself imposes significant burdens on government officials, the Court has refined the procedures for determining good faith in order to sift out insubstantial claims. Such claims not only subject the official to the high cost of litigation but, more important, tend to distract the official from his or her governmental duties. Furthermore, the threat of suit impedes discretionary decision-making and may discourage talented candidates from accepting government service. *See Harlow v. Fitzgerald* (S.Ct.1982).

Wood v. Strickland (S.Ct.1975) provides a background for understanding the problem. In that case, two students were summarily suspended from high school by the board of education. The Court held that a board member would be liable for damages under § 1983 "if he knew or reasonably should have known that the action ... would violate the constitutional rights of the student affected, or if he took the action with the malicious intention to cause a deprivation of constitutional rights or other injury to the student."

While the objective component of the *Wood* rule presented a number of problems, the subjective component proved to be even more troublesome. By merely alleging malice, litigants were able to create a factual issue that would require extensive discovery and possibly a trial on the merits. The Supreme Court addressed this problem in *Harlow v. Fitzgerald* (S.Ct.1982) and concluded that "bare allegations of malice should not suffice to subject government officials either to the costs of trial or to the burdens of broad-reaching discovery." The Court said that on motion for summary judgment the trial judge should ascertain the current law and determine whether it was established at the time of the action in question: "government officials performing discretionary functions generally are shielded from liability for civil damages insofar as their conduct does not violate clearly established statutory or constitutional rights of which a reasonable person would have known." Until that threshold requirement is met, discovery is not allowed. It seems clear under *Harlow* that if the law is unsettled an official will be immune even when his actions are malicious. The *Harlow* case was reinforced by later decisions which held that a rejection of an official's immunity defense is subject to an immediate appeal, *Mitchell v. Forsyth* (S.Ct.1985), and that the subjective beliefs of an officer are irrelevant. *Anderson v. Creighton* (S.Ct.1987) (applying the *Harlow* rule to inferior officers).

§ 48. MUNICIPAL LIABILITY

The Court revisited the issue of municipal liability under § 1983 in *Monell v. Department of Social Services* (S.Ct.1978). That case involved an allegation that the City of New York required pregnant employees to leave their jobs before it was medically necessary. In overturning *Monroe's* ruling on municipal immunity, the Court re-examined the legislative history of § 1983 and concluded that since municipalities can cause the same harm as natural persons and since § 1983 was intended to be broadly construed, "there is no reason to suppose that municipal corporations would have been excluded from the sweep of [the statute]." But although the term "person" in § 1983 was thus found to include municipal corporations, the *Monell* case nevertheless defined municipal liability differently from the liability of natural persons. The Court said that local governments could not be sued under § 1983 on a respondeat superior theory for injuries inflicted by their employees or agents: "Instead, it is when execution of a government's policy or custom, whether made by its lawmakers or by those whose edicts or acts may fairly be said to represent official policy, inflicts the injury that the government as an entity is responsible under § 1983."

Since a municipality can be held liable only for official policy or custom, the question of how official policy is created has become a crucial issue. The Court discussed this issue in a series of recent cases. In *Pembaur v. Cincinnati* (S.Ct.1986), the plaintiff alleged that his fourth amendment rights were violated when police officers used an ax to chop down a door in his office building in order to serve capias warrants on witnesses subpoenaed by the grand jury. The police took this action after conferring with the county prosecutor, who said, "Go in and get them." Upon finding this statement by the prosecutor sufficient to establish official policy, a plurality of the Court said: "municipal liability under § 1983 attaches where—and only where—a deliberate choice to follow a course of action is made from among various alternatives by the ... officials responsible for establishing final policy with respect to the subject matter in question...."

Two years later, the Court addressed the question of *which* official is responsible for establishing "final policy". In *City of St. Louis v. Praprotnik* (S.Ct.1988), a municipal employee claimed that he had been transferred, and subsequently laid off, in retaliation for appealing a job suspension. A plurality of the Court said that the identification of officials having "final policymaking authority" was a matter of state law and that the City's charter appeared to give authority to set employment policy to the Civil Service Commission and to the mayor and aldermen, rather than to the supervisors who had caused the transfer and layoff. The opinion concluded that when a supervisor's discretionary decisions are "subject to review" by authorized policymakers, the latter officials have the final policymaking authority even if they ordinarily defer to the supervisor.

Finally, the Court imposed a stringent requirement of culpability and causation in *Board of County Commissioners v. Brown* (S.Ct.1997). A 5–4 majority ruled that a "policy" giving rise to municipal liability could not be established merely by showing that a sheriff's decision to hire a deputy without adequate screening was attributable to the municipality. Instead, the plaintiff would have to "demonstrate that, through its deliberate conduct, the municipality was the 'moving force' behind the injury alleged." In *Brown*, the plaintiff could not establish municipal liability unless she proved that the sheriff "should have concluded that [his deputy's] use of excessive force would be a plainly obvious consequence of the hiring decision." The Court believed that rigorous culpability and causation standards were needed because every injury inflicted by a municipal employee "can be traced to a hiring decision in a 'but for' sense."

A municipality can also be held liable under § 1983 for injuries resulting from a failure to train its employees properly. However, liability in such cases is limited to situations in which "a municipality's failure to train its employees in a relevant respect evidences a 'deliberate indifference' to the rights of its inhabitants...." *City of Canton v. Harris* (S.Ct.1989). On the other hand a municipality, unlike individual officers, is immune to claims for punitive damages, at least in the absence of "an extreme situation where ... taxpayers are directly responsible for perpetrating an outrageous abuse of constitutional rights." *City of Newport v. Fact Concerts, Inc.* (S.Ct.1981). But a municipality is not entitled, in cases involving claims for compensatory damages, to any qualified immunity based on the good faith of its officials. *Owen v. City of Independence* (S.Ct.1980).

Unlike municipalities, neither the states nor state officers acting in an official capacity are "persons" within the meaning of § 1983. *Will v. Michigan Dept. of State Police* (S.Ct.1989). But state officers can ordinarily be sued for injunctive or declaratory relief because actions for prospective relief are not treated as actions against the state, *Idaho v. Coeur d'Alene Tribe* (S.Ct.1997); and state officers are also liable for damages when sued in their personal rather than their official capacity. *Hafer v. Melo* (S.Ct.1991). Congress has power under § 5 of the fourteenth amendment to abrogate the states' immunity from claims for damages "as a means of enforcing the substantive guarantees of the fourteenth amendment." *Fitzpatrick v. Bitzer* (S.Ct. 1976). However, Congress does not have power under the commerce clause to abrogate the states' immunity from actions for damages—an immunity which is ultimately grounded in the eleventh amendment. *Seminole Tribe of Florida v. Florida* (S.Ct.1996).

§ 49. PROTECTED INTERESTS

On its face § 1983 appears to incorporate federal constitutional rights by reference. Because of its comprehensive nature, § 1983 threatened to turn virtually every grievance against the government into a potential constitutional issue. The Court had two ways in which it could deal with this perceived threat. First, § 1983 could be construed more narrowly than the Constitution by rejecting a literal interpretation of the statute. See Monaghan, Of "Liberty and Property", 62 Cornell L.Rev. 405 (1977). Alternatively, the scope of the underlying constitutional rights could be restricted. The Court, as earlier discussed, has pursued the latter course by limiting the interests protected under the fourteenth amendment. (See §§ 9, 11 above.) For example, the Court has held that the availability of a postdeprivation remedy for loss of property rights may be sufficient to satisfy the requirements of due process. *Hudson v. Palmer* (S.Ct.1984) ("an unauthorized intentional deprivation of property by a state employee does not constitute a violation of the procedural requirements of the due process clause ... if a meaningful postdeprivation remedy for the loss is available"). See also *Paul v. Davis* (S.Ct. 1976). This focus on the adequacy of state law remedies is difficult to reconcile with the ruling in *Monroe v. Pape* that § 1983 "is *supplementary* to the state remedy." (Emphasis added.) See *Zinermon v. Burch* (S.Ct.1990) (attempting to limit *Hudson* to cases in which the state could not have anticipated a deprivation and there was no feasible predeprivation remedy).

Nonconstitutional interests are also protected by § 1983, which safeguards rights "secured by the Constitution and laws...." In *Maine v. Thiboutot* (S.Ct.1980), the Court held that § 1983 "encompasses claims based on purely statutory violations of federal law...." Later decisions, however, appear to have cut back on *Thiboutot*. In *Middlesex County Sewerage Authority v. National Sea Clammers Association* (S.Ct.1981), the Court said that the existence of "comprehensive enforcement mechanisms" in the statute in question demonstrated that Congress intended "to supplant any remedy that otherwise would be available under § 1983." See also *Pennhurst State School and Hospital v. Halder-*

man (S.Ct.1981). Not surprisingly, lower courts have fallen into conflict on the question of which federal statutory rights are protected by § 1983. See Brown, *Whither Thiboutot?: Section 1983, Private Enforcement, and the Damages Dilemma,* 33 DePaul L.Rev. 31 (1983).

§ 50. THE RELATIONSHIP BETWEEN STATE LAW AND § 1983

Although state courts may entertain § 1983 suits, *Maine v. Thiboutot* (S.Ct.1980), most § 1983 litigation is brought in federal courts. Yet many issues that regularly arise in the course of such litigation are not addressed in § 1983. Often federal and state laws intersect, and it is necessary to decide which law governs and what that law provides.

"Deficiencies" in Federal Law. When § 1983 is "deficient" or "not adapted" to an issue, courts are directed by statute to apply state law, provided the state law is not inconsistent with federal law. 42 U.S.C.A. § 1988. For example, there is no federal statute of limitations governing suits under § 1983. The Court has, accordingly, looked to state law to cure that deficiency. In an effort to achieve uniformity and ease of administration, the Supreme Court held that the state statute of limitations governing personal injury claims will apply to suits under § 1983. *Wilson v. Garcia* (S.Ct.1985). If a state has multiple statutes of limitations for personal injury actions, the general statute of limitations on personal injury claims will govern in § 1983 cases. *Owens v. Okure* (S.Ct.

1989) (declining to apply a state statute of limitations for intentional torts to an action based on police brutality). State law also controls the tolling of the statute of limitation. See *Johnson v. Railway Express Agency* (S.Ct.1975). However, federal law has been held to preempt state notice-of-claim requirements in § 1983 litigation, even when the action is brought in state court. *Felder v. Casey* (S.Ct.1988) (state statute requiring notice of claims against government agencies or officers within 120 days of an alleged injury held invalid as applied to § 1983 actions).

Since federal law calls for "deficiencies" to be cured by referring to state law, federal courts generally are not free to fashion their own common law rules in § 1983 litigation. *Robertson v. Wegmann* (S.Ct.1978) illustrates the point. The *Wegmann* case raised the question whether a district judge "was required to adopt as federal law a Louisiana survivorship statute, which would have caused [the] cause of action to abate, or was free instead to create a federal common-law rule allowing the action to survive." The Supreme Court first found that federal law was deficient as to whether a § 1983 claim survives the death of the plaintiff. It turned next to state law and determined that the state statute, under which the plaintiff's cause of action would survive only in favor of members of his immediate family, was not inconsistent with the policies of § 1983. Under these circumstances, the Court ruled that state law must be applied, although the holding of the case was limited "to situations in which no claim is made that state law generally is inhospitable to survival of § 1983 actions...."

Habeas Corpus and Res Judicata. Read literally, § 1983 could be used by a state prisoner as an alternative to habeas corpus in seeking release from prison. Since § 1983, unlike the habeas corpus statute, does not require exhaustion of state remedies, a prisoner could circumvent state procedures by filing suit under § 1983 rather than petitioning for habeas. In order to forestall this result, the Court held in *Preiser v. Rodriguez* (S.Ct.1973) that habeas corpus is the exclusive federal remedy for obtaining release from unconstitutional imprisonment: "a § 1983 action is a proper remedy for a state prisoner who is making a constitutional challenge to the conditions of his prison life, but not to the fact or length of his custody." See also *Heck v. Humphrey* (S.Ct.1994) (a prisoner, who seeks to recover damages for a constitutional violation which would "necessarily imply the invalidity" of a conviction, must prove that the conviction has been called into question by a federal writ of habeas corpus or by a state tribunal).

The Court has also held that res judicata principles apply to § 1983 actions even when federal habeas relief is unavailable. Thus, a state prisoner was precluded from litigating fourth amendment claims in a § 1983 action despite the fact that those claims could not be heard on a petition for habeas, *Stone v. Powell* (S.Ct.1976), because state courts had afforded a full and fair opportunity to litigate the issues. *Allen v. McCurry* (S.Ct.1980). The same principle of preclusion applies when a litigant has wrongfully failed to raise a § 1983 claim in a previous state court proceeding. *Migra v. Board of Education* (S.Ct.1984). The rulings of state administrative agencies do not have res judicata effect, although decisions by state courts reviewing an administrative rulings do have such effect. *Kremer v. Chemical Construction Corp.* (S.Ct.1982). However, the prior state court proceeding must be adjudicative of the § 1983 issue in order for res judicata to apply. For example, a guilty plea in state court will not preclude a criminal defendant from bringing a § 1983 action to vindicate his constitutional rights if those rights could not be litigated in the criminal proceeding. *Haring v. Prosise* (S.Ct.1983) (guilty plea did not determine the legality of a search of the defendant's apartment).

Release–Dismissal Agreements. In *Newton v. Rumery* (S.Ct.1987), the Court addressed the question whether a judge "properly may enforce an agreement in which a criminal defendant releases his right to file a § 1983 action in return for a prosecutor's dismissal of pending criminal charges." Although a release-dismissal agreement is a formal contract and contractual matters are usually controlled by state law, the validity of a waiver of § 1983 claims is governed by federal law. The Court, rejecting a suggestion that release-dismissal agreements are invalid per se, noted that "In many cases a defendant's choice to enter into a release-dismissal agreement will reflect a highly rational judgment that the certain benefits of escaping criminal prosecution exceed the speculative benefits of prevailing in a civil action." In *Rumery,* the litigant was a sophisticated businessman, was represented by counsel and took several days to arrive at his decision to waive § 1983 claims. The Court held that release-dismissal agreements should be enforced at least where, as in the instant case, the "agreement [is] voluntary...., there is no evidence of prosecutorial misconduct, and ... enforcement of [the] agreement would not adversely affect the relevant public interests." Five members of the Court, in two separate opinions, expressed the view that the defendant in a § 1983 action should have the burden of proving the validity of release-dismissal agreements.

§ 51. ATTORNEY'S FEES

In actions to enforce § 1983, a court "in its discretion may allow the prevailing party ... a reasonable attorney's fee as part of the costs." 42 U.S.C.A. § 1988. Although the statutory provision for attorney's fees appears to be discretionary and to apply alike to plaintiffs and defendants, it has not been interpreted literally. The Supreme Court has said that a prevailing plaintiff "should ordinarily recover an attorney's fee unless special circumstances would render such an award unjust." *Newman v. Piggie Park Enterprises* (S.Ct.1968). A prevailing defendant, on the other hand, will not be awarded attorney's fees unless the court finds that " 'the plaintiff's action was frivolous, unreasonable, or without foundation....' " *Hughes v. Rowe* (S.Ct.1980). Both the Court's reluctance to award fees to defendants and the Court's insistence on routine awards for prevailing plaintiffs are based on the statutory purpose of facilitating the enforcement of civil rights.

A public official's immunity under § 1983 does not extend to attorney's fees unless the official is immune to the underlying cause of action. Thus when a state supreme court acted in a legislative capacity, no attorney's fees could be recovered from members of the court; but when the same court acted in an enforcement capacity, attorney's fees could be recovered. *Supreme Court of Virginia v. Consumers Union* (S.Ct.1980). And when a federal court has properly enjoined a state judge's unconstitutional actions, the judge will be liable for attorney's fees, even though she would have been immune to a claim for damages and the award of fees may have substantially the same effect as an award of damages. *Pulliam v. Allen* (S.Ct.1984). However, a defendant cannot be held liable for attorney's fees unless he is held liable on the merits of the cause of action. See *Kentucky v. Graham* (S.Ct. 1985) (attorney's fees cannot be recovered from a governmental entity when a plaintiff prevails only against public officials in their personal capacities).

In order to be awarded attorney's fees, a litigant must be a "prevailing party." Under this requirement, a plaintiff must obtain some relief on the merits of at least one claim before fees can be recovered. It is not enough that the plaintiff receive a favorable judicial statement of law in the course of litigation if the judgment itself is unfavorable. See *Hewitt v. Helms* (S.Ct.1987) (attorney's fees denied where official immunity prevented a judgment for damages and no other relief was sought); *Hanrahan v. Hampton* (S.Ct.1980) (reversal of a judgment which had directed verdicts for defendants was insufficient to make plaintiff a prevailing party). Even a declaratory judgment in favor of the plaintiffs will not justify an award of attorney's fees unless "it affects the behavior of the defendant toward the plaintiff." *Rhodes v. Stewart* (S.Ct.1988) (where non-class action was brought by two prison inmates, one of whom died and the other of whom was released from prison before issuance of court order, neither could be deemed a prevailing party). But the Court has rejected a suggestion that litigants must prevail on the "central issue" in a law suit; it is enough that a party " 'succeed on any significant issue in the litigation, which achieves some of the benefit [he] sought in bringing the suit.' " *Texas State Teachers v. Garland Indep. School Dist.* (S.Ct.1989).

The amount to be awarded as attorney's fees is determined by a variety of factors, including the extent of the plaintiff's success in the litigation. However, the fee need not be proportionate to the damages recovered and in some cases may far exceed the amount of damages. See *City of Riverside v. Rivera* (S.Ct.1986) (approving attorney's fees of $245,456 after recovery of $33,350 in damages). Accordingly, a contingent fee agreement with the plaintiff will not operate as a ceiling on the amount a court may award. *Blanchard v. Bergeron* (S.Ct. 1989). The Court has said that "The most useful starting point for determining the amount of a reasonable fee is the number of hours reasonably expended ... multiplied by a reasonable hourly rate." *Hensley v. Eckerhart* (S.Ct.1983). This figure, commonly called the "lodestar," must be based on "prevailing market rates in the relevant community." *Blum v. Stenson* (S.Ct.1984). Although some cases may involve a substantial risk of nonrecovery, courts cannot enhance a fee award beyond the lodestar amount to reflect the fact that attorneys were retained on a contingent fee basis. *Burlington v. Dague* (S.Ct.1992).

APPENDIX

SELECTED CONSTITUTIONAL AND STATUTORY PROVISIONS

THE CONSTITUTION OF THE UNITED STATES

Amendment I

Congress shall make no law respecting an establishment of religion, or prohibiting the free exercise thereof; or abridging the freedom of speech, or of the press; or the right of the people peaceably to assemble, and to petition the Government for a redress of grievances.

Amendment IV

The right of the people to be secure in their persons, houses, papers, and effects, against unreasonable searches and seizures, shall not be violated, and no Warrants shall issue, but upon probable cause, supported by Oath or affirmation, and particularly describing the place to be searched, and the persons or things to be seized.

Amendment V

No person shall be held to answer for a capital, or otherwise infamous crime, unless on a presentment or indictment of a Grand Jury, except in cases arising in the land or naval forces, or in the Militia, when in actual service in time of War or public danger; nor shall any person be subject for the same offense to be twice put in jeopardy of life or limb; nor shall be compelled in any criminal case to be a witness against himself, nor be deprived of life, liberty, or property, without due process of law; nor shall private property be taken for public use, without just compensation.

AMENDMENT VI

In all criminal prosecutions, the accused shall enjoy the right to a speedy and public trial, by an impartial jury of the State and district wherein the crime shall have been committed, which district shall have been previously ascertained by law, and to be informed of the nature and cause of the accusation; to be confronted with the witnesses against him; to have compulsory process for obtaining Witnesses in his favor, and to have the Assistance of Counsel for his defence.

AMENDMENT VII

In Suits at common law, where the value in controversy shall exceed twenty dollars, the right of trial by jury shall be preserved, and no fact tried by a jury, shall be otherwise re-examined in any Court of the United States, than according to the rules of the common law.

Amendment VIII

Excessive bail shall not be required, nor excessive fines imposed, nor cruel and unusual punishments inflicted.

Amendment IX

The enumeration in the Constitution, of certain rights, shall not be construed to deny or disparage others retained by the people.

Amendment X

The powers not delegated to the United States by the Constitution, nor prohibited by it to the States, are reserved to the States respectively, or to the people.

Amendment XIII

Section 1. Neither slavery nor involuntary servitude, except as a punishment for crime whereof the party shall have been duly convicted shall exist within the United States, or any place subject to their jurisdiction.

Section 2. Congress shall have power to enforce this article by appropriate legislation.

Amendment XIV

Section 1. All persons born or naturalized in the United States and subject to the jurisdiction thereof, are citizens of the United States and of the State wherein they reside. No State shall make or enforce any law which shall abridge the privileges or immunities of citizens of the United States; nor shall any State deprive any person of life, liberty, or property, without due process of law; nor deny to any person within its jurisdiction the equal protection of the laws.

Section 2. Representatives shall be apportioned among the several States according to their respective numbers, counting the whole number of persons in each State, excluding Indians not taxed. But when the right to vote at any election for the choice of electors for President and Vice President of the United States, Representatives in Congress, the Executive and Judicial officers of a State, or the members of the Legislature thereof, is denied to any of the male inhabitants of such State, being twenty-one years of age, and citizens of the United States, or in any way abridged, except for participation in rebellion, or other crime, the basis of representation therein shall be reduced in the proportion which the number of such male citizens shall bear to the whole number of male citizens twenty-one years of age in such State.

Section 5. The Congress shall have power to enforce, by appropriate legislation, the provisions of this article.

Amendment XV

Section 1. The right of citizens of the United States to vote shall not be denied or abridged by the

United States or by any State on account of race, color, or previous condition of servitude.

Section 2. The Congress shall have power to enforce this article by appropriate legislation.

Amendment XIX

The right of citizens of the United States to vote shall not be denied or abridged by the United States or by any State on account of sex.

Congress shall have power to enforce this article by appropriate legislation.

Amendment XXIV

Section 1. The right of citizens of the United States to vote in any primary or other election for President or Vice President, for electors for President or Vice President, or for Senator or Representative in Congress, shall not be denied or abridged by the United States or any State by reason of failure to pay any poll tax or other tax.

Section 2. The Congress shall have power to enforce this article by appropriate legislation.

Amendment XXVI

Section 1. The right of citizens of the United States, who are eighteen years of age or older, to vote shall not be denied or abridged by the United States or by any State on account of age.

Section 2. The Congress shall have power to enforce this article by appropriate legislation.

THE CIVIL RIGHTS ACT OF 1964 (42 U.S.C.A.)

DISCRIMINATION IN PLACES OF PUBLIC ACCOMMODATION

§ 2000a. Prohibition against discrimination or segregation in places of public accommodation—Equal access

(a) All persons shall be entitled to the full and equal enjoyment of the goods, services, facilities, privileges, advantages, and accommodations of any place of public accommodation, as defined in this section, without discrimination or segregation on the ground of race, color, religion, or national origin.

(b) Each of the following establishments which serves the public is a place of public accommodation within the meaning of this subchapter if its operations affect commerce, or if discrimination or segregation by it is supported by State action:

(1) any inn, hotel, motel, or other establishment which provides lodging to transient guests, other than an establishment located within a building which contains not more than five rooms for rent or hire and which is actually occupied by the proprietor of such establishment as his residence;

(2) any restaurant, cafeteria, lunchroom, lunch counter, soda fountain, or other facility principally engaged in selling food for consumption on the

premises, including, but not limited to, any such facility located on the premises of any retail establishment; or any gasoline station;

(3) any motion picture house, theater, concert hall, sports arena, stadium or other place of exhibition or entertainment; and

(4) any establishment (A)(i) which is physically located within the premises of any establishment otherwise covered by this subsection, or (ii) within the premises of which is physically located any such covered establishment, and (B) which holds itself out as serving patrons of such covered establishment.

. . .

(e) The provisions of this subchapter shall not apply to a private club or other establishment not in fact open to the public, except to the extent that the facilities of such establishment are made available to the customers or patrons of an establishment within the scope of subsection (b) of this section.

Pub.L. 88–352, Title II, § 201, July 2, 1964, 78 Stat. 243.

DISCRIMINATION IN FEDERALLY ASSISTED PROGRAMS

§ 2000d. Prohibition against exclusion from participation in, denial of benefits of, and discrimination under Federally assisted programs on ground of race, color, or national origin

No person in the United States shall, on the ground of race, color, or national origin, be excluded from participation in, be denied the benefits of, or be subjected to discrimination under any program or activity receiving Federal financial assistance.

Pub.L. 88–352, Title VI, § 601, July 2, 1964, 78 Stat. 252.

§ 2000d–1. Federal authority and financial assistance to programs or activities by way of grant, loan, or contract other than contract of insurance or guaranty; rules and regulations; approval by President; compliance with requirements; reports to Congressional committees; effective date of administrative action

Each Federal department and agency which is empowered to extend Federal financial assistance to any program or activity, by way of grant, loan, or contract other than a contract of insurance or guaranty, is authorized and directed to effectuate the provisions of section 2000d of this title with respect to such program or activity by issuing rules, regulations, or orders of general applicability which shall be consistent with achievement of the objectives of the statute authorizing the financial assistance in connection with which the action is taken. No such rule, regulation, or order shall become effective unless and until approved by the President. Compliance with any requirement adopted pursuant to this section may be effected (1) by the termination of or refusal to grant or to continue assistance under such program or activity to any recipient as to whom there has been an express finding on the record, after opportunity for hearing, of a failure to comply with such requirement, but such termination or refusal shall be limited to the particular political entity, or part thereof, or other recipient as to whom such a finding has been made and, shall be limited in its effect to the particular program, or part thereof, in which such noncompliance has been so found, or (2) by any other means authorized by law: *Provided, however,* That no such action shall be taken until the department or agency concerned has advised the appropriate person or persons of the failure to comply with the requirement and has determined that compliance cannot be secured by voluntary means....

Pub.L. 88–352, Title VI, § 602, July 2, 1964, 78 Stat. 252.

§ 2000d–2. Judicial review; Administrative Procedure Act

Any department or agency action taken pursuant to section 2000d–1 of this title shall be subject to such judicial review as may otherwise be provided by law for similar action taken by such department or agency on other grounds. In the case of action, not otherwise subject to judicial review, terminating or refusing to grant or to continue financial assistance upon a finding of failure to comply with any requirement imposed pursuant to section 2000d–1 of this title, any person aggrieved (including any State or political subdivision thereof and any agency of either) may obtain judicial review of such action in accordance with chapter 7 of title 5, and such action shall not be deemed committed to unreviewable agency discretion within the meaning of that chapter.

Pub.L. 88–352, Title VI, § 603, July 2, 1964, 78 Stat. 253.

§ 2000d–7. Civil rights remedies equalization

(a) General provision

(1) A State shall not be immune under the Eleventh Amendment of the Constitution of the United States from suit in Federal court for a violation of section 504 of the Rehabilitation Act of 1973 [29 U.S.C.A. § 794], title IX of the Education Amendments of 1972 [20 U.S.C.A. § 1681 et seq.], the Age Discrimination Act of 1975 [42 U.S.C.A. § 6101 et seq.], title VI of the Civil Rights Act of 1964 [42 U.S.C.A. § 2000d et seq.], or the provisions of any

other Federal statute prohibiting discrimination by recipients of Federal financial assistance.

(2) In a suit against a State for a violation of a statute referred to in paragraph (1), remedies (including remedies both at law and in equity) are available for such a violation to the same extent as such remedies are available for such a violation in the suit against any public or private entity other than a State.

Pub.L. 99–506, Title X, § 1003, Oct. 21, 1986, 100 Stat. 1845.

EQUAL EMPLOYMENT OPPORTUNITY (TITLE VII, AS AMENDED)

§ 2000e. Definitions

For the purposes of this subchapter—

(a) The term "person" includes one or more individuals, governments, governmental agencies, political subdivisions, labor unions, partnerships, associations, corporations, legal representatives, mutual companies, joint-stock companies, trusts, unincorporated organizations, trustees, trustees in cases under Title 11, or receivers.

(b) The term "employer" means a person engaged in an industry affecting commerce who has fifteen or more employees for each working day in each of twenty or more calendar weeks in the current or preceding calendar year, and any agent of such a person, but such term does not include (1) the United States, a corporation wholly owned by the Government of the United States, an Indian tribe, or any department or agency of the District of Columbia subject by statute to procedures of the competitive service (as defined in section 2102 of Title 5), or (2) a bona fide private membership club (other than a labor organization) which is exempt from taxation under section 501(c) of Title 26, except that during the first year after March 24, 1972, persons having fewer than twenty-five employees (and their agents) shall not be considered employers.

(c) The term "employment agency" means any person regularly undertaking with or without compensation to procure employees for an employer or to procure for employees opportunities to work for an employer and includes an agent of such a person.

(d) The term "labor organization" means a labor organization engaged in an industry affecting commerce, and any agent of such an organization, and includes any organization of any kind, any agency, or employee representation committee, group, association, or plan so engaged in which employees participate and which exists for the purpose, in whole or in part, of dealing with employers concerning grievances, labor disputes, wages, rates of pay, hours, or other terms or conditions of employment, and any conference, general committee, joint or system board, or joint council so engaged which is subordinate to a national or international labor organization.

. . .

(f) The term "employee" means an individual employed by an employer, except that the term "employee" shall not include any person elected to public office in any State or political subdivision of any State by the qualified voters thereof, or any person chosen by such officer to be on such officer's personal staff, or an appointee on the policy making level or an immediate adviser with respect to the exercise of the constitutional or legal powers of the office. The exemption set forth in the preceding sentence shall not include employees subject to the civil service laws of a State government, governmental agency or political subdivision. With respect to employment in a foreign country, such term includes an individual who is a citizen of the United States.

. . .

(k) The terms "because of sex" or "on the basis of sex" include, but are not limited to, because of or on the basis of pregnancy, childbirth, or related medical conditions; and women affected by pregnancy, childbirth, or related medical conditions shall be treated the same for all employment-related purposes, including receipt of benefits under fringe benefit programs, as other persons not so affected but similar in their ability or inability to work, and nothing in section 2000e–2(h) of this title shall be interpreted to permit otherwise. This subsection shall not require an employer to pay for health insurance benefits for abortion, except where the life of the mother would be endangered if the fetus were carried to term, or except where medical complications have arisen from an abortion: Provided, That nothing herein shall preclude an employer from providing abortion benefits or otherwise affect bargaining agreements in regard to abortion.

. . .

As amended Pub.L. 102–166, Title I, §§ 104, 109(a), Nov. 21, 1991, 105 Stat. 1074, 1077.

§ 2000e–1. Applicability to foreign and religious employment

(a) Inapplicability of subchapter to certain aliens and employees of religious entities

This subchapter shall not apply to an employer with respect to the employment of aliens outside any State, or to a religious corporation, association, educational institution, or society with respect to the employment of individuals of a particular religion to perform work connected with the carrying on by such corporation, association, educational institution, or society of its activities.

. . .

As amended Pub.L. 102–166, Title I, § 109(b), Nov. 21, 1991, 105 Stat. 1077.

§ 2000e–2. Unlawful employment practices

(a) It shall be an unlawful employment practice for an employer—

(1) to fail or refuse to hire or to discharge any individual, or otherwise to discriminate against

any individual with respect to his compensation, terms, conditions, or privileges of employment, because of such individual's race, color, religion, sex, or national origin; or

(2) to limit, segregate, or classify his employees or applicants for employment in any way which would deprive or tend to deprive any individual of employment opportunities or otherwise adversely affect his status as an employee, because of such individual's race, color, religion, sex, or national origin.

(b) It shall be an unlawful employment practice for an employment agency to fail or refuse to refer for employment, or otherwise to discriminate against, any individual because of his race, color, religion, sex, or national origin, or to classify or refer for employment any individual on the basis of his race, color, religion, sex, or national origin.

(c) It shall be an unlawful employment practice for a labor organization—

(1) to exclude or to expel from its membership, or otherwise to discriminate against, any individual because of his race, color, religion, sex, or national origin;

(2) to limit, segregate, or classify its membership or applicants for membership, or to classify or fail or refuse to refer for employment any individual, in any way which would deprive or tend to deprive any individual of employment opportunities, or would limit such employment opportunities or otherwise adversely affect his

status as an employee or as an applicant for employment, because of such individual's race, color, religion, sex, or national origin; or

(3) to cause or attempt to cause an employer to discriminate against an individual in violation of this section.

. . .

(e) Notwithstanding any other provision of this subchapter, (1) it shall not be an unlawful employment practice for an employer to hire and employ employees, for an employment agency to classify, or refer for employment any individual, for a labor organization to classify its membership or to classify or refer for employment any individual, or for an employer, labor organization, or joint labor-management committee controlling apprenticeship or other training or retraining programs to admit or employ any individual in any such program, on the basis of his religion, sex, or national origin in those certain instances where religion, sex, or national origin is a bona fide occupational qualification reasonably necessary to the normal operation of that particular business or enterprise, and (2) it shall not be an unlawful employment practice for a school, college, university, or other educational institution or institution of learning to hire and employ employees of a particular religion if such school, college, university, or other educational institution or institution of learning is, in whole or in substantial part, owned, supported, controlled, or managed by a particular religion or by a particular religious corporation, association, or society, or if the curriculum of such school, college, university, or other educational institution or institution of learning is directed toward the propagation of a particular religion.

. . .

(h) Notwithstanding any other provision of this subchapter, it shall not be an unlawful employment practice for an employer to apply different standards of compensation, or different terms, conditions, or privileges of employment pursuant to a bona fide seniority or merit system, or a system which measures earnings by quantity or quality of production or to employees who work in different locations, provided that such differences are not the result of an intention to discriminate because of race, color, religion, sex, or national origin, nor shall it be an unlawful employment practice for an employer to give and to act upon the results of any professionally developed ability test provided that such test, its administration or action upon the results is not designed, intended or used to discriminate because of race, color, religion, sex or national origin. It shall not be an unlawful employment practice under this subchapter for any employer to differentiate upon the basis of sex in determining the amount of the wages or compensation paid or to be paid to employees of such employer if such differentiation is authorized by the provisions of section 206(d) of Title 29.

(i) Nothing contained in this subchapter shall apply to any business or enterprise on or near an

Indian reservation with respect to any publicly announced employment practice of such business or enterprise under which a preferential treatment is given to any individual because he is an Indian living on or near a reservation.

(j) Nothing contained in this subchapter shall be interpreted to require any employer, employment agency, labor organization, or joint labor-management committee subject to this subchapter to grant preferential treatment to any individual or to any group because of the race, color, religion, sex, or national origin of such individual or group on account of an imbalance which may exist with respect to the total number or percentage of persons of any race, color, religion, sex, or national origin employed by any employer, referred or classified for employment by any employment agency or labor organization, admitted to membership or classified by any labor organization, or admitted to, or employed in, any apprenticeship or other training program, in comparison with the total number or percentage of persons of such race, color, religion, sex, or national origin in any community, State, section, or other area, or in the available work force in any community, State, section, or other area.

. . .

(*l*) It shall be an unlawful employment practice for a respondent, in connection with the selection or referral of applicants or candidates for employment or promotion, to adjust the scores of, use different cutoff scores for, or otherwise alter the results of, employment related tests on the basis of race, color, religion, sex, or national origin.

(m) Except as otherwise provided in this subchapter, an unlawful employment practice is established when the complaining party demonstrates that race, color, religion, sex, or national origin was a motivating factor for any employment practice, even though other factors also motivated the practice.

. . .

As amended Pub.L. 102–166, Title I, §§ 105(a), 106, 107(a), 108, Nov. 21, 1991, 105 Stat. 1074–76.

THE VOTING RIGHTS ACT OF 1965, AS AMENDED (42 U.S.C.A.)

§ 1973. Denial or abridgement of right to vote on account of race or color through voting qualifications or prerequisites

(a) No voting qualification or prerequisite to voting, or standard, practice, or procedure shall be imposed or applied by any State or political subdivision in a manner which results in a denial or abridgement of the right of any citizen of the United States to vote on account of race or color, or in contravention of the guarantees set forth in section 1973b(f)(2) of this title, as provided in subsection (b) of this section.

(b) A violation of subsection (a) of this section is established if, based on the totality of circumstances, it is shown that the political processes leading to nomination or election in the State or political subdivision are not equally open to participation by members of a class of citizens protected by subsection (a) of this section in that its members have less opportunity than other members of the electorate to participate in the political process and to elect representatives of their choice. The extent to which members of a protected class have been elected to office in the State or political subdivision is one circumstance which may be considered: *Provided,* That nothing in this section establishes a right to have members of a protected class elected in numbers equal to their proportion in the population.

As amended Pub.L. 97–205, § 3, June 29, 1982, 96 Stat. 134.

§ 1973a. Proceeding to enforce the right to vote—suspension of use of tests and devices which deny or abridge the right to vote

(b) If in a proceeding instituted by the Attorney General or an aggrieved person under any statute to enforce the voting guarantees of the fourteenth or fifteenth amendment in any State or political subdivision the court finds that a test or device has been used for the purpose or with the effect of denying or abridging the right of any citizen of the United States to vote on account of race or color, or in contravention of the voting guarantees set forth in section 1973b(f)(2) of this title, it shall suspend the use of tests and devices in such State or political subdivisions as the court shall determine is appropriate and for such period as it deems necessary.

As amended 1978 Reorg. Plan No. 2, § 102, eff. Jan. 1, 1979, 43 F.R. 36037, 92 Stat. 3783.

§ 1973b. Suspension of the use of tests or devices in determining eligibility to vote

(a) Action by state or political subdivision for declaratory judgment of no denial or abridgement; three-judge district court; appeal to Supreme Court; retention of jurisdiction by three-judge court

(1) To assure that the right of citizens of the United States to vote is not denied or abridged on account of race or color, no citizen shall be denied the right to vote in any Federal, State, or local election because of his failure to comply with any test or device in any State with respect to which the determinations have been made under the first two sentences of subsection (b) of this section or in any political subdivision of such State (as such subdivision existed on the date such determinations were made with respect to such State), though such determinations were not made with respect to such subdivision as a separate unit, or in any political subdivision with respect to which such determinations have been made as a separate unit, unless the United States District Court for the District of Columbia issues a declaratory judgment under this section. No citizen shall be denied the right to vote in any Federal, State, or local election because of

his failure to comply with any test or device in any State with respect to which the determinations have been made under the third sentence of subsection (b) of this section or in any political subdivision of such State (as such subdivision existed on the date such determinations were made with respect to such State), though such determinations were not made with respect to such subdivision as a separate unit, or in any political subdivision with respect to which such determinations have been made as a separate unit, unless the United States District Court for the District of Columbia issues a declaratory judgment under this section. A declaratory judgment under this section shall issue only if such court determines that during the ten years preceding the filing of the action, and during the pendency of such action—

(A) no such test or device has been used within such State or political subdivision for the purpose or with the effect of denying or abridging the right to vote on account of race or color or (in the case of a State or subdivision seeking a declaratory judgment under the second sentence of this subsection) in contravention of the guarantees of subsection (f)(2) of this section;

(B) no final judgment of any court of the United States, other than the denial of declaratory judgment under this section, has determined that denials or abridgements of the right to vote on account of race or color have occurred anywhere in the territory of such State or political subdivision or (in the case of a State or subdivision seeking a declaratory judgment under the second sentence of this subsection) that denials or abridgements of the right to vote in contravention of the guarantees of subsection (f)(2) of this section have occurred anywhere in the territory of such State or subdivision and no consent decree, settlement, or agreement has been entered into resulting in any abandonment of a voting practice challenged on such grounds; and no declaratory judgment under this section shall be entered during the pendency of an action commenced before the filing of an action under this section and alleging such denials or abridgements of the right to vote;

. . .

(b) Required factual determinations necessary to allow suspension of compliance with tests and devices; publication in Federal Register

The provisions of subsection (a) of this section shall apply in any State or in any political subdivision of a state which (1) the Attorney General determines maintained on November 1, 1964, any test or device, and with respect to which (2) the Director of the Census determines that less than 50 per centum of the persons of voting age residing therein were registered on November 1, 1964, or that less than 50 per centum of such persons voted in the presidential election of November 1964. On and after August 6, 1970, in addition to any State or political subdivision of a State determined to be subject to subsection (a) of this section pursuant to

APPENDIX

the previous sentence, the provisions of subsection (a) of this section shall apply in any State or any political subdivision of a State which (i) the Attorney General determines maintained on November 1, 1968, any test or device, and with respect to which (ii) the Director of the Census determines that less than 50 per centum of the persons of voting age residing therein were registered on November 1, 1968, or that less than 50 per centum of such persons voted in the presidential election of November 1968. On and after August 6, 1975, in addition to any State or political subdivision of a State determined to be subject to subsection (a) of this section pursuant to the previous two sentences, the provisions of subsection (a) of this section shall apply in any State or any political subdivision of a State which (i) the Attorney General determines maintained on November 1, 1972, any test or device, and with respect to which (ii) the Director of the Census determines that less than 50 per centum of the citizens of voting age were registered on November 1, 1972, or that less than 50 per centum of such persons voted in the Presidential election of November 1972.

. . .

(f) Congressional findings of voting discrimination against language minorities; prohibition of English-only elections; other remedial measures

. . .

(2) No voting qualification or prerequisite to voting, or standard, practice, or procedure shall be

imposed or applied by any State or political subdivision to deny or abridge the right of any citizen of the United States to vote because he is a member of a language minority group.

. . .

As amended Pub.L. 97–205, § 2(a)–(c), June 29, 1982, 96 Stat. 131–33.

§ 1973c. Alteration of voting qualifications and procedures; action by state or political subdivision for declaratory judgment of no denial or abridgement of voting rights; three-judge district court, appeal to Supreme Court

Whenever a State or political subdivision with respect to which the prohibitions set forth in section 1973b(a) of this title based upon determinations made under the first sentence of section 1973b(b) of this title are in effect shall enact or seek to administer any voting qualification or prerequisite to voting, or standard, practice, or procedure with respect to voting different from that in force or effect on November 1, 1964, or whenever a State or political subdivision with respect to which the prohibitions set forth in section 1973b(a) of this title based upon determinations made under the second sentence of section 1973b(b) of this title are in effect shall enact or seek to administer any voting qualification or prerequisite to voting, or standard, practice, or procedure with respect to voting different from that in force or effect on November 1,

1968, or whenever a State or political subdivision with respect to which the prohibitions set forth in section 1973b(a) of this title based upon determinations made under the third sentence of section 1973b(b) of this title are in effect shall enact or seek to administer any voting qualification or prerequisite to voting, or standard, practice, or procedure with respect to voting different from that in force or effect on November 1, 1972, such State or subdivision may institute an action in the United States District Court for the District of Columbia for a declaratory judgment that such qualification, prerequisite, standard, practice, or procedure does not have the purpose and will not have the effect of denying or abridging the right to vote on account of race or color, or in contravention of the guarantees set forth in section 1973b(f)(2) of this title, and unless and until the court enters such judgment no person shall be denied the right to vote for failure to comply with such qualification, prerequisite, standard, practice, or procedure: *Provided,* That such qualification, prerequisite, standard, practice, or procedure may be enforced without such proceeding if the qualification, prerequisite, standard, practice, or procedure has been submitted by the chief legal officer or other appropriate official of such State or subdivision to the Attorney General and the Attorney General has not interposed an objection within sixty days after such submission, or upon good cause shown, to facilitate an expedited approval within sixty days after such submission, the Attorney General has affirmatively indicated that such objection will not be made. Neither an affirmative indication by the Attorney General that no objection will be made, nor the Attorney General's failure to object, nor a declaratory judgment entered under this section shall bar a subsequent action to enjoin enforcement of such qualification, prerequisite, standard, practice, or procedure. In the event the Attorney General affirmatively indicates that no objection will be made within the sixty-day period following receipt of a submission, the Attorney General may reserve the right to reexamine the submission if additional information comes to his attention during the remainder of the sixty-day period which would otherwise require objection in accordance with this section. Any action under this section shall be heard and determined by a court of three judges in accordance with the provisions of section 2284 of Title 28 and any appeal shall lie to the Supreme Court.

As amended Pub.L. 94–73, Title II, §§ 204, 206, Title IV, § 405, Aug. 6, 1975, 89 Stat. 402, 404.

THE CIVIL RIGHTS ACT OF 1968 (42 U.S.C.A.)

§ 3601. Declaration of policy

It is the policy of the United States to provide, within constitutional limitations, for fair housing throughout the United States.

Pub.L. 90–284, Title VIII, § 801, Apr. 11, 1968, 82 Stat. 81.

§ 3603. Effective dates of certain prohibitions

. . .

(b) Nothing in section 3604 of this title (other than subsection (c)) shall apply to—

(1) any single-family house sold or rented by an owner: *Provided,* That such private individual owner does not own more than three such single-family houses at any one time: *Provided further,* That in the case of the sale of any such single-family house by a private individual owner not residing in such house at the time of such sale or who was not the most recent resident of such house prior to such sale, the exemption granted by this subsection shall apply only with respect to one such sale within any twenty-four month period: *Provided further,* That such bona fide private individual owner does not own any interest in, nor is there owned or reserved on his behalf, under any express or voluntary agreement, title to or any right to all or a portion of the proceeds from the sale or rental of, more than three such single-family houses at any one time: *Provided further,* That after December 31, 1969, the sale or rental of any such single-family house shall be excepted from the application of this subchapter only if such house is sold or rented (A) without the use in any manner of the sales or rental facilities or the sales or rental services of any real estate broker, agent, or salesman, or of such facilities or services of any person in the business of selling or renting dwellings, or of any employee

or agent of any such broker, agent, salesman, or person and (B) without the publication, posting or mailing, after notice, of any advertisement or written notice in violation of section 3604(c) of this title; but nothing in this proviso shall prohibit the use of attorneys, escrow agents, abstractors, title companies, and other such professional assistance as necessary to perfect or transfer the title, or

(2) rooms or units in dwellings containing living quarters occupied or intended to be occupied by no more than four families living independently of each other, if the owner actually maintains and occupies one of such living quarters as his residence.

(c) For the purposes of subsection (b) of this section, a person shall be deemed to be in the business of selling or renting dwellings if—

(1) he has, within the preceding twelve months, participated as principal in three or more transactions involving the sale or rental of any dwelling or any interest therein, or

(2) he has, within the preceding twelve months, participated as agent, other than in the sale of his own personal residence in providing sales or rental facilities or sales or rental services in two or more transactions involving the sale or rental of any dwelling or any interest therein, or

(3) he is the owner of any dwelling designed or intended for occupancy by, or occupied by, five or more families.

Pub.L. 90–284, Title VIII, § 803, Apr. 11, 1968, 82 Stat. 82.

§ 3604. Discrimination in sale or rental of housing and other prohibited practices

As made applicable by section 3603 of this title and except as exempted by sections 3603(b) and 3607 of this title, it shall be unlawful—

(a) To refuse to sell or rent after the making of a bona fide offer, or to refuse to negotiate for the sale or rental of, or otherwise make unavailable or deny, a dwelling to any person because of race, color, religion, sex, or national origin.

(b) To discriminate against any person in the terms, conditions, or privileges of sale or rental of a dwelling, or in the provision of services or facilities in connection therewith, because of race, color, religion, sex, or national origin.

(c) To make, print, or publish, or cause to be made, printed, or published any notice, statement, or advertisement, with respect to the sale or rental of a dwelling that indicates any preference, limitation, or discrimination based on race, color, religion, sex, or national origin, or an intention to make any such preference, limitation, or discrimination.

(d) To represent to any person because of race, color, religion, sex, or national origin that any dwelling is not available for inspection, sale, or rental when such dwelling is in fact so available.

(e) For profit, to induce or attempt to induce any person to sell or rent any dwelling by representations regarding the entry or prospective entry into the neighborhood of a person or persons of a particular race, color, religion, sex, or national origin.

. . .

As amended Pub.L. 100–430, §§ 6(a)–(b)(2), (e), 15, Sept. 13, 1988, 102 Stat. 1620, 1622, 1623, 1636.

§ 3605. Discrimination in financing of housing

(a) In general

It shall be unlawful for any person or other entity whose business includes engaging in residential real estate-related transactions to discriminate against any person in making available such a transaction, or in the terms or conditions of such a transaction, because of race, color, religion, sex, handicap, familial status, or national origin.

(b) "residential real estate-related transaction" defined

As used in this section, the term "residential real estate-related transaction" means any of the following:

(1) the making or purchasing of loans or providing other financial assistance—

(A) for purchasing, constructing, improving, repairing, or maintaining a dwelling; or

(B) secured by residential real estate.

(2) The selling, brokering, or appraising of residential real property.

(c) Appraisal exemption

Nothing in this subchapter prohibits a person engaged in the business of furnishing appraisals of real property to take into consideration factors other than race, color, religion, national origin, sex, handicap, or familial status.

As amended Pub.L. 100–430, § 6(c), Sept. 13, 1988, 102 Stat. 1622.

§ 3606. Discrimination in provision of brokerage services

After December 31, 1968, it shall be unlawful to deny any person access to or membership or participation in any multiple-listing service, real estate brokers' organization or other service, organization, or facility relating to the business of selling or renting dwellings, or to discriminate against him in the terms or conditions of such access, membership, or participation, on account of race, color, religion, sex, or national origin.

Pub.L. 90–284, Title VIII, § 806, Apr. 11, 1968, 82 Stat. 84; Pub.L. 93–383, Title VIII, § 808(b)(3), Aug. 22, 1974, 88 Stat. 729.

§ 3607. Exemptions

(a) Religious organizations and private clubs

Nothing in this subchapter shall prohibit a religious organization, association, or society, or any nonprofit institution or organization operated, supervised or controlled by or in conjunction with a religious organization, association, or society, from limiting the sale, rental or occupancy of dwellings which it owns or operates for other than a commercial purpose to persons of the same religion, or from giving preference to such persons, unless membership in such religion is restricted on account of race, color, or national origin. Nor shall anything in this subchapter prohibit a private club not in fact open to the public, which as an incident to its primary purpose or purposes provides lodgings which it owns or operates for other than a commercial purpose, from limiting the rental or occupancy of such lodgings to its members or from giving preference to its members.

. . .

As amended Pub.L. 104–76, §§ 2, 3, Dec. 28, 1995, 109 Stat. 987.

§ 3615. Effect on State laws

Nothing in this subchapter shall be construed to invalidate or limit any law of a State or political subdivision of a State, or of any other jurisdiction in which this subchapter shall be effective, that grants, guarantees, or protects the same rights as are granted by this subchapter; but any law of a State, a political subdivision, or other such jurisdiction that purports to require or permit any action that would be a discriminatory housing practice under this subchapter shall to that extent be invalid.

Pub.L. 90–284, Title VIII, § 816, formerly § 815, Apr. 11, 1968, 82 Stat. 89; renumbered § 816, Pub.L. 100–430, § 8(1), Sept. 13, 1988, 102 Stat. 1625.

§ 3617. Interference, coercion, or intimidation

It shall be unlawful to coerce, intimidate, threaten, or interfere with any person in the exercise or enjoyment of, or on account of his having exercised or enjoyed, or on account of his having aided or encouraged any other person in the exercise or enjoyment of, any right granted or protected by section 3603, 3604, 3605, or 3606 of this title.

As amended Pub.L. 100–430, §§ 8(1), 10, Sept. 13, 1988, 102 Stat. 1625, 1635.

AGE DISCRIMINATION IN EMPLOYMENT ACT (29 U.S.C.A.)

§ 623. Prohibition of age discrimination

(a) Employer practices

It shall be unlawful for an employer—

(1) to fail or refuse to hire or to discharge any individual or otherwise discriminate against any individual with respect to his compensation, terms, conditions, or privileges of employment, because of such individual's age;

(2) to limit, segregate, or classify his employees in any way which would deprive or tend to deprive

any individual of employment opportunities or otherwise adversely affect his status as an employee, because of such individual's age; or

(3) to reduce the wage rate of any employee in order to comply with this chapter.

(b) Employment agency practices

It shall be unlawful for an employment agency to fail or refuse to refer for employment, or otherwise to discriminate against, any individual because of such individual's age, or to classify or refer for employment any individual on the basis of such individual's age.

(c) Labor organization practices

It shall be unlawful for a labor organization—

(1) to exclude or to expel from its membership, or otherwise to discriminate against, any individual because of his age;

(2) to limit, segregate, or classify its membership, or to classify or fail or refuse to refer for employment any individual, in any way which would deprive or tend to deprive any individual of employment opportunities, or would limit such employment opportunities or otherwise adversely affect his status as an employee or as an applicant for employment, because of such individual's age;

(3) to cause or attempt to cause an employer to discriminate against an individual in violation of this section.

. . .

(e) Printing or publication of notice or advertisement indicating preference, limitation, etc.

It shall be unlawful for an employer, labor organization, or employment agency to print or publish, or cause to be printed or published, any notice or advertisement relating to employment by such an employer or membership in or any classification or referral for employment by such a labor organization, or relating to any classification or referral for employment by such an employment agency, indicating any preference, limitation, specification, or discrimination, based on age.

(f) Lawful practices; age an occupational qualification; other reasonable factors; laws of foreign workplace; seniority system; employee benefit plans; discharge or discipline for good cause

It shall not be unlawful for an employer, employment agency, or labor organization—

(1) to take any action otherwise prohibited under subsections (a), (b), (c), or (e) of this section where age is a bona fide occupational qualification reasonably necessary to the normal operation of the particular business, or where the differentiation is based on reasonable factors other than age, or where such practices involve an employee in a workplace in a foreign country, and compliance with such subsections would cause such employer, or a corporation controlled by such employer, to violate the laws of the country in which such workplace is located;

(2) to take any action otherwise prohibited by subsections (a), (b), (c), or (e) of this section—

(A) to observe the terms of a bona fide seniority system that is not intended to evade the purposes of this chapter, except that no such seniority system shall require or permit the involuntary retirement of any individual specified by section 631(a) of this title because of the age of such individual; or

(B) to observe the terms of a bona fide employee benefit plan—

(i) where, for each benefit or benefit package, the actual amount of payment made or cost incurred on behalf of an older worker is no less than that made or incurred on behalf of a younger worker, as permissible under section 1625.10, title 29, Code of Federal Regulations (as in effect on June 22, 1989); or

(ii) that is a voluntary early retirement incentive plan consistent with the relevant purpose or purposes of this chapter.

Notwithstanding clause (i) or (ii) of subparagraph (B), no such employee benefit plan or voluntary early retirement incentive plan shall excuse the failure to hire any individual specified by section 631(a) of this title, because of the age of such individual. An employer, employment agency, or labor organization acting under subparagraph (A), or under clause (i) or (ii) of subparagraph (B), shall have the burden of proving that such actions are lawful in any civil enforcement proceeding brought under this chapter; or

(3) to discharge or otherwise discipline an individual for good cause.

. . .

As amended Pub.L. 104–208, Div. A, Title I, § 101(a) [Title I, § 119, Subsec. 1(b)], Sept. 30, 1996, 110 Stat. 3009–23.

. . .

§ 626. Recordkeeping, investigation, and enforcement

. . .

(c) Civil actions; persons aggrieved; jurisdiction; judicial relief; termination of individual action upon commencement of action by Commission; jury trial

(1) Any person aggrieved may bring a civil action in any court of competent jurisdiction for such legal or equitable relief as will effectuate the purposes of this chapter: *Provided,* That the right of any person to bring such action shall terminate upon the commencement of an action by the Equal Employment Opportunity Commission to enforce the right of such employee under this chapter.

(d) Filing of charge with Commission; timeliness; conciliation, conference, and persuasion

No civil action may be commenced by an individual under this section until 60 days after a charge alleging unlawful discrimination has been filed with the Equal Employment Opportunity Commission.

. . .

Pub.L. 90–202, § 7, Dec. 15, 1967, 81 Stat. 604; Pub.L. 95–256, § 4(a), (b)(1), (c)(1), Apr. 6, 1978, 92 Stat. 190, 191; 1978 Reorg.Plan No. 1, § 2, eff. Jan. 1, 1979, 43 F.R. 19807, 92 Stat. 3781.

. . .

§ 631. Age limits

(a) Individuals at least 40 years of age

The prohibitions in this chapter shall be limited to individuals who are at least 40 years of age.

. . .

(c) Bona fide executives or high policymakers

(1) Nothing in this chapter shall be construed to prohibit compulsory retirement of any employee who has attained 65 years of age and who, for the 2–year period immediately before retirement, is employed in a bona fide executive or a high policymaking position, if such employee is entitled to an immediate nonforfeitable annual retirement benefit from a pension, profit-sharing, savings, or deferred compensation plan, or any combination of such plans, of the employer of such employee, which equals, in the aggregate, at least $44,000.

. . .

As amended Pub.L. 101–239, Title VI, § 6202(b)(3)(C)(ii), Dec. 19, 1989, 103 Stat. 2233.

THE REHABILITATION ACT
(29 U.S.C.A.)

§ 794. Nondiscrimination under Federal grants and programs

(a) Promulgation of rules and regulations

No otherwise qualified individual with a disability in the United States, as defined in section 706(8) of this title, shall, solely by reason of her or his disability, be excluded from the participation in, be denied the benefits of, or be subjected to discrimination under any program or activity receiving Federal financial assistance or under any program or activity conducted by any Executive agency or by the United States Postal Service. The head of each such agency shall promulgate such regulations as may be necessary to carry out the amendments to this section made by the Rehabilitation, Comprehensive Services, and Developmental Disabilities Act of 1978. Copies of any proposed regulation shall be submitted to the appropriate authorizing committees of the Congress, and such regulation may take effect no earlier than the thirtieth day after the date on which such regulation is so submitted

. . .

(d) Standards used in determining violation of section

The standards used to determine whether this section has been violated in a complaint alleging employment discrimination under this section shall be the standards applied under title I of the Americans with Disabilities Act of 1990 (42 U.S.C.A. 1211 et seq.) and the provisions of sections 501 through 504, and 510, of the Americans with Disabilities Act of 1990 (42 U.S.C.A. 12201–12204 and 12210), as such sections relate to employment.

As amended Pub.L. 102–569, Title I, § 102(p)(32), Title V, § 506, Oct. 29, 1992, 106 Stat. 4360, 4428; Pub.L. 103–382, Title III, § 394(i)(2), Oct. 20, 1994, 108 Stat. 4029.

§ 706. Definitions

. . .

(8)(A) Except as otherwise provided in subparagraph (B), the term "individual with a disability" means any individual who (i) has a physical or mental impairment which for such individual constitutes or results in a substantial impediment to employment and (ii) can benefit in terms of an employment outcome from vocational rehabilitation services provided pursuant to subchapter I, III, VI, or VIII of this chapter.

(B) Subject to subparagraphs (C), (D), (E), and (F), the term "individual with a disability" means, for purposes of sections 701, 713, and 714 of this title, and subchapters II, IV, V, and VII of this chapter, any person who (i) has a physical or mental impairment which substantially limits one or more of such person's major life activities, (ii) has a record of such impairment, or (iii) is regarded as having such an impairment.

. . .

(D) For the purpose of sections 793 and 794 of this title, as such sections relate to employment, such term does not include an individual who has a currently contagious disease or infection and who, by reason of such disease or infection, would constitute a direct threat to the health or safety of other individuals or who, by reason of the currently contagious disease or infection, is unable to perform the duties of the job.

(E) For the purposes of sections 791, 793, and 794 of this title—

(i) for purposes of the application of subparagraph (B) to such sections, the term "impairment" does not include homosexuality or bisexuality; and

(ii) therefore, the term "individual with a disability" does not include an individual on the basis of homosexuality or bisexuality.

(F) For the purposes of sections 791, 793, and 794 of this title, the term "individual with a disability" does not include an individual on the basis of—

(i) transvestism, transsexualism, pedophilia, exhibitionism, voyeurism, gender identity disorders not resulting from physical impairments, or other sexual behavior disorders;

(ii) compulsive gambling, kleptomania, or pyromania; or

(iii) psychoactive substance use disorders resulting from current illegal use of drugs.

. . .

As amended Pub.L. 101–336, Title V, § 512, July 26, 1990, 104 Stat. 376; Pub.L. 102–569, Title I, § 102(a)–(n), (p)(3), Oct. 29, 1992, 106 Stat. 4347–56; Pub.L. 103–73, Title I, §§ 102(1), 103, Aug. 11, 1993, 107 Stat. 718; Pub.L. 103–218, Title IV, § 404, Mar. 9, 1994, 108 Stat. 97.

§ 794a. Remedies and attorneys' fees

(a)(1) The remedies, procedures, and rights set forth in section 717 of the Civil Rights Act of 1964 (42 U.S.C.A. 2000e–16 [42 U.S.C.S. § 2000e–16]), including the application of sections 706(f) through 706(k) (42 U.S.C.A. 2000e–5(f) through (k) [42 U.S.C.S. § 2000e–5(f)–(k)]), shall be available, with respect to any complaint under section 501 of this Act [29 U.S.C.S. § 791], to any employee or applicant for employment aggrieved by the final disposition of such complaint, or by the failure to take final action on such complaint. In fashioning an equitable or affirmative action remedy under such section, a court may take into account the reasonableness of the cost of any necessary work place accommodation, and the availability of alternatives therefor or other appropriate relief in order to achieve an equitable and appropriate remedy.

(2) The remedies, procedures, and rights set forth in title VI of the Civil Rights Act of 1964 [42 U.S.C.S. §§ 2000d et seq.] shall be available to any person aggrieved by any act or failure to act by any recipient of Federal assistance or Federal provider

of such assistance under section 504 of this Act [29 U.S.C.S. § 794].

(b) In any action or proceeding to enforce or charge a violation of a provision of this title [29 U.S.C.S. §§ 790 et seq.], the court, in its discretion, may allow the prevailing party, other than the United States, a reasonable attorney's fee as part of the costs.

Sept. 26, 1973, P.L. 93–112, Title V, § 505, as added Nov. 6, 1978; P.L. 95–602, Title I, § 120, 92 Stat. 2982.

CIVIL RIGHTS ATTORNEY'S FEES AWARD ACT OF 1976
(42 U.S.C.A. SEC. 1988)

§ 1988. Proceedings in vindication of civil rights

(a) Applicability of statutory and common law

The jurisdiction in civil and criminal matters conferred on the district courts by the provisions of titles 13, 24, and 70 of the Revised Statutes for the protection of all persons in the United States in their civil rights, and for their vindication, shall be exercised and enforced in conformity with the laws of the United States, so far as such laws are suitable to carry the same into effect; but in all cases where they are not adapted to the object, or are deficient in the provisions necessary to furnish suitable remedies and punish offenses against law, the common law, as modified and changed by constitution and statutes of the State wherein the court having jurisdiction of such civil or criminal cause is to be held, so far as the same is not inconsistent with the Constitution and laws of the United States, shall be extended to and govern the said courts in the trial and disposition of the cause, and, if it is of a criminal nature, in the infliction of punishment on the party found guilty.

(b) Attorney's fees

In any action or proceeding to enforce a provision of sections 1981, 1981a, 1982, 1983, 1985, and 1986 of this title, title IX of Public Law 92–318 [20 U.S.C.A. § 1681 et seq.], the Religious Freedom Restoration Act of 1993 [42 U.S.C.A. § 2000b et seq.], title VI of the Civil Rights Act of 1964 [42 U.S.C.A. § 2000d et seq.], or section 13981 of this title, the court, in its discretion, may allow the prevailing party, other than the United States, a reasonable attorney's fee as part of the costs, except that in any action brought against a judicial officer for an act or omission taken in such officer's judicial capacity such officer shall not be held liable for any costs, including attorney's fees, unless such action was clearly in excess of such officer's jurisdiction.

(c) Expert fees

In awarding an attorney's fee under subsection (b) of this section in any action or proceeding to enforce a provision of section 1981 or 1981a of this title, the court, in its discretion, may include expert fees as part of the attorney's fee.

As amended Pub.L 102–166, Title I, §§ 103, 113(a), Nov. 21, 1991, 105 Stat. 1074, 1079; Pub.L. 103–

141, § 4(a), Nov. 16, 1993, 107 Stat. 1489; Pub.L. 103–322, Title IV, § 40303, Sept. 13, 1994, 108 Stat. 1942; Pub.L. 104–317, Title III, § 309(b), Oct. 19, 1996, 110 Stat. 3853.

THE RECONSTRUCTION STATUTES
CRIMINAL PROVISIONS (18 U.S.C.A.)

§ 241. Conspiracy against rights

If two or more persons conspire to injure, oppress, threaten, or intimidate any person in any State, Territory, Commonwealth, Possession, or District in the free exercise or enjoyment of any right or privilege secured to him by the Constitution or laws of the United States, or because of his having so exercised the same; or

If two or more persons go in disguise on the highway, or on the premises of another, with intent to prevent or hinder his free exercise or enjoyment of any right or privilege so secured—

They shall be fined under this title or imprisoned not more than ten years, or both; and if death results from the acts committed in violation of this section or if such acts include kidnapping or an attempt to kidnap, aggravated sexual abuse or an attempt to commit aggravated sexual abuse, or an attempt to kill, they shall be fined under this title or imprisoned for any term of years or for life, or both, or may be sentenced to death.

As amended Pub.L. 103–322, Title VI, § 60006(a), Title XXXII, §§ 320103(a), 320201(a), Title XXXIII, § 330016(1)(L), Sept. 13, 1994, 108 Stat. 1970,

2109, 2113, 2147; Pub.L. 104–294, Title VI, §§ 604(b)(14)(A), 607(a), Oct. 11, 1996, 110 Stat. 3507, 3511.

§ 242. Deprivation of rights under color of law

Whoever, under color of any law, statute, ordinance, regulation, or custom, willfully subjects any person in any State, Territory, Commonwealth, Possession, or District to the deprivation of any rights, privilege, or immunities secured or protected by the Constitution or laws of the United States, or to different punishments, pains, or penalties, on account of such person being an alien, or by reason of his color, or race, than are prescribed for the punishment of citizens, shall be fined under this title or imprisoned not more than one year, or both; and if bodily injury results from the acts of a dangerous weapon, explosives, or fire, shall be fined under this title or imprisoned not more than ten years, or both; and if death results from the acts committed in violation of this section or if such acts include kidnapping or an attempt to kidnap, aggravated sexual abuse or an attempt to commit aggravated sexual abuse, or an attempt to kill, shall be fined under this title, or imprisoned for any term of years or for life, or both, or may be sentenced to death.

As amended Pub.L. 103–322, Title VI, § 60006(b), Title XXXII, §§ 320103(a), 32103(b), Title XXXIII, § 330016(1)(H), Sept. 13, 1994, 108 Stat. 1970, 2109, 3113, 2147, Pub.L. 104–294, Title VI,

§§ 604(b)(14)(B), 607(a), Oct. 11, 1996, 110 Stat. 3507, 3511.

CIVIL PROVISIONS (42 U.S.C.A.)

§ 1981. Equal rights under the law

(a) Statement of equal rights

All persons within the jurisdiction of the United States shall have the same right in every State and Territory to make and enforce contracts, to sue, be parties, give evidence, and to the full and equal benefit of all laws and proceedings for the security of persons and property as is enjoyed by white citizens, and shall be subject to like punishment, pains, penalties, taxes, licenses, and exactions of every kind, and to no other.

. . .

(c) Protection against impairment

The rights protected by this section are protected against impairment by nongovernmental discrimination and impairment under color of state law.

As amended Pub.L. 102–166, Title I, § 101, Nov. 21, 1991, 105 Stat. 1071.

§ 1982. Property rights of citizens

All citizens of the United States shall have the same right, in every State and Territory, as is enjoyed by white citizens thereof to inherit, purchase, lease, sell, hold, and convey real and personal property.

R.S. § 1978.

§ 1983. Civil action for deprivation of rights

Every person who, under color of any statute, ordinance, regulation, custom, or usage of any State or Territory or the District of Columbia, subjects, or causes to be subjected, any citizen of the United States or other person within the jurisdiction thereof to the deprivation of any rights, privileges, or immunities secured by the Constitution and laws, shall be liable to the party injured in an action at law, suit in equity, or other proper proceedings for redress, except that in any action brought against a judicial officer for an act or omission taken in such officer's judicial capacity, injunctive relief shall not be granted unless a declaratory decree was violated or declaratory relief was unavailable. For the purpose of this section, any Act of Congress applicable exclusively to the District of Columbia shall be considered to be a statute of the District of Columbia.

As Amended Pub.L. 104–317, Title III, § 309(c), Oct. 19, 1996, 110 Stat. 3853.

§ 1985. Conspiracy to interfere with civil rights

. . .

(3) If two or more persons in any State or Territory conspire or go in disguise on the highway or on the premises of another, for the purpose of depriving, either directly or indirectly, any person or class of persons of the equal protection of the laws, or of equal privileges and immunities under the laws; or

for the purpose of preventing or hindering the constituted authorities of any State or Territory from giving or securing to all persons within such State or Territory the equal protection of the laws; or if two or more persons conspire to prevent by force, intimidation, or threat, any citizen who is lawfully entitled to vote, from giving his support or advocacy in a legal manner, toward or in favor of the election of any lawfully qualified person as an elector for President or Vice President, or as a Member of Congress of the United States; or to injure any citizen in person or property on account of such support or advocacy; in any case of conspiracy set forth in this section, if one or more persons engaged therein do, or cause to be done, any act in furtherance of the object of such conspiracy, whereby another is injured in his person or property, or deprived of having and exercising any right or privilege of a citizen of the United States, the party so injured or deprived may have an action for the recovery of damages, occasioned by such injury or deprivation, against any one or more of the conspirators.

R.S. § 1980.

*

INDEX

References are to Pages

ABORTION
Consent provisions, 29–30
Government funding, 29, 30–32
Informational requirements, 29, 33–34
Limiting Roe, 36–39
Right to terminate pregnancy, 15–17
Viability testing, 34–36

ACCESS TO THE COURTS
Civil cases, 162–164
Counsel, 161–162, 164
Transcripts, 159–160

ACTIONS UNDER 42 U.S.C. § 1983
Generally, Ch. 8
Attorney's fees, 253–254, 268–271
Deficiencies in federal law, 264–266
Eleventh amendment, 261–262
Exhaustion requirements, 253
Federal officials, 256
Habeas corpus, 266–267
Immunities, 254–262
Municipal liability, 252, 258–262
Notice requirements, 265
Personal liability, 252–254
Protected interests, 262–264
Release-dismissal agreements, 267–268
Res judicata, 266–267

ACTIONS UNDER 42 U.S.C. § 1983—Cont'd
State law, 264–266
Statutes of limitations, 264–265

AFFIRMATIVE ACTION
See Compensatory Treatment of Racial Minorities; Sex Discrimination

ALIENS
Access to government resources, 134–137
Distinction between federal and state regulation, 137
Education, 137
Occupational restrictions, 135–136
Ownership of land, 135
Suspect classification, 134

APPORTIONMENT
See Legislative Apportionment

BADGES OF SLAVERY, 224–225

BENIGN QUOTAS
See Compensatory Treatment of Racial Minorities; Sex Discrimination

BILL OF RIGHTS
Applicability to the states, 3–6
Penumbra, 11–13
Standard for enforcement, 5–6, 10–11

BONA FIDE OCCUPATIONAL QUALIFICATIONS, 232–235

BUSING
See Desegregation

CIVIL RIGHTS LEGISLATION
See also Employment Discrimination
Post–Brown statutes, 226–229
Reconstruction statutes, 244–251
Suits under 42 U.S.C. § 1983, see Ch. 8

COMPENSATORY TREATMENT OF RACIAL MINORITIES
Case law, 96–110
Congressional power, 109–110
General policy considerations, 110–113
Layoffs, 104–105
Minority set-asides, 106–110
University admissions, 102–104, 111–112

CONGRESSIONAL IMPLEMENTATION OF CONSTITUTIONAL RIGHTS, 212–216

CONGRESSIONAL MODIFICATION OF CONSTITUTIONAL RIGHTS, 216–221

CONGRESSIONAL POWER OVER PRIVATE DISCRIMINATION
Commerce clause, 223–224
Conspiracies, 222–223
Rights of national citizenship, 211
Thirteenth Amendment, 224–225

COUNSEL, RIGHT TO, 161–162, 164

DELIBERATE SPEED
See Desegregation

DESEGREGATION
Ambiguities of Swann, 80–83
Anti-busing legislation, 87–89
Congressional reaction to Swann, 87
"Deliberate speed," 75–77
Evasive schemes, 77
Northern de jure segregated districts, 83–87
Partially segregated areas, 90–93

DISCRIMINATION
Generally, Chs. 4, 5, 7, 8
Access to the courts, 159–164
Aliens, 134–137
Fundamental interests, 164–170
Illegitimacy, 138–144
Past residence, 158–159
Purposeful, 65–70, 229–235
Racial, 65–93, 96–113
Sex, 113–131
Sexual orientation, 174–175
Travel, 154–159
Voting, 146–154, 177–183, 226–228
Wealth, 132–134

DISTINCTION BETWEEN PERSONAL AND ECONOMIC FREEDOMS, 17–19

DUE PROCESS
See also Abortion; Hearing, Right to
Generally, Chs. 2, 3
Applicability of, 20–28, 41–46

DUE PROCESS—Cont'd
Liberty of contract, 8–10
Natural law, 7–8
Standard of review, 10–11, 19–28

DURATIONAL RESIDENCE REQUIREMENTS
See Travel, Right to

EDUCATION
See also Segregation
Aid to private schools, 77, 201–203
Alienage, 137, 169–170
Finance, 166–167
Students' rights, 57–58, 59–60

ELECTIONS
See Legislative Apportionment; Public Function Doctrine; Voting

EMPLOYMENT DISCRIMINATION
Against sub-classes, 230–232
Bona fide occupational qualifications, 232–235
Discriminatory impact, 240–244
Procedures for redress, 239–240
Proof 235–240
Purposeful discrimination, 229–235
Reconstruction statutes, 245–246
Remedies, 237–239

ENTITLEMENT DOCTRINE, 41–45

EQUAL PROTECTION
Generally, Chs. 4, 5
Equal Rights Amendment, 129–131
Peremptory challenge, 69–70
Purposeful discrimination, 65–70

FUNDAMENTAL INTERESTS. 164–170

GENDER-BASED CLASSIFICATIONS
See Sex Discrimination

GERRYMANDERING
See Legislative Apportionment

HEARING, RIGHT TO
See also Irrebuttable Presumptions: Public Employment; Seizure of Property
Injury to reputation, 51–53

HEARING, RIGHT TO—Cont'd
Legislative control, 44–46
Legitimate claim of entitlement, 41–44
Prisoners, 53–54
Type required, 57–60

HOUSING
Fundamental interest analysis, 164–166
Legislation, 223–224, 226, 248–249
Restrictive covenants, 194–198

ILLEGITIMACY, 138–144

INDIANS, 131

INDIGENTS
See Wealth Classifications

IRREBUTTABLE PRESUMPTIONS, 60–63

JUDICIAL ENFORCEMENT OF DISCRIMINATION, 194–198

LEGISLATIVE APPORTIONMENT
Equal population requirement, 177–178
Gerrymandering, 68, 100–101, 181–183
Local governmental units, 178–179
Permissible departures from equality, 179–181

LIBERTY OF CONTRACT
See Due Process

NATURAL LAW
See Due Process

NINTH AMENDMENT, 13–15

POLITICAL PARTIES
Ballot access, 150–152
Campaign financing, 153–154
Party affiliation requirements, 151–152
White primaries, 186–187

PRIVACY, RIGHT TO,
Abortion, 15–17, 29–39
Homosexuality, 22–26
Personal autonomy, 21–28
The "right to die", 26–28

PRIVILEGES AND IMMUNITIES, 1–3

PUBLIC EMPLOYMENT, 44–46, 54–56

PUBLIC FUNCTION DOCTRINE
Company towns, 188
Elections, 186–187
Parks, 189–190
Rationale, 190–194
Shopping centers, 188–189
Utilities, 192

RACIAL CLASSIFICATIONS
See also Desegregation
Compensatory treatment, 96–113
Purposeful discrimination, 65–70, 230–231
Separate-but-equal doctrine, 70–72

RATIONALITY TEST
"Newer" equal protection, 175–177
Traditional standard, 64–65, 164–165, 171–172
Variations in application, 172–175

REAPPORTIONMENT
See Legislative Apportionment

RESTRICTIVE COVENANTS
See Judicial Enforcement of Discrimination

SEGREGATION
See also Desegregation
De facto, 73–74, 93–96
Separate-but-equal doctrine, 70–74

SEIZURE OF PROPERTY, 46–51

SEX DISCRIMINATION
Compensatory treatment, 122–127
Education, 120–122
Equal Rights Amendment, 129–131
Family rights, 127–129
Pregnancy-related disabilities, 130–131
Selective service, 119–120
Standard of review, 113–122
Statutory rape, 118–119
Unique physical characteristics, 130–131

SIGNIFICANT STATE INVOLVEMENT
Aid, 201–202
Approval, 207–209

SIGNIFICANT STATE INVOLVEMENT—Cont'd
Authorization, 205, 208
Encouragement, 199–201
Joint participation, 205–206
Leasing public building, 198–199, 206–209
Licensing, 206–209
Regulation, 206–209

STATE ACTION
See also Judicial Enforcement of Discrimination; Public Function Doctrine; Significant State Involvement
Generally, Ch. 6
Balancing theory, 196–197, 209–210
Basis for requiring, 184–186
Power theory, 190–193
Thirteenth Amendment, 224

SUSPECT CLASSIFICATIONS
See also Compensatory Treatment of Racial Minorities; Segregation
Generally, Ch. 4
Age, 133–134
Alienage, 134–137
Illegitimacy, 138–144
Mental retardation, 173–174
Race, 65–70, 102–110
Sex, 113–131
Wealth, 132–134

TITLE VII
See Employment Discrimination

TRAVEL, RIGHT TO
Durational residence requirements, 155–158
Government prohibitions, 154–155

VOTING
See also Legislative Apportionment
Ballot access, 150–151
Campaign financing, 153–154
Disqualification of criminals, 150
Durational residence requirements, 149–150
Legislation, 226–228
Party affiliation requirements, 151–153
Poll tax, 146
Property qualifications, 148–149
Special purpose districts, 148–149, 178–179

VOTING—Cont'd
Standard of review, 146–148

WEALTH CLASSIFICATIONS
Generally, 132–134
Civil justice, 162–164
Criminal appeals, 159–162
Education, 166–167, 170
Social welfare, 164–166
Travel, 155–159
Voting, 146

†